SPIRIT: 101

Transcending, understanding, living within and among the human condition; becoming and being who you really are and created to be.

RAMON LAZARUS

BALBOA.PRESS
A DIVISION OF HAY HOUSE

Balboa Press books may be ordered through booksellers or by contacting:

Balboa Press
A Division of Hay House
1663 Liberty Drive
Bloomington, IN 47403
www.balboapress.com
844-682-1282

Because of the dynamic nature of the Internet, any web addresses or links contained in this book may have changed since publication and may no longer be valid. The views expressed in this work are solely those of the author and do not necessarily reflect the views of the publisher, and the publisher hereby disclaims any responsibility for them.

The author of this book does not dispense medical advice or prescribe the use of any technique as a form of treatment for physical, emotional, or medical problems without the advice of a physician, either directly or indirectly. The intent of the author is only to offer information of a general nature to help you in your quest for emotional and spiritual well-being. In the event you use any of the information in this book for yourself, which is your constitutional right, the author and the publisher assume no responsibility for your actions.

Any people depicted in stock imagery provided by Getty Images are models, and such images are being used for illustrative purposes only.
Certain stock imagery © Getty Images.

Print information available on the last page.

ISBN: 979-8-7652-4980-2 (sc)
ISBN: 979-8-7652-4982-6 (hc)
ISBN: 979-8-7652-4981-9 (e)

Library of Congress Control Number: 2024903501

Balboa Press rev. date: 03/19/2024

CONTENTS

PREFACE

This book will awaken one's consciousness and awareness as pertains to beingness. It will inspire and empower the reader and provide a perspective or viewpoint on how life-forms see themselves in relation to themselves, others, and God; how they relate to themselves; and how others and God relate to them. It will increase one's vitality and establish a positive attitude and sense of well-being.

This book is not intended to replace, prescribe, or dispense medical advice or recommend any technique for the treatment of any medical diagnosis, condition, or problem absent a physician directly or indirectly. The intent of the book is to offer general information to be used to increase vitality and spiritual, emotional, and physical well-being. If you use any of the information in this book, the author and the publisher do not assume responsibility for your usage or actions.

The book is to be used with the page titled "Conflict Resolution" as a guide to help readers identify areas within themselves they may choose to address to work toward resolution in establishing well-being and vitality.

ACKNOWLEDGMENTS

With great appreciation and gratitude, I would like to thank all who have contributed to my life thus far, from family to neighbors to teachers of every kind, especially those I have learned from directly or indirectly as a result of being led to compile and write the papers for this book. This book is a labor of love of the calling that chose me to become a doctor and a healer in the service of others and to find help for them when no other could provide the help they sought. Finally, thanks to the Most High God and Jesus Christ, who live on thrones in heaven and whose Spirit is busy helping others through their intentions and prayers every day.

ACKNOWLEDGMENTS

INTRODUCTION

This book is not about the projection of the ego through the intellect, with its observations and aspirations of the soul and spirit. It comes from actual mystical experiences of the soul at all levels of beingness, incorporating the process with insight directly from such experiences integrated and incarnated with revelation and realization realized and understood about all aspects of being that apply and relate to God, the human condition, and how the human condition relates to becoming and being a creation of God.

This book is based upon the living Word of God and not an opinion, as an opinion is a by-product of an ego when it is trying to determine with belief as fact and fantasy, guessing at an outcome based upon its own incomplete, uncertain experience, trying to bridge the gap in its lack of understanding about a particular topic or subject.

The living Word of God is interested in the truth of a subject or unifying divisions or apparent conflicts between life-forms and souls to discern what is true in love and ascertain an appropriate conclusion to a given dilemma and action to be taken, if any, based upon spiritual insight, knowledge, and wisdom pertaining to all it potentially or will effect. The purpose of such deliberations is to guide those involved to the truth they seek from a state of either dysfunction or wholeness and reveal it in such a way to each indwelling life-form that there can be no mistake as to the content, context, realization, understanding, integration, and assimilation of such knowledge.

This will be experienced by all individual life-forms or souls in such a way as to expand and enlighten where they are when they receive it, where it wishes to lead or guide them, and how to get there using free will to activate their due process of being or their God-given right to know who they really are and are created to be.

This book is based upon spiritual knowledge and wisdom through the Most High God, Jesus Christ, and the Holy Spirit, obtained by integrating and incarnating my heart and soul. It is a journey through the peace of heaven and the brokenness of hell to become the person I was created to be in love, truth, wisdom, and justice.

CONFLICT RESOLUTION

1. Identify the issue. What is it about?

2. Identify the emotions and feelings. For example, are you sad or angry or frightened?

3. Make "I am" statements: "I am _____ [fill in the blank with emotions or feelings]." Do this until there are no more feelings left about the issue. Ask, "What else?" Doing this will work through ego defense mechanisms, getting to the core feeling.

4. Once done, ask, "Who are you?"

5. Ask, "How old are you?"

6. Ask, "What did you see and hear?"

7. Ask, "What did you experience?" This could be external, internal, or both. The answers to this and the above questions will identify dissociated thought forms that led you away from who you are in Christ. It could be a statement like "I'm all alone" or "Nobody loves me." Identify the source the statement came from. Was it yourself or others?

8. Ask Christ to help you reclaim love through Jesus's name and blood.

9. Embrace your inner child with Jesus, and forgive him or her. If the response to who you are is God speaking to you, simply acknowledge it, be still, and realize it. If the response to who you are is not of God, then continue with questions to reveal the source, and claim Jesus Christ's name, precious blood, and precious water; God's presence; and Jesus's resurrection to reclaim ground given or a stronghold out of dysfunction to wholeness. Refer to this page before and after reading a chapter for related relatability and resonance in resolving potential conflicts and establishing vitality and well-being.

The chapters of this book are composed of two master's degree theses and six doctoral dissertation submissions to a metaphysical university system. They passed the review process of the respective metaphysical universities they were submitted to. The thesis and dissertation material is based upon years of personal and professional experience. The process of writing the chapters of the book took eight years to accomplish. Reading this book is an investment in one's self and future, spiritually speaking. It will foster growth, challenge outdated false beliefs, help to ease and dissolve emotional blocks, and help to convert one's own personal knowledge into wisdom through the realizations obtained through the spiritual transformational process. It also will help to fulfill one's spiritual duty of taking responsibility for one's thoughts, emotions, feelings, attitudes, behaviors, and conduct, leading to becoming God's masterpiece of who you really are and were created to be. With each realization and revelation, healing is inevitably possible, along with restored health, vitality, well-being, a positive outlook or attitude, and a return to joy and gratitude, which, together with appreciation, lead to happiness and contentment.

Christ Consciousness and the Kingdom of Heaven

A Thesis Submitted in Partial Fulfillment of
the Requirements for the Degree of Master of
Metaphysical Science in the Department of Graduate
Studies of the University of Metaphysics

RAMON LAZARUS
MARCH 25, 2015

INTRODUCTION

Christ consciousness is the operating system of the soul. Its purpose is to establish being by guiding the soul to merge with the heart, dissolving the ego and bringing the integrated soul and incarnated heart into the kingdom of heaven, where the soul is reconnected and whole and real.

It consists of the Christ light of creation, the living Word of God, and purified true spirit. It also utilizes the archetypes of priest, prophet, and king. It is the goal of the true Christian and mystic alike. The way to the kingdom of heaven (higher consciousness) is Jesus Christ Himself (John 14:6 NKJV). More specifically, it is "to allow God to transform us inwardly by the complete renewing of our minds" (Romans 12:2 NKJV) so that we, like Saint Paul, can honestly say "we have the mind of Christ" (1 Corinthians 2:16 NKJV). This "putting on the mind which was in Christ Jesus" (Philippians 2:5 NKJV)—that is, Christ consciousness—is the goal of the Christian spiritual path (Marion xiii).

According to Jim Marion, a contemporary Christian mystic, the principal goal of every Christian should be the realization of the kingdom of heaven. In the Sermon on the Mount, Jesus described the type of people who inhabit the kingdom of heaven, namely the meek, the merciful, the peacemakers, and the pure in heart (Matthew 5:1–10 NKJV). He told us we should seek first the kingdom of heaven (Matthew 6:3 NKJV). Christ consciousness is important for fulfillment of the soul and entry into the kingdom of heaven. It is for everyone. "Jesus Himself constantly expressed His love of beings and life in feasts, and again and again spoke of the Kingdom as a feast or banquet to which God was inviting everyone" (Harvey 13).

Christ consciousness is the guiding force to the realization of the kingdom of heaven. The process is clear. It is an internal phenomenon or to be experienced within one's self—"the Kingdom of Heaven is within" (Luke 17:21 NKJV). Whatever produces a meditative state in an individual with an intent to awaken the soul will activate the process, consciousness, the awareness of Christ consciousness, and the destination and consciousness of the kingdom of heaven. During awakening, higher consciousness, or Christ consciousness, is activated and released, giving the individual an expanded awareness with multidimensional aspects. There is a oneness with Christ that communicates through thought and feeling, and the light, the awareness, illuminates the heart and mind to navigate the interior landscape, using the individual's free will to methodically maneuver toward the kingdom of heaven. The living Word of God communicates directly with the individual and through intuition. From Christ consciousness, we glean and gain insight to navigate every choice we will face from the perspective that is Christ. Christ consciousness is one with all of creation and God. It is divinity in human form. "Awareness is aware of its own awareness and omni presence. Existence and its expression as both form and formless is God and prevail equally in all objects, persons, plants, and animals. Everything is united by the divinity of existence" (Hawkins 24).

Christ consciousness, being creation itself, is in "...the present and the now. This now is continuous so that neither beginnings or endings are possible" (Hawkins 29). Charlene M. Proctor mentions Christ consciousness, describing it as follows: "an intelligence that is present in all creation, a pure reflection of spirit in the created realm" (18). Christ consciousness in the kingdom of heaven has been around since before the beginning of time—going back to creation itself and before. Mystics, saints, sages, avatars, and holy people have experienced and witnessed this consciousness. There are many accounts of it. They all point to becoming one with God through the experience of Christ consciousness to reach the kingdom of heaven, which Jim Marion describes as the *nondual level—* reaching oneness with God. It is a spiritual education in being, as it was meant to be, created by God from the beginning of creation. We are meant "to become one with God's infinite intelligence, which is embedded in every particle of creation" (Proctor 18). This process of Christ consciousness in reaching the kingdom of heaven is a mystical process, and therefore, it is of a much higher nature than mainstream science and can only be quantified and qualified by those of a mystical nature with metaphysical science to understand and make sense of its applications to everyday interpretations and meanings as to how to proceed with what is useful to the person who wishes to choose such an endeavor. This process, according to Proctor, "is already present within us… Our entire life is a conversation with the Presence, who is showing us how to become that which we already are, which is divine. It's the entire reason we are here" (17–18).

Being one with God in oneness, according to Proctor, is as follows: "It is a complete harmonic convergence with the Divine, where we draw ourselves back to conscious oneness with all creation. It is our realization of God's own reflection in the son of man, in all of humankind. To have the Christ light within or have 'Christ in you' is to obtain that level of consciousness" (14). Proctor, like Marion and Harvey, describes this phenomenon and process as internal or within: "The Christ realization is an internal experience" (15). "The Kingdom of Heaven is a kingdom that you and I can find and see only by going deep within ourselves" (Marion 3). It is found at the point where the beginning of the consciousness of mind begins before falling off into unconscious sleep. It is right at that point where the unconscious and conscious mind meet and overlap when one is falling asleep, waking up, or meditating. "The Kingdom is inside you. … It is our inmost consciousness" (Harvey 15).

Christ consciousness and the kingdom of heaven are our individual and collective states of being to be established for meaning and purpose in our lives. Christ consciousness represents the fulfillment of the soul incarnated and merged with the heart to bring together oneness with God and all other life-forms in creation. It is an enlightening experience from awakening to realization of both the Christ consciousness and the nondual level of the kingdom of heaven. For some, this initiation or awakening may come about quickly, while for others, it may come about more gradually and methodically. As Proctor puts it, "it's about experiencing truth in our own individual consciousness. Birthing the Christ self means we have cleaned house and can now live with a balanced life in the present moment. We volunteer to surrender our old thought patterns, uncover our egos, and take a long, hard look at them so we can let go of… negative conditions" (15). She adds, "It actually takes a lot of courage to do this. We examine our faulty beliefs, for example we are sinners or inherently bad, and make a conscious choice to change our outlook and self- perception" (15).

Christ consciousness's purpose is to shine the light of awareness, bring light to the darkness, illuminate that darkness, and reveal truth. It is important because its primary task is to deal with the ego and its illusions. Embarking on an inner adventure will reveal Christ consciousness and the kingdom of heaven, but it will also reveal the ego. Christ consciousness will reveal every false belief and illusion, both individually and collectively, when applied to understanding conflicts or differences. It will provide understanding and promote love, unity, and wholeness within an individual or among individuals. Wholeness comes as a result of working through the ego and reconnecting with God on the other side of the process.

REVIEW OF THE LITERATURE

A review of the literature reveals that Christ consciousness in the kingdom of heaven has been around since the beginning of creation and is a state of being and consciousness that is real, not based upon belief. Here are a few examples from the Bible:

> In the beginning was the word and the word was with God, and the word was God. (John 1:1 NKJV)

> He was in the beginning with God. (John 1:2 NKJV)

> I am the Way, the Truth, and the Life. No one comes to the Father except through Me. (John 14:6 NKJV)

Charlene Proctor writes, "Birthing Christ consciousness within the human body is natural, because God's omnipresent intelligence exists in every particle of creation. ... According to Jesus, all people who become united with Christ consciousness can be called sons of God, when they know God is in them and they are part of God" (29).

Jim Marion writes, "To put on the mind of Christ, therefore, is to experience this non dual consciousness (awareness) for ourselves. And, once we do put on the mind of Christ, we, like Jesus, will see the Kingdom of Heaven all around us here and now" (11).

Andrew Harvey writes, "The door into the Kingdom- into a unitive, interconnected relationship of divine human charity with all things and beings and into the life of total service and celebration of others that must flow from it lies always open" (14).

Valerie Hunt writes, "When God is experienced, this event is as real as any sensory perception of one's own self. In those instances, we have victory over death and pain. We are in touch with the ongoing-ness of the soul. We understand the divine plan and our role in it. We come closer to perfection, and we are worthy[of] being called God's co-creator" (311).

David Hawkins writes about the enlightenment of Christ consciousness and being in the presence of God, referring to it as "the Presence." He describes *beingness* as follows: "Instead of thinking-ness, there is a self-revealing knowingness that imparts complete understanding and is self-explanatory by its self-effulgent essence. It is as though everything speaks silently and presents itself in its entirety in the absolute beauty of its perfection" (26). Hawkins further elaborates on the Presence, saying "the suffusion of the Presence throughout the totality and essence of all that exists is exquisite in its gentleness, and its touch is like a meltingness"(26)." The inner self is its core. In the ordinary world, only the surface of things can be touched, but in the Presence, the innermost essence of everything is interspersed with every other thing. This touch, which is the Hand of God, in its soft gentleness, is at the same time an expression and the abode of infinite power. In its contact with the inner essence of everything, one is aware that the Presence is being felt by every other thing, object, or person" (26). It is understood by the author's use in the composition of this paper that the soul; Christ consciousness; and subsequent oneness with God, the Presence, and the kingdom of heaven are the perspective and experience from which they all write, and there are many others in and out of religion on the same subject. I have chosen these authors because they represent a contemporary mystical perspective on an old and timeless practice: that of the soul and its Christ consciousness, its fulfillment in the kingdom of heaven, and its oneness with God.

Christ consciousness and the soul are the heart of spirituality. Spirituality is the domain of the soul. Religion is the domain of the ego. "The Declaration of Independence spells out that this is a nation whose government derives its authority from the spiritual principles of the Creator" (Hawkins 69). Charlene M. Proctor writes, "In 1797, during John Adams's administration, the Senate unanimously ratified the Treaty of Peace and Friendship, which states in Article XI that' the government of the United States is not in any sense founded on the Christian religion'" (4). Hawkins further adds, "By exploiting trivialities at the cost of ignoring the main thrust of spiritual truth, religions contribute to their own downfall and that of all humanity. Much that is revered as church doctrine is really the product of the ego" (73).

With Christ consciousness and its fulfillment in becoming one with God, there is a requisite of facing and appropriately dealing with the ego to reach the desired and destined spiritual maturity. Jim Marion writes,

> Non dual consciousness that is the vision of the Kingdom of Heaven is the highest stage in the growth of human consciousness from infancy to full spiritual maturity. By the process of inner growth in spiritual awareness, a path of constant inner realization, we gradually come to see our own union with God in Christ so that, at the final stage of non dual awareness, God alone and His Kingdom remain. (13)

This passage by Marion eludes to a process consisting of several levels of psychological and spiritual development in consciousness and leading to the kingdom of heaven. Proctor also makes reference to growth: "We have to clean ourselves out in order to make room for something better. It's a vigorous exercise, the most painful part of which is facing our ego and our suffering" (1). Harvey adds, "No one not even the greatest mystic, can know beforehand what such a stripping inevitably entails; its agony is too extreme for the mind to imagine and its torture reaches more deeply and finally into the ultimate recesses of being than any previous form of suffering" (83). This growth will further be explored in the findings section of this paper.

Further review of the literature reveals more on the topic of Christ consciousness. Proctor writes, "Christ consciousness [call it Krishna, Buddha or Mohammed consciousness it is all the same depending upon your wisdom tradition] is the highest form of consciousness a human can express or experience. It is God firmly seated in your individual consciousness, such that you are aware of the Presence of God within you, but it is not your individual ego thinking that you are God" (85). Norman Paulsen defines Christ consciousness in three stages:

1. One who sees the Presence and feels the essence of the divine inner sun rising on the horizon at midnight.
2. One who experiences the Presence of the divine inner sun as in a swoon one instant and hears the voice thereof speaking from all eternity.
3. One who experiences the Presence of the divine inner sun, the body of Christ, face-to-face; experiences so-called physical death; enters that Presence; sees all that light and life have become; and returns to reclaim the body after minutes, hours, or days. (200)

Paulsen is an adept who gives detailed insight cosmically into Christ consciousness. He gives descriptive accounts of his experience with what he calls the divine mother, the divine father, and the Christ child, I Am That I Am. Paulsen writes,

> Yes, I am that I am, mother and father, had awakened from the dream of eternal ever new joy and bliss, and had given birth to the consciousness and light of creation, the Christ. This divine living, offspring of pure consciousness and light is now known as the Light of God, the Great Central Sun, the inner penetrating body of Christ, the essence of our divine mother and father, I am that I am. (287)

Paulsen explains in detail the creation of creation energetically and cosmically around the divine twin stars: "The eight dual expanding spheres or dimensions of consciousness were impregnated with the very essence of divine personality, the twelve energies of virtue! The Kingdom of God, with realms of creation, began to manifest around each of the divine twin stars" (284). Paulsen further elaborates on creation:

> Let there be light; and there was light! The first creation of light like a sun, was now glowing within incandescent brilliance as it expanded and floated in the midst of

the vast cosmic sea of that-ness. The divine projections
for the newly born great expanding sphere of creation,
encompassing the eight inner penetrating realms of the
Kingdom of God were completed. Divine spirit, mother
and father would now move outward and dance in
the images of creation being projected by their divine
offspring, the Christ child! (286–87)

Paulsen's account of Christ consciousness from his experience is a
firsthand account learned from a teacher who had obtained Christ
consciousness. Paulsen learned from Paramahansa Yogananda, a twentieth-
century mystic and holy man. Paulsen simply did as Yogananda instructed
and, with some practice, achieved Christ consciousness and entered the
kingdom of heaven. Both Marion and Proctor also mention Yogananda
in their books as one who has achieved Christ consciousness and entered
the kingdom of heaven.

Christ consciousness and the kingdom of heaven are not part of the
body but are of spirit. They are everyone's birthright and the spiritual
destination of every person ever created. Paulsen's account mentioned
previously describes just how intimate the encounter and experience are
and how personal they can be also. Christ consciousness is the living
Word of God. It is the infinite intelligence of the universe in spirit, soul,
and mind, individualized for the purpose of bringing divinity into human
form to lead, teach, heal, transform, and live in harmony with others as a
realization of that divinity. "Essentially, we are sparks, or individualized
ideas, of the Divine Presence that exists within all creation. But just as
human intelligence is needed to create anything purposeful, vibration
and consciousness need intelligence for matter to evolve. Hence, God's
intelligence is present within all vibratory creation and is called Christ
consciousness" (Proctor 26). "It is more of a universal, cosmic principle
than a person" (Proctor 26). Christ consciousness is both mystical and
spiritual. "Mysticism is a deep level of spirituality where one fully sinks
into the experience of God's love" (Proctor 54). "Spirituality is… about
directly experiencing the truth of spiritual teachings in a process of personal
transformation" (Proctor 55). Spirituality can also be illuminating and
learned from by direct experience, giving new spiritual teaching besides

those that one has learned from. Christ consciousness is enlightening or can be enlightenment itself. "Enlightenment means awakening to our God self within" (Proctor 56). There is a oneness with all life, as well as a yearning to make that oneness known to others and enjoy the bliss of that oneness while also desiring to make a positive contribution from that oneness. In Christ consciousness's enlightenment, one "grasps that God is present in everything and everyone but there will always be more to learn" (Proctor 57). The journey or process of Christ consciousness is ongoing toward its destination.

Jim Marion further describes Christ consciousness: "At this level the Christian is identified with his or her true Christ self, which is seen as in a spiritual union with God the Creator. At this level one can truthfully say, "I live now not I, but Christ lives in me" (183), as Saint Paul said. The person with Christ consciousness sees all other human beings as the Christ and treats them accordingly. According to Marion, the causal level is the first level of consciousness of the human as a realized divinity, and it is consciousness at the level of the soul or individualized spirit. Auricly Marion writes, "The crown chakra opens dramatically with the result that the head is now circled by a halo. The heart center or chakra also fully opens and we become vessels of tremendous love and compassion" (184). Marion further explains the causal level thusly:" the word *causal* is used because this is the level of causes, the archetypal principles or ideal patterns by and from which the lower planes of existence (astral and physical) are built... These principles are the cause of all the other lesser forms that spring from them. This is the level of the Logos, the eternal Word of God (John 1:1–3), through whom, as the firstborn of creation (Colossians 1:15–20), all else in creation comes" (184). What Marion describes here is Christ consciousness from a consciousness point of view, evolved-spirituality point of view, and metaphysical point of view. The next step, as Marion points out, is actually not a level at all but what he describes as the fulfillment of the Christ consciousness into the kingdom of heaven. Jesus said, "The Father and I are one," referring to this level. "Non-dual consciousness or the Kingdom of Heaven marks the end of all division between 'creature' and 'creator'" (Marion 197).

This review of the literature of includes authors Charlene M. Proctor, PhD; Jim Marion; Andrew Harvey; Valerie V. Hunt; Norman Paulsen;

and David R. Hawkins, MD, PhD. They and the Holy Bible all point out that Christ consciousness is a real state of consciousness and actually the merging of divinity and humanity into one being. Several of the authors also mention that it is a mystical experience leading to growth and transformation. Christ consciousness is real, based not upon belief, dogma, or doctrine but upon universal love and intelligence from God.

FINDINGS

Based on the review of the literature, Christ consciousness and the kingdom of heaven are real from a mystical perspective. Material mainstream science has not yet caught up to metaphysical science as far as proving Christ consciousness and the kingdom of heaven exist. Energy-field findings by Valerie Hunt have led to new information in extrasensory human capacity and higher consciousness and the mystical connections of spirit. She was the first to discover vibration patterns during pain, disease, and illness in emotional and spiritual states. She has found scientific evidence of individualized field signatures and subtle energetic happenings between people and within groups. I will present some of her work with case studies in this chapter. Other findings reveal that there are many levels of consciousness to transcend or work through till one arrives at Christ consciousness and the kingdom of heaven. The ego is also part of the process, with its illusions. Jim Marion and David Hawkins offer maps or paths to validate the necessary steps to successfully arrive at Christ consciousness in the kingdom of heaven. Valerie Hunt's work in and with field consciousness is important not only for understanding mind, body, and soul interrelatedness and interaction but also for showing or displaying Christ consciousness as a healing modality. The following is an excerpt from her discovery.

> Information that emerges from higher consciousness states helps to explain the profound emotional connection with traumatic episodes, intense spiritual experiences, and threats to the soul. Although these emotions are similar

to those connected to physical existence, they are simpler, purer, and possess greater charge. When not released at the source level of higher consciousness, the effects of these energies seem to filter down to be discharged at the personality body level of existence. Thus higher emotions often become locked in to the material closed reality system. In contrast to the emotions at the material body level, in altered states there is evidence of an open emotional system that is dynamically in-touch with deep needs and subtle happenings in the universe. Here in the no time/ space realm, one discovers free emotional energy, a super consciousness state, the home of the peak experiences that we never forget. Here the closed system opens, revealing a broad continuum of emotions that explain things we knew about ourselves, particularly the schisms in our awareness. I began to see the current model of emotion in a broader context when I realized that the emotions connected with the self are the synthesizing mechanism of the body, and the emotions connected with the soul are the organizing medium for the mind. ... Ideally, we should be able to focus consciousness on any portion of the spectrum without losing our identity within the larger system. We should be able to remain grounded in earth reality while another part of our awareness is soaring to higher states. (108–9)

This is her discovery regarding mind, body, and soul and their relationship to emotional energy and healing work. It is important to mention here the impact in understanding repressed emotions. "Repressed emotions create huge gaps in the frequency spectra; these are sometimes called 'chakra blocks.' This is the source of psychosomatic disorders" (Hunt 112). This is important to metaphysicians because metaphysicians are uniquely gifted and talented to be able to help people with these and other conditions.

The following case studies are examples of Christ consciousness in action on the part of Valerie Hunt in helping others to achieve wholeness.

I recall working with a 35 year old illiterate woman sent to me from UCLA Neuro-Psychiatric Institute. She could neither read or write. Her psychiatrist asked me to help determine whether she was a deep mystic or psychotic. He said that she had been hypnotically regressed to age 5, where she got stuck and would not communicate. They had had difficulty bringing her out of that hypnotic state. When I first saw her, she announced that she was a mystic, to which I responded, "so am I we should have a good time together.".... When she appeared comfortable, ... I suggested "let's take a consciousness trip." I explained that she should close her eyes and start imagining that she was walking on a path, and then to look around and describe what she saw. After some rambling, she saw herself as a young girl with a whole rack of new, little girl clothes of all colors and styles. When asked which of these she wanted to put on she chose a black and red one, not colors chosen by most little girls. She put it on and went back to a play area. There she found a boy who was "playing around". Instantly her vibrations shot up, leaving a vacuum. She escaped something frightening by entering another state of consciousness. I made contact with her in her higher state and suggested that she was "out of her body" and should come back so that we could work. Finally, I was able to gradually lower both of our vibrations and literally, while talking with her, to" walk her back down" in consciousness. Soon she again remembered the little boy and started to vibrationally escape... I told her that she was going away so often that I needed her help. I asked her to grab one of her feet in her imagination when she started to escape, while I would grab the other. Together we would keep her grounded. She quickly learned to monitor herself to see when she was about to pop out of her body. She was then to pull both feet downward... Throughout a long session, we discovered that the age 5 episode was a sexual attack where, to protect her from her rage, she went into a high mystical state which she enjoyed so much that she did not tell anyone about either experience. Furthermore, if she stayed in that mystic state she could not remember the attack. She also verbalized that she did not want to read or write because it was not fun. I told her psychiatrist that the emotional program of her consciousness and the electromagnetic field had blocked their diagnosis and treatment. It should be easier now that we had made some connection. (128–29)

This case study shows how Christ consciousness can help someone within a lifetime to obtain healing and wholeness if he or she chooses to do so. This next case study shows how Christ consciousness can access trauma from other lifetimes or, as Valerie Hunt calls them, life-hoods.

Another woman was referred by a local priest because of her intense debilitating fear that neither she nor a psychiatrist had been able to change by working on the many material problems in her life. Intuitively, I suspected that she had been insane in some other life-hood, although this was not the present diagnosis. When she started imaging and going up in vibration, she poured out of the crown chakra until I could no longer feel her energy field, as though it had slipped from her body. This condition existed off and on for many days. When I brought down her vibration by contacting her field, it was like trying to ground a helium balloon. In this state individuals do not know the way back and many do not will to return. Different from comatose patients with a weak will, they have an energized will which misdirects all their energy into the altered state. Finally, I helped this woman to know how to put on the brakes so as not to lose consciousness. We walked up and down the vibrational consciousness scale until material imagery came. There were many skirmishes with life-hoods, none settling on any significant information until we hit pay dirt. She laboriously relived being a wizened old woman in Egypt who at one time had been a simple mystic who channeled information that the priests had rejected. When they threw her out of the temple she went to live in a small rock cave. There she became insane… Gradually she began to recognize this horrible experience and to acknowledge how her spiritual nature had been rejected when she was a temple priestess. She confided that she had always been afraid of insanity and had known that she was insane before. Indeed, her life has changed, her mystic nature is returning and her fears have lessened. More importantly, she no longer fears insanity, for she had relived insanity and returned. We helped her to reprogram her energy field. In the process of reprogramming she found the emotion which organized the field and the behavior which resulted. (130)

Both of these case studies show how important Christ consciousness is in helping people to heal, become whole, and become Christ consciousness themselves if that is what they choose. As has been discovered so far in the findings of this paper, Christ consciousness and the kingdom of heaven are the highest levels of consciousness. They are real and needed to deal with and heal from trauma or encounters with lower consciousness or the lowest-consciousness being, the ego. I believe that all trauma, in one lifetime or another, was subject to another's unconsciousness of ego, which resulted in the deficit experienced by the individual with the wound.

David Hawkins's map, or scale, of consciousness includes the full spectrum of consciousness, from the lowest to the highest. The consciousness scale in his book *Letting Go* lists eight emotions that are below significance and deal with the ego. They are as follows:

1. The emotion of humiliation at the level of shame, with a life view that is miserable and a God view that is despising.
2. The emotion of blame at the level of guilt, with a life view that is evil and a God view that is vindictive.
3. The emotion of despair at the level of apathy, with a life view that is hopeless and a God view that is condemning.

4. The emotion of regret at the level of grief, with a life view that is tragic and a God view that is disdainful.

5. The emotion of anxiety at the level of fear, with a life view that is frightening and a God view that is punitive.

6. The emotion of craving at the level of desire, with a life view that is disappointing and a God view that is denying.

7. The emotion of hate at the level of anger, with a life view that is antagonistic and a God view that is vengeful.

8. The emotion of scorn at the level of pride, with a life view that is demonic and a God view that is indifferent. (336)

Those who are ego-driven and controlled by their egos have all these negative lower-consciousness emotions contributing to their unconsciousness. Hawkins describes this dynamic, from which we can glean insight: "We typically feel so much guilt about anger that we find it necessary to make the object of our anger wrong so that we can say our anger is' justified'... It is common for people to repress their anger, aggression, and inner hostility; they view it as unpleasant, undignified and even as a moral failure or spiritual set back" (124).

As we have learned from the findings earlier in this chapter, repression of feelings or emotions leads to illness. The bottom of the spectrum of consciousness is responsible for man's inhumanity to man through shame and despair. Hawkins, in his book *Transcending the Levels of Consciousness: The Stairway to Enlightenment*, discusses the unconsciousness of the consciousness of the ego: "Shame is used as a tool of cruelty, and its victims often become cruel. Shamed children are cruel to animals and cruel to each other" (33). Hawkins further elaborates on shame: "Shame is also reflective of self hatred that, when turned outward, can result in severe, even homicidal aggression" (35). Hawkins briefly discusses despair: "Despair is characterized by helplessness and hopelessness and is therefore described as a dispirited state and hellish to endure" (34). This finding of the ego and its lower nature of unconsciousness shows just how inhumane acts of evil committed by one human toward another can be and how it leads to repressed emotions and has karmic implications as far as trying to resolve and heal.

The ego provides the substance, or fuel, as it is dissolved in God's presence, causing realizations and insights into transformation about self, God, and the world, leading to wholeness. Before we leave the ego and transcend it to higher levels, Christ consciousness, and the kingdom of heaven, we will look briefly at one of the functions the ego uses to maintain itself: the creation of illusion. One illusion we will look at is a religious one that many Christians have: believing that Jesus Christ is their Lord and Savior. That statement implies "Jesus Christ has done everything for me by dying on the cross, resurrecting, and ascending into heaven; and I, being a believer, am absolved of everything." Jim Marion calls the notion of being saved, for those who use that term, arrogant and also mentions that many Christians do indeed believe everything has been done for them. Andrew Harvey has this to say about it:

> The Savior Icon, in other words, is a later' inspiration' of the early Christian church, reeling under the impact of Jesus' life and of the transmission of His mystical force and essence that continued after the crucifixion and resurrection; it has nothing to do with Jesus' own vision of Himself and of His mission… Knowing Jesus in this way challenges the beliefs not only of all fundamentalist churches but also of those who place emphasis on Jesus Christ as the unique and all powerful savior. (6)

Harvey further adds that this illusion prevents people from taking appropriate responsibility for their lives. He writes, "Jesus places the responsibility for the 'real life' squarely on the shoulders of each human being; He does not claim to be the Savior who will initiate everyone into this 'abundant life': He is the sign that such a life is possible, but the work and sacrifice and passionate search for awakening have to be chosen and undertaken individually by each person" (17). This and other illusions have led to atrocities being committed against humanity in the name of God. The Crusades fought centuries ago were based upon similar illusions. Christ consciousness and the kingdom of heaven are needed to navigate through and transcend the ego and its illusions to become who we were created to be.

Continuing with David Hawkins's map of the scale of consciousness, picking up where we left off, let's look at the following:

1. The emotion of affirmation at the level of courage, with a life view that is feasible and a God view that is permitting. (This level Hawkins called significant because it begins the continued upward ascent in consciousness to enlightenment and Christ consciousness in the kingdom of heaven.)
2. The emotion of trust at the level of neutrality, with a life view that is satisfactory and a God view that is enabling.
3. The emotion of optimism at the level of willingness, with a life view that is hopeful and a God view that is inspiring.
4. The emotion of forgiveness at the level of acceptance, with a life view that is harmonious and a God view that is merciful.
5. The emotion of understanding at the level of reason, with a life view that is meaningful and a God view that is wise.
6. The emotion of reverence at the level of love, with a life view that is benign and a God view that is loving.
7. The emotion of serenity at the level of joy, with a life view that is complete and a God view that is one.
8. The emotion of bliss at the level of peace, with a life view that is perfect and a God view that is all being.
9. The emotion of ineffability at the level of enlightenment, with a life view that is God view itself. (336)

This scale by Hawkins, although linear, describes both the linear scale and the nonlinear scale of consciousness. Other findings include one from Jim Marion, who discovered there are several levels of consciousness of the human personality. They are as follows: "the archaic consciousness of infants, the magical consciousness of children, mythic consciousness, rational consciousness, vision-logic consciousness, psychic consciousness, subtle consciousness, and the consciousness of a human as a realized divinity: Christ consciousness and non dual consciousness" (Marion). We have already reviewed Christ consciousness and nondual consciousness and awareness. We will briefly address the other levels leading up to Christ consciousness and nondual consciousness.

Marion points out four principles that govern the spiritual path from start to finish:

1. All growth in consciousness is a process of inner realization.
2. All inner realizations are the results of personal experience 'meditated upon' in some fashion.
3. All growth in consciousness is a lessening of self-centeredness, a death to the old self-centered way of looking at the world and a simultaneous 'rebirth' into a less self-centered way of seeing things.
4. As a person's consciousness goes up the spiritual ladder from level to level, the person's consciousness becomes less and less attached to physical matter. (34)

The archaic consciousness of infants deals with the child learning to separate physically and emotionally from its mother and lasts until age three years. "Magical consciousness is the emergence of the mind in a child as something separate from its physical/emotional being where the child is learning to distinguish between its own emerging mental images and symbols and the external world, lasts until age 7 years" (Marion 37–38). Mythic consciousness is the level of consciousness of the child from about age seven to adolescence. "It is the first of the mental levels. It is the consciousness of the child's emerging mind or ego. The child at this level believes that the God in the sky much like its parents, can work every sort of miracle to meet the child's needs" (Marion 41). Rational consciousness, the second of the mental levels, is the dominant consciousness of the present age and is the level of consciousness more or less attained by the average adult in contemporary society. "In today's world, the passage from mythic into rational consciousness is the primary spiritual task of adolescence. During this stage a child develops an ability to reason beyond the concrete rules and roles of the mythic level and learn to handle abstract ideas and grasp universal principles" (Marion 49). Vision-logic consciousness is the highest of the three mental levels of consciousness. "It is the consciousness of many great artists, writers, scientists and philosophers. Vision logic's primary characteristics are the identification of the self with the abstract mind and the ability to think from many different perspectives. It is global in its interest in and concern for other persons" (Marion 63). In psychic consciousness, we no longer identify the self with the rational mind. "Instead, we identify the self with the inner witness that observes body, emotions, and mind. This inner witness is the permanent self, the part of the self beyond space time… Senses such as clairaudience and clairvoyance that roughly parallel the physical ones and which are referred to in the New Testament" (Marion 69). Subtle consciousness is the last level at which our self will be identified with our human personality. At the subtle level, our consciousness becomes capable of receiving direct communications from the causal level, the level of the soul. "We gain immediate contact with our Guardian Angel, our own spiritual master and Jesus Himself. All three of these serve as messengers (angels) of the true self and guide us towards our final individuation as a human being" (Marion 105).

It is important to note here that every soul is at or in a different level or stage of growth or development. Where one awakens may be different from where one ends up. At some point, depending on free will, all the stages or levels referenced in this paper will be gone through and integrated on both a personality level and a soul level. The integration of the personality may take months to a couple of years. The integration of the soul usually takes several years.

DISCUSSION

The literature on Christ consciousness and the kingdom of heaven is clear. It gives metaphysical, mystical evidence of such states of consciousness and reveals an infinite, divine intelligence that is not only contacted but also manifesting and integrated as well. Christ consciousness involves becoming a divine human or a human being instead of being just human. Christ consciousness and the kingdom of heaven are real states of consciousness leading to spiritual growth, understanding, and wholeness. To achieve such a state, find a method that induces a meditative state. This can be obtained by yoga, meditation, body work, or any of a number of healing techniques available from someone who practices metaphysical techniques.

For me, cranial sacral therapy produced a meditative state in which I became almost instantly enlightened fifteen years ago with Christ consciousness. I found the awakening refreshing and desired more as far as learning, understanding, and growth was concerned. Enlightenment is living in the resurrection versus the crucifixion as far as consciousness is concerned. Intuition and insight are truly worth their weight in gold.

After one awakens, there is a natural spiritual desire to continue following the path of Christ, which quickly becomes an act of free will that must be chosen again and again to continue on the path to fulfillment. This act of free will to choose, along with intention, actively pursues love and truth and has a learning curve involved to continue evolving toward Christ consciousness and the kingdom of heaven. In addition to what is cited in this paper, both Jim Marion and Andrew Harvey discuss at length the suffering, or dark night, of the soul that is involved with such growth. It can be excruciating and debilitating, totally disrupting a person's life and his or her ability to function in the world. This can include physical or mental illnesses and disturbances at various levels of development, including psychotic episodes as well as addictions and neuroses. It is not to be taken lightly and will require some kind of help at some point in the process. It is an endeavor to be taken consciously with guidance from God in establishing connection with Him or Her to initiate, guide, and complete the process from beginning to end.

Christ consciousness in the kingdom of heaven is God's intended destination for us spiritually while we are alive in the body. Without Christ consciousness and the kingdom of heaven, life would eventually become dark, twisting, and evil, with no hope, from being at the total mercy of the ego. If awakening doesn't happen through first establishing connection with God, then the Christ consciousness's integration and incarnation will accelerate and not allow the process of unconscious material of the ego to process in a conscious manner, leading to anti-Christ people, such as Adolph Hitler. Jesus Christ's life, as portrayed in the New Testament, started with awakening (His baptism), His time awakened in His healing ministry, integration (crucifixion), incarnation (resurrection), and ascension (fulfillment of the Christ consciousness), returning to the kingdom of heaven as a fully realized divinity. This process continues to this day, but it is an internal experience leading to transformation of both inner and outer aspects of being, as learned about in this paper. Intelligence and creative force in Christ consciousness and the kingdom of heaven involve being one with God, all of life, all life-forms, and all of creation. Created and Creator are one.

Dr. Masters describes, in his *Master's Degree Curriculum*, this oneness "as the innermost nature of mind and it has many names: Nirvana by the Buddhist, Samadhi by the Hindu, Christ consciousness by the Christian mystic and cosmic consciousness by the philosopher" (Masters 1:8). Dr. Masters continues with the practical application of Christ consciousness, or the inner mind, as he states, "The work of the metaphysician is to bring knowledge of this inner mind to others. Truly a person can be transformed into a better, more aware, more loving and productive individual through such an experience. All lesser practices of metaphysics should have this inner experience as the ultimate goal" (Masters 1:9). "The Kingdom of Heaven, metaphysically speaking, is not an after death place, but this higher inner mind into which a person may enter and commune and become one with the infinite mind" (Masters 1:9). In *Mystical Insights*, Dr. Masters describes persons with Christ consciousness thusly: "enlightened persons go about their days bringing or expressing greater love and creativity in whatever they are involved".

SUMMARY AND CONCLUSION

Christ consciousness and the kingdom of heaven are real and needed to become whole, whether people realize it or not. The implications and applications are as infinite as Christ consciousness itself. For those who do realize, it is an amazing experience and a true expression of an authentic spiritual Christian path, fulfilling Saint Paul's statement that we are to share in Christ's suffering as well as the joy it brings. Those who don't realize needlessly suffer at the hands of their unconsciousness and the ego's lower consciousness, harming others and themselves as they purposelessly search outside themselves for their lower ego desires. For most people, it is a conscious undertaking, and conscious suffering is what Christ consciousness and the kingdom of heaven bring. Unconscious suffering does not count, because it involves the ego not getting its own way and is different from the soul and its suffering. Christ consciousness and the kingdom of heaven's fulfillment produces the people and human beings God, our parents, the world, and we always hoped we would become. Each one who goes through this process will have a purposeful and meaningful life that is part of God, the universe, and all created things. We can use our gifts to share with one another, sharing in the joy of; living life connected and whole, one with God and one another; creating with God and life; and healing all unconsciousness, humanness, and brokenness in all life.

WORKS CITED

Harvey, Andrew. *Son of Man: The Mystical Path to Christ.* New York, NY: Penguin Putnam, 1998.

Hawkins, David. *The Eye of the Eye: From Which Nothing Is Hidden.* W. Sedona, AZ: Veritas Publishing, 2001.

———. *Letting Go.* United States: Hay House, 2012.

———. *Transcending the Levels of Consciousness: The Stairway to Enlightenment.* W. Sedona, AZ: Veritas Publishing, 2006.

The Holy Bible: New King James Version. Thomas Nelson, 1984.

Hunt, Valerie V. *Infinite Mind: Science of the Human Vibrations of Consciousness.* Malibu, California: Malibu Publishing Company, 1996.

Marion, Jim. *Putting On the Mind of Christ: The Inner Work of Christian Spirituality.* Charlottesville, VA: Hampton Roads Publishing Company, 2011.

Masters, Paul Leon. *Master's Degree Curriculum.* 2 vols. Burbank, CA: Printing, 2011.

Paulsen, Norman. *Christ Consciousness: The Emergence of the Pure Self Within.* Buellton, CA: Solar Logos Foundation, 2002.

Proctor, Charlene M. *The Oneness Gospel.* Minneapolis, MN: Two Harbors Press, 2011.

2

Total Integration of Being

A Dissertation Submitted in Fulfillment of the
Requirements for the Degree of Doctor of
Metaphysical Science on Behalf of the Department
of Graduate Studies of the University of Sedona

RAMON LAZARUS
OCTOBER 27, 2015

INTRODUCTION

Total integration of being is the emergence, convergence, and integration of the soul, mind, body, and heart. It is free of ego constraints, configurations, and constructs obtained in the process of indoctrination into unconsciousness, humanness, and brokenness, or what is known psychologically and spiritually as the ego. It is a psychophysical, psychospiritual, parapsychological, and psychological process.

The parable of the sower and the seed artfully describes and depicts the fragmentation of being—the mind, heart, and soul as separate parts intertwined with the ego—as well as the finished product, which is total integration of being. The following verses and their metaphysical interpretations come from the King James Version of the Holy Bible.

> The seed is the word of God. Those by the wayside are the ones who hear; then the devil comes and takes away the word out of their hearts, lest they should believe and be saved. (Luke 8:11–12)

These verses represent a soul troubled and disconnected because of ego. The devil, through negative feelings of unconsciousness, drowns out and doubts the Word of God.

> But the ones on the rock are those who, when they hear, receive the Word with joy; and these have no root, who believe for a while and in time of temptation fall away. (Luke 8:13)

This verse represents a hardened heart that has built up layers of feelings of brokenness that form a barrier around and in the heart, keeping the Word of God from taking root.

> And the ones that fell among thorns are those who, when they have heard, go out and are choked with cares, riches and pleasures of life, and bring no fruit to maturity. (Luke 8:14)

This verse represents a cluttered mind with feelings of humanness that don't allow the Word of God to be nurtured and cultivated.

> But the ones that fell on the good ground are those who, having heard the Word with a noble and good heart, keep it and bear fruit with patience. (Luke 8:15)

This verse represents total integration of being, wherein soul, heart, and mind are free from their ego constraints, configurations, and constructs and merged by Christ consciousness and God's Word into unity and atonement with God.

Verses 16 through 18 further describe the person and soul who have achieved this total integration of being and its impact on one's life and others in the world.

> No one, when he has lit a lamp, covers it with a vessel or puts it under a bed, but sets it on a lamp stand, that those who enter may see the light. (Luke 8:16)

This verse describes the soul shining in the heart, illuminating the mind of itself and all others it comes in contact with.

> For nothing is secret that will not be revealed, nor anything hidden that will not be known and come to light. (Luke 8:17)

This verse describes the process of how God and His living Word work within the individual soul who has obtained total integration of being. The light of the soul reveals a little at a time so it can be made aware and realize knowledge and truth in a context that applies to both the individual soul and others with love from God's presence.

> Therefore take heed how you hear. For whoever has, to
> him more will be given; and whoever does not have, even
> what he seems to have will be taken from him. (Luke 8:18)

This verse represents God's abundance. Those who act upon and live by it will be given more in abundance—whatever that abundance might be, whether wisdom, knowledge, or truth. Total integration of being is the state of being Jesus Christ referred to when He said, "I have come to give them life abundantly." His example of His life represents the most efficient and methodical way to achieve such a state of being.

With this overview and introduction in mind, we will take a closer look at the process and steps included in the total integration of being, or the emergence, convergence, and integration of the soul, heart, and mind in regard to the ego. But first, we will define some terms in regard to the ego and how they relate to not only the ego but also the process of total integration of being.

Unconsciousness, for purposes of this paper, will be defined as denial, forgetfulness, and ignorance and corresponds to the soul and the illusion of imperfection. It covers chakras one through four upon awakening and embodiment and chakra two upon integration.

Brokenness refers to the feelings associated with being broken, which include despair, powerlessness, hopelessness, and unworthiness. This happens as a result of the powers and principalities and causes disintegration of the heart, disincarnation of the soul, and formation of ego. It corresponds to the heart and the illusion of perfection. It covers chakras four through seven upon awakening and embodiment and chakra one upon integration.

Humanness refers to emotions that protect brokenness and overcompensate for powerlessness, including primary emotions of fear and anger as well as blame and unforgiveness. It includes addictions. It corresponds to the mind and the illusion of separation from God. It covers chakras one through seven upon awakening and embodiment and chakra three upon integration.

Wound is a site of damage done to soul, heart, or mind. It can be physical, mental, or emotional or give the illusion of affecting the spirit, or it can be any combination thereof, including all mentioned.

Thinking is the primary defense mechanism of the ego. It acts as a distraction from the wound and self and includes habits and behaviors.

Voice of illusion refers to Lilith's voice as she went through her descent into hell and became unconscious, disincarnated, and disintegrated. It is confronted along with the illusion of illusions upon integration and incarnation.

Illusion of illusions refers to the final or first illusion upon which all other illusions have their basis in error or ego. It's the basis of false self. The unconscious, disincarnate, disintegrated Lilith represents the illusion of illusions.

Lilith was Adam's first wife before Eve. Lilith and Adam were created equally from the earth but were in conflict as far as their relationship was concerned. The conflict resulted in Lilith taking the blame for Adam, who objected to dealing with his feelings of unconsciousness, humanness, and brokenness. Lilith's descent to earth became hell, where she manifested Adam's internal disowned feelings, which became the first negative dysfunctional projection. Lilith became the first broken heart and lost soul and the first soul to awaken after entering time and space. Her journey and story represent the soul's journey to wholeness from creation and to fulfillment and becoming real, a human being, with the help of Jesus Christ and His soul's journey from creation, awakening, embodiment, crucifixion, resurrection, and ascension.

Illusion is something that appears real and desirable to the ego but, in actuality, is opposite of what it appears to be. It is used to mask and cover up a wound and is the primary building block of the ego to establish the illusion of separation from God. It is the perceptual mechanism of the ego experience.

Projection, according to *Dorland's Medical Dictionary*, is an unconscious defense mechanism in which a person attributes to someone else unacknowledged ideas, thoughts, feelings, and impulses that he or she finds undesirable or unacceptable in him- or herself (1362:4).

Spiritual bypass, as defined by Charles Whitfield, MD, in his book *The Power of Humility*, is a bypassing or ignoring of the lower levels to get to the higher levels of consciousness.

REVIEW OF LITERATURE

As we have seen with the parable of the seed, there is a fragmented state of being, and there is a whole state of being, as stated by Jesus Christ speaking from His Christ consciousness. Jesus Christ gives further instructions regarding this topic in Matthew 22:37–39: "You shall love the Lord your God with all your heart, all your mind and all your soul. ... Love your neighbor as yourself" (NKJV). These verses give insight into the fragmented ego and its primary basic function of projection to alleviate its pain and suffering in a dysfunctional way. Matthew 7:3 states, "Why point out the speck in your brother's eye, when you have a board in your own?" Jesus's admonishment to love God with all your heart, mind, and soul reveals that each component of being must be loved, which means being relinquished, cared for, and worked through to be released from the ego. To love your neighbor as yourself means you do not project onto others the negativity and pain you have inside from being fragmented and broken.

Jesus, in Matthew 7:3, says to do your own inner spiritual growth work first before negatively projecting it onto another, and if you do this, then you will be heard and received without conflict. This process of growth and integration is summed up in Matthew 10:39, which states, "He who loses his life for my sake will find it." This translates to "Whoever gives up his ego will find his soul and true purpose." Jesus Christ references the journey of evolution and spiritual growth in Luke 9:23, wherein He says, "You must pick up your cross and follow Me." Here Jesus is describing not only the journey from beginning to end but also what kind of journey it is. It will be difficult, requiring discomfort and involving suffering that is not pleasant. The cross represents the convergence point for the integration of heart, soul, and mind, relinquishing the ego and being liberated from it. Those who live in the shadow of the crucifixion are orientated with their egos and are preoccupied with death. Those who live in the resurrection are orientated with their souls and are preoccupied with life and their purpose. The process of fragmentation to wholeness usually takes years and involves lengthy contemplations and reflections to fully realize its importance and significance to self, others, and God.

The ego has its origin in wounding. Without a wound, there would be no ego. Wounding and ego configuration are done by the principalities and powers of this world, which indoctrinate all souls on earth. Andrew Harvey, a mystic, describes this process in his book *Son of Man*. All souls who are to follow Christ consciousness and follow God's will by integrating and incarnating will "risk persecution, humiliation, and perhaps even death at the hands of those authorities and those 'principalities and powers' that are dedicated to keeping the human race un-divinized and enslaved" (165). Harvey also comments on this further, quoting Jesus from the Gospel of Thomas: "Blessed are they who have been persecuted within themselves. It is they who truly come to know the Father. ... Blessed is the person who has suffered and found life"(108).

Integration to wholeness includes the necessary suffering to go through and be free of the ego, with its feelings of unconsciousness, humanness, and brokenness, which are painful and difficult to experience and process because of their intensity and their lower, dense vibrational energies and frequencies. These energies and frequencies cause pain and misery and are traumatic enough to cause disintegration and fragmentation of mind, heart, and soul to the point of annihilation. It is no small task to take on this kind of undertaking, and it is impossible without God and Christ's help. This process described here is internal, with its origin in spirit, and covers all dimensions and levels of consciousness. It is traumatic because we go through it conscious and awake when it happens, and we have to be willing to process it and face it at the point of breaking and bring awareness and consciousness to the part of ourselves that becomes fragmented and lost. The good news is that we go through it only once. However, the processing of it frightens us and gives us cause for apprehension.

The process of wounding, as described herein, is a modification of a model developed by Charles Whitfield, MD, and outlined in *Codependence*

(27–28). The powers and principalities project their energies onto the whole human being, the child. The human being or child, in a need to stabilize itself, takes in and accepts the projected energies, along with the voice of illusion, which provides a narrative or a story of overcompensation, and the child idealizes those involved. Because this causes the human being to be vulnerable, it causes the true self to be wounded so often that to protect its true nature, it defensively submerges or fragments or splits off itself deep within the unconscious part of its psyche. The child takes in what it is told and stores it in its unconscious and conscious mind. The energies that project into the child create tension, and there is also tension created from the true self to come alive and to evolve. Charles Whitfield, a psychotherapist, in his book *Codependence*, has this to say: "At the same time, the ego attacks the true self thus forcing it to stay submerged keeping self-esteem low. The child's grieving of its losses and traumas are not supported. This resulting "psychopathology" or" lesion" has been called a schizoid compromise, ... and a splitting off of the true self" (28). This results in developmental delays or difficulties; arrested development or failure to thrive; psychological, emotional, mental, and spiritual problems; and a wide array of illnesses. Keeping the true self submerged or fragmented with unsupported negative stimuli and behaviors leads to codependency.

Recovery from such an ordeal requires Christ consciousness and God as well as support from loving people and a shifting of orientation from ego to soul. Our self of infancy before the powers and principalities wound us gets lost and fragmented, and we work hard to recover from and reclaim it. The inner child, as defined by Charles Whitfield in *Healing*, is our "real or higher self" (9). Because of the breaking process, this inner child, or higher self, gets stifled or denied. "When this vital part of each of us is not nurtured and allowed freedom of expression, a false or codependent self or ego emerges" (Whitfield 9). The breaking or fragmentation process is a projection of negative energy onto us and into us; it is a violation of our boundaries. As a result, we, in turn, project onto others in our lives and environments from our egos. When an ego projects, it causes pain and suffering for the object it is projecting onto and into. In *Boundaries*, Whitfield says, "With awareness of your inner life and clear boundaries and limits, you can handle or at times even prevent such a boundary invasion, and thus avoid unnecessary pain and suffering" (8). Whitfield's assessment goes on to include "their pain/confusion or attempts at control or manipulation, maybe theirs, not yours" (8).

It is important to distinguish necessary suffering from unnecessary suffering. Unnecessary suffering is from ego projection, and necessary suffering comes from being liberated from the ego. Danah Zohar, in her book *SQ: Connecting with Our Spiritual Intelligence*, defines *spiritual illness*: "Spiritual illness is a condition of being fragmented, especially from the center of the self. Spiritual health is a condition of center wholeness. Spiritual intelligence, SQ is the means by which we can move from one to the other, the means by which we can heal ourselves" (185). Spiritual illness involves being fragmented and cut off from one's self, others, and God. This inability not to feel is not genetic, inborn, or from karma. It is for the strict purpose of being broken and configured with an ego to experience separateness through the illusion of illusions and the illusion of separation to become a particle in the mind of God. The trauma of spiritual illness is incapacitating. Basic functioning on a day-to-day basis is a challenge. It brings a mix of emotions, feelings, and experiences consisting of, but not limited to, the catatonia of illness to the sublime perfection of God. Sometimes it is difficult to distinguish the two because for true integration, it is necessary to have both experiences simultaneously to differentiate the two and begin dissolving the one into the other. All higher faculties and dimensionality of soul, spirit, heart, mind, and God are employed and used to their highest degree of functioning to unify and unite each fragment, heal it, and reassemble it with all aspects of form, function, and performance. "Spiritual intelligence is the soul's intelligence. It is the intelligence with which we heal ourselves and with which we make ourselves whole" (Zohar 9). A soul with Christ consciousness knows how to be aware and discern every kind of malady known to man as created by the ego. It knows exactly what needs to go where and in which proportion and will recreate a new form better than the old one that was fragmented.

Given the sovereignty of God and Christ consciousness, the work of integration is not easy. Jim Marion, in his book *Putting on the Mind of Christ*, gives insight as to why integration, specifically the dark night of the soul, involves great suffering: "What one must remember is that we are not dealing here with the integration or individuation of the personality. We are dealing here with integration... at the level of the soul" (122).

The dark night also causes psychic suffering because it is transpersonal: "The Christian in the Dark Night, like Jesus on the Cross, is allowed to participate in the redemptive work of the Christ. That is, we take into our psyche, as we move through the transpersonal planes of consciousness, a measure of the world's negativity, and we transmute that negativity back into the basic stuff of the universe,... love" (Marion 123).

The breaking process involves suppression and depression of emotions and fragmented parts of our souls, which complicates the healing process. Jim Marion comments on this:

> Further it is true that these repressed negative parts of the self are sometimes magnetically linked to the energies of other dark negative entities that share the same low vibrations. The dark entities to which these damaged soul parts can be linked include negative thought forms, discarnate human beings who, have not found their way to the light and perhaps even real demons. (98)

This time of the dark night of the soul can go on for years. Jim Marion describes how this inner state can affect one's outer world." Because of all the negativity being transmuted by being released into conscious awareness, all sorts of negative things tend to occur in our outer lives. This is because negative thoughts and negative emotions,(conscious or unconscious), produce, by the laws of manifestation, negative external consequences in a person's life" (102).

People who are unconscious and have this internal process activated by other built-in mechanisms of being and don't tune in and pay attention to what is going on inside themselves internally will be at the mercy of what is going on inside them as well as outside them. If they have internal violence going on inside, on the outside, they may come in contact with violence. In *Transcending*, David Hawkins, MD, PhD, a psychiatrist and well-known author on enlightenment, has this to say about the dark night of the soul: "The ego's basic illusion is that it is God and that without it, death will occur. Thus what is described as the Dark Night of the Soul is actually the Dark Night of the Ego. ... Paradoxically the Dark Night of the Soul is often a sign of significant spiritual progress for it is not really the soul but the ego that is in the dark" (38). The dark night of the soul is a cleansing or purification of all creations of the ego. It is intense and requires suffering because the ego not only believes in its own creations but also thinks they are real. Everything the ego creates is illusion. What the ego believes is illusion. What the ego thinks is illusion. Illusion is a false belief in itself. It is so difficult that one may spend a lifetime, or a good part of it, living and perceiving from this viewpoint of the ego before there is a change in consciousness and awareness. With the passage of time, the ego becomes complacent and resigned to decline in life. As a result of this complacency and resignation, God designed awakening points or intervals into each life and lifetime.

These awakening points or intervals are aligned with the planets in astrology and with the chakras. The chakras all develop with their own amount of development and time. Developmentally, the time intervals are less for younger years, and once mature, with established development in chakras one through seven, they repeat in development every seven years, according to Cyndi Dale, author of *The Complete Book of Chakra Healing*.

Barbara Hand Clow, an author and astrologer, discovered a consistent pattern with her work in astrology. She found that certain aspects in her clients' charts corresponded to certain life events. She found that a Saturn return—which is one cycle around the sun, or twenty-eight years for the planet Saturn—corresponded with a change in a person's life around age twenty-eight, within one to three years of such a time. This change involves a physical challenge as far as increasing consciousness is concerned. Her next aspect was a Uranus opposition, which occurred at about age thirty-eight years, which is half an orbit around the sun for the planet Uranus. This involved some kind of emotional challenge as far as consciousness is concerned. Next, she discovered a return, or full cycle of orbit, for the planet Chiron, whose time span is about fifty to fifty-one years and corresponds to a challenge in a change of consciousness itself. These awakening points or intervals are designed to prompt the soul to awaken and become conscious and aware of itself—to get busy or, as Jesus Christ said, "be about My Father's business." It is important to note that once the configuration of an ego has been established and accepted—and all are—metaphysical and psychospiritual energy flow through the perfect system of creation to the individual, who is altered and changed. Certain faculties and functions cease to give the illusion of being separate from creation to have that experience and later, if chosen, become enlightened.

Shakuntala Modi, MD, a psychiatrist and the author of *Remarkable Healings*, has found past lives play an important role in the problems of her patients' conflicts in their lives. According to her patients' reports, "...the subconscious mind, which is in fact the soul, not only has the knowledge of the source of their emotional, mental, and physical difficulties and conflicts, but also provide solutions for the problems and even healing" (183). Dr. Modi has also found that under hypnosis, her patients "...claim that their souls are fragmented due to some emotional, mental, or physical trauma. They often report their souls are not complete or whole and use terms such as broken, divided, split, fractured, or fragmented, to indicate that parts or pieces of their souls are missing" (368). Dr. Modi's practice deals with retrieving patients' lost or fragmented soul parts, bringing light to the deception or ego that caused them, and restoring the fragmented parts back to her clients, resolving and processing the trauma and then cleansing the persons to remove any dark or negative energy or influence, restoring the persons back to their purpose.

Sal Rachele, the author of *Soul Integration*, has this to say about reclaiming lost soul fragments: "The key to soul integration is to reclaim your lost soul fragments. That means becoming aware of all the traumatic experiences you have ever had in this lifetime or in past lifetimes" (195). With Christ consciousness, this is almost automatic, depending on the stamina and willingness of the individual involved. The wisdom of the psyche discerns with the soul and heart which experiences can be handled and which ones need to be released more gradually. Rachele has found in his work that forgiveness and release work are the best ways to reclaim lost soul fragments. "With emotional clearing you need to fully feel, experience and express your feelings, while at the same time becoming detached from them. You must view them from a higher perspective. Forgiveness is similar in that you must be present to all the feelings within before you can truly forgive" (196). Rachele also uses guided meditation and positive affirmations to claim protection and do the work of reclaiming the soul fragments and dealing with negative energies and entities. Doing integration work involves dealing with negative feelings. They can only be dealt with by having awareness and discernment to determine what is true from what is false.

In *Letting Go*, David Hawkins, MD, gives a general characterization of the average person who is resigned to growth: "We carry around with us a huge reservoir of accumulated negative feelings, attitudes, and beliefs. The accumulated pressure makes us miserable and is the basis of many of our illnesses and problems. We are resigned to it and explain it away as the human condition" (9). The human condition is marked by the collective predominance of the ego because of fear, anger, and ignorance and an inability to do anything about it. Hawkins states in his book *Letting Go*, "It is the accumulated pressure of feelings that cause thoughts. One feeling, for instance, can create literally thousands of thoughts over a period of time" (9).

Ego thinks; the soul feels. The ego thinks thoughts to distract itself from the feelings inside it. The soul feels and is interested in being so it can use awareness and discern what it is feeling. Hawkins's observation of feelings causing thoughts is in accord with scientific research. The Gray-La Violette scientific theory integrates psychology and neurophysiology. "Their research demonstrated that feeling tones organize thoughts and memory" (Hawkins 10). The accumulated accumulation of feelings is what causes stress in the ego. These feelings play out in the outer or external and, because of blame, are associated with projection. The ego thinks all its problems are outside itself, so that is where the ego thinks the problem is. Hawkins's approach to dealing with feelings, as given in *Letting Go*, is revealing and insightful: "Letting Go involves being aware of a feeling, letting it come up, staying with it, and letting it run its course without wanting to make it different or do anything about it" (19–20). Hawkins also adds not to judge and to allow oneself to have feelings about the negative feelings. There will also be feelings about having feelings. In this way, by allowing feelings to come up and to be processed out, the destruction of the ego and its vicious cycle of sin, death, and karma begins. This process decompresses the ego and dissipates the energy in it to release, and at the same time, with awareness and discernment, it allows contextualization and deep meaning to be given to and gleaned from not only the feelings themselves but also the process of processing them and how they relate to the integration process overall. By continually doing this little by little, spiritual growth work will eventually go through and process all feelings that are compressed and backlogged in the psyche. The process can be slow at times and fast at others, depending upon the nature and energy of the feelings involved; whether or not there are complications connected with them, such as a repressed emotion, an entity, a demon, or a spirit; and whether or not a feeling is entangled. This process is how God makes up for lost time and is a period of tremendous learning and insight.

To recap, using awareness and discernment along with God's guidance, intuition, and discernment allows a feeling to come up. Feel it if necessary, without judgement, and allow it to be. Determine if it is yours or someone else's. If it is someone else's, choose forgiveness; include God, yourself, your parents, and the world; and surrender it to God. If the feeling is yours, allow the feeling to come up; be with it the best you can without judgment; choose forgiveness of God, yourself, your parents, and the world; and surrender it to God. This appropriate handling of feelings honors creation, God, others, the world, and all sentient beings in the universe. This method or process is a more comprehensive and thorough way of taking responsibility for one's unfinished business than psychotherapy. Hawkins puts it this way: "The objective of psychotherapy is to replace unsatisfactory mental programs with more satisfactory ones. In contrast, the object of letting go is the elimination of limiting mental and emotional programs"(233). The goal of psychotherapy is management of conditions, wherein letting go is freedom from what is being managed.

Daniel Goleman, in his book *Emotional Intelligence*, shares his insights on emotions that help with mitigating feelings: "When some feature of an event seems similar to an emotionally charged memory from the past, the emotional mind responds by triggering the feelings that went with that remembered event" (295). Emotions are the protectors of our feelings. In ego dysfunction, they project onto circumstances and others. When used with Christ consciousness and awareness, they determine which associations are coordinated to be processed as far as feelings and emotions are concerned. This also lines up with what Hawkins has to say about feelings: many feelings cause many thoughts in a high proportion.

Aminah Raheem, PhD, is the originator of transpersonal integration, a holistic, psychospiritual approach that works through the body's chakra and meridian energy systems and the psyche to include the soul. She describes spiritual emergence: "The person who experiences a spiritual emergence, or crisis that can look like a psychotic episode may seek a transpersonal therapist who is familiar with spiritual developments" (189). Metaphysicians can offer insight, understanding, comfort, and healing in this area. Whether the spiritual emergence is a psychosis or looks like one, we can be of enormous benefit to someone going through this kind of ordeal.

Psychosis, as explained and defined by Shakuntala Modi, MD, occurs when the repression mechanism of the subconscious gets released and too much information gets out too fast, overwhelming persons to the point where they cannot function. It is possible to have a spiritual emergence and have psychosis at the same time. If this is the case, it is possible to cotreat a patient as long as the psychosis is stabilized by some method, usually medication, so the patient can begin to sort out and work through his or her unresolved issues and feelings and not be overwhelmed by them to the point of not being able to function. Spiritual emergence can also cause a nonfunctioning state. It is not uncommon for psychosis and spiritual emergence to be experienced at the same time. This often is the case when one is broken.

The configuring of the ego to disintegration, fragmentation, and annihilation of the soul simultaneously corresponds to the divine and the process of enlightenment. In the split second of being broken, when the ego forms and the divine is revealed, both heaven and hell are experienced at the same time. Because the ego is programmed to project outwardly and the voice of illusion has already blamed God for its pain, God is feared, and heartbreak settles in. Upon the soul's awakening and the establishment of Christ consciousness, this process is reversed, and God is experienced as loving and supportive, leaving the work of integration of ego into soul to the free will of the individual when the time is right. Hawkins comments in his book *The Eye of the I* on fearing God: "Another reason the ego is tenacious is its fear of God. This fear is aided and abetted by the prevalent misinformation about the nature of God and on whom, in this process of personification, all kinds of anthropomorphic defects are projecting, which distort man's imagination about the nature of deity itself" (129).

A psychotic break is a tearing of the veil that separates ego from soul and is part of the process of integration and incarnation. When Jesus Christ died on the cross, the veil was torn, and the temple—the ego, comprised of feelings of unconsciousness, humanness, and brokenness—was destroyed. The internal pressure of the ego trying to keep itself in tact along with the soul's determination to emerge created a supernatural force that created the destruction so something new could be born. Since God is everywhere and Christ is the first begotten of light, darkness is not complete without the light. Since Christ consciousness begins at creation but is eclipsed by ego shadow and darkness, during breaking, it shines again. At the point of breaking, everything that happens, including fragmentation, is kept track of and accounted for in the exact way in which everything is broken and disassembled. Because of breaking, we are vulnerable not only to what we gave in to in order to believe the ego to begin with but also to all other energies associated with it. The recovery process is long and deliberate so that we learn what we need to be whole and live our life's purpose.

Carl Jung, a great twentieth-century psychologist, "suffered something like a schizophrenic breakdown that troubled him for seven years" (Zohar 109). Artists and creative people alike have a tendency toward psychiatric illness, which is associated with a form of suffering. As we have studied, spiritual emergence and illness can come about and happen to anyone at any time, and metaphysicians need to be ready to assist those who find themselves in the process of either or both.

The ego-based closed system bypasses the etheric brain, which is the spiritual brain activated by kundalini energy. This is Hawkins's model of spiritual bypass, as given in *Discovery*: "In deprogramming the experiencer from the evolutionary development of the ego with its multifunction complexity, it can be seen why spiritual evolution takes time plus effort, awareness, and high motivation" (113). Hawkins adds that the kundalini rises through the chakras and transforms, changing the physiology and dynamics of the brain, including hemispheric dominance. Consequently, there is a shift in brain hormones and neurotransmitters from ego-based left-brain stress hormones to right-brain spiritual, positive, peace-based hormones or endorphins (114). It is the difference between ego (disease) and spirit (health). This bypassing of the etheric brain is a psychophysical and psychospiritual spiritual bypass. As can be seen from Hawkins's model of spiritual bypass, it is a phenomenon that transcends the physical and psychological aspects of beingness. This aspect is an unconscious spiritual bypass, a disconnect from the ethereal brain. A conscious spiritual bypass involves choosing to avoid growth. It is an attempt to ignore or deny the lower level of consciousness to get to the higher level of consciousness as defined by Charles Whitfield. In *The Power*, Whitfield adds that this is the case from "…being prematurely born again to having a spiritual awakening and focusing only on the 'light' or focusing on psychic ability as a major part of our identity" (45). Consequences of a spiritual bypass are numerous dysfunctions, "including active codependence or conflict: denial of the richness of our inner life, …to control oneself or others" (45).

Jeff Foster, in his book *The Deepest Acceptance*, echoes the same insights as Whitfield. He states his definition of a spiritual bypass: "The phenomenon of using spiritual concepts to deny unacceptable human emotions and feelings has often been called spiritual bypassing" (126). The ego bypasses spirit both consciously and unconsciously. It is a multilayered approach rooted in illusion's manipulation of free will and choice, as if there isn't one. It offers something in the place of choice, trying to see it as the truth, using the illusion of free will. True free will is discovered after soul awakening when working through unresolved issues and unresolved feelings with both Christ consciousness and the ego present at the same time. A spiritual bypass only allows for the ego to be present, and the soul or spirit is made into an illusion, a mere memory of knowing about God but not having experienced God.

The psychopathology of the ego is where the ego envies the soul, both its etiology and composition and its God. The ego, because of its envy, likes to create masks or illusions to try to compete with the soul. These masks are based on errors and half truths in an attempt by the ego to guess about the soul, using incomplete data regarding what it thinks it knows about the soul. The ego draws a conclusion based upon its guess and thinking to fool itself into believing its true basis upon its own illusion-based etiology. It does this to avoid itself and its contents, which are painful. When this decision to avoid itself is made, it is an unconscious mechanism, a default setting to experience elation at not having to face itself, creating a bypass and mistakenly thinking it is God or the Holy Spirit. This psychopathology of the ego takes place in most churches every weekend.

With the illusion of being, when confronted with truth, the ego will have a split-second delay from spiritually bypassing but choose, because of its default setting, illusion. It chooses illusion not by choice but by its programming and habit. When spiritually bypassing, the ego will create an illusion complete with a narrative of an explanation that brings it comfort and maintains its illusory nature. The ego tells itself what it wants to hear, which correlates to the voice of illusion and its default setting of separation from God and nature, an error to justify its existence to itself and keep the illusion of being intact. Spiritual bypassing is the illusion of growth. Projection is the avoidance of growth, and blame involves refusing to take responsibility for growth.

Once the chakras are cleared—and, in the case of Mary Magdalene, seven demons representing the seven cardinal sins—the soul is established as the point of reference or being. As it lives, moves, and has its beingness, it begins the process of consciousness and individuation toward becoming one with God. *The Gospel of Mary Magdalene* by Jean-Yves Leloup relays a conversation Mary Magdalene had with Jesus regarding a vision she saw of His resurrected body. She asked Jesus through which medium or state of being she saw Him. She asked whether it was through the soul or through the spirit. "Jesus replied back to her, it was neither but something called the *nous* which is between the two" (117). Leloup describes the *nous* as the intermediary between soul and spirit, consisting of mind but also having a component of spirit. Leloup describes it as the link through which phenomena and animation of both animate and inanimate phenomena or God occur. This is important because it allows for a communication to take place between God and man that is an actual experience of past, present, or future events as seen by the mind of God and experienced in the created as God. It is a conscious, aware phenomenon and part of integration of soul, body (heart), and mind under the direction of Christ consciousness.

In *The Gospel of Thomas* by Jean-Yves Leloup, the disciple Thomas quotes Jesus Christ on integration: "When you make the two into one, when you make the inner like the outer and the high like the low; when you make male and female into a single one, so that male is not male and the female is not female; when you have eyes in your eyes, a hand in your hand, a foot in your foot and an icon in your icon, then you will enter the kingdom of heaven" (19). The concept of making the two into one refers to the heart and soul integrating as one flesh and spirit. The concept of making the inner like the outer refers to the unity of integrated experience, in which the inner world and outer world are one. The concept of making the high like the low refers to the ascent in consciousness to the upper room merging heaven and earth. "[Making] male and female into a single one, so that the male is not male and the female is not female" is a reference to the integration of opposites reconciled and whole, as represented by the sacred androgyne, as manifested as an angel of light directly created from God's presence. Having "eyes in your eyes" means the eyes of the heart and soul see things as God sees them, and the "hand in your hand and the foot in your foot" refers to the occupation of the body by the soul and the spirit, which completely fill the body from head to toe and through the arms to the hands. When all these things are merged and integrated, as well as others not mentioned, then there is total integration of being, through which one enters the kingdom while on earth with soul, heart, and mind one with each other and God.

DISCUSSION

Being broken causes fear and anger and begins the constructs of a fear-based God and judgment from that God. Thinking begins based upon the premise "God allowed it to happen, so I must have done something to deserve it." Fear of judgment and fear of God are created and eventually lead to all other fears. This continues and spirals through our DNA to create the narrative for all the perceptions we would have if it weren't for Christ and Christ consciousness. Thinking becomes a defense mechanism to direct focus away from the brokenness to other thoughts that seek to find comfort in whatever will work to alleviate the pain and suffering created by brokenness. This focus away from one's self in brokenness leads to searching outside oneself in the world. Being broken creates the illusion of isolation and separation from God. Thinking continues and says, "What kind of God would allow this to happen to me?" Since brokenness creates fear and fear is the predominant thought, then a God of fear is created to compete with the real God and create doubt, because thinking is based upon a self that's broken, isolated, alone, and fearful. One believes God allowed this to happen, so blame is created, and God gets blamed for the brokenness. Pride, in its own creation, leads to contempt, rebellion, and disobedience. Anger against God is created, and subsequent rebellion against God forms. Because of how unpleasant the negative feelings are and how uncomfortable the tension they create is, thinking tries to displace them or project them onto God and others. Anger toward God turns to resentment, creating pride. Ego forms with an *either-or* mentality, a duality. Thinking becomes the priority of ego. Thinking continues because God is God, and He allowed it to happen, so it must be true. This thinking convinces us, through this logic, to accept thinking versus feeling. Ego defense mechanisms are created with brokenness; therefore, feelings support ego thinking. Out of ego, competitive thinking arises—temptations that compete with feeling to avoid the experience of brokenness. Because Christ comes at the point of breaking, the ego competes with thinking against feeling. Thinking that God is responsible for our brokenness favors a false God and a secular existence without God. One says, "God didn't help me in my time of need, so why should I help Him?" Feeling leads to Christ and God. Thinking leads to Satan.

Denial forms as a last gasp of the soul in rejecting brokenness and forms the limen between the conscious and subconscious minds. Because the person starts to believe his or her own thinking from brokenness, denial of the truth is reinforced and fortified. Denial of the truth is favored over the truth because illusion has been accepted as reality, and that reality is preferred over the discomfort of brokenness. Pride further develops because the thinking initiated by the voice of illusion creates thinking that rationalizes incorrectly that God allowed something negative to happen to a person; therefore, he or she must have done something to deserve it. Furthermore, one might say, "God is angry at me. Since God knows all, if He is angry at me, then God is against me for some reason." Thinking further rationalizes with something like the following:

> Why has this happened to me? I haven't done anything wrong. I trusted God. God doesn't care about me. I am on my own. I can't depend on God, so I don't trust God. This can't be happening to me. God is everything. I believe in a God who wouldn't do that to me. So God, as I formerly knew Him, can't be trusted. He isn't real and is false. I believe in a different God. My God is better than the old God I used to know, and this God wouldn't allow anything bad to happen to me. This God is all-powerful in control, will not bow down to the old God, and doesn't deal with the things of the old God. I will share this new God with others and tell others how great He is and how He cares for me and never allows anything bad to happen to me. He is the center of the universe and of my being.

This new God will be bigger and greater than the old God, and I will worship Him. The old God rejected me, so I will reject others who do not worship my God. Those who worship the old God I formerly knew can't be trusted, because the old God can't be trusted. This new God is perfect and will never treat me badly, and if I follow Him and keep Him happy, I will never be punished again. If I am good enough, He will give me all that I want, and I will be happy if I do not anger Him or give Him reason to reject me. So I will become perfect like Him, the way I created Him. I will no longer experience negativity or be imperfect. This is a win-win between me and God and is our new covenant, which shall not be broken. To break it would mean eternity in hell and suffering with no hope, with Satan in control of my life. The voice of illusion told Adam and Eve they were naked in the Garden of Eden.

This is just a sampling of ego configuration and programming associated with being broken.

All souls are broken, lose their ability to be, and are fitted with an ego during infancy. It happens at the time when parents choose to vaccinate their babies. This physical indoctrination to the planet with immunization to overwhelm the child mentally and physically has a component that is emotionally and spiritually overwhelming as well. The powers, principalities, and dark rulers of the world, allowed by God to run it, are both the initiation and the process of being introduced to the world and being configured with an ego after the soul becomes broken. It is a horrendous and traumatic experience to go through and recover from things you're not allowed to be made aware of and process until later in life. This is the basis for most, if not all, disease, physical, emotional, and spiritual. The powers and principalities are both energy and spirit of a lower, dense quality and nature. When they swarm and attack to break a heart and soul, these energies are harsh and cause chaos, fragmentation, disintegration, and disincarnation, establishing wounds on any or all levels of mind and disrupting being. This is done until all negative feelings and emotions are experienced, but not processed, to contrast divinity and offer an alternative to God as an attractive choice, with no apparent consequences for that choice. If a soul knew ahead of time what the consequences of that choice would be in all likelihood, it would not choose it. This plausible deniability has a purpose and allows souls, if they make a choice they regret, to have an easier time in forgiving themselves, because they were unconscious and programmed and configured in such a way that they simply did not know the truth; it was kept from them in such a way that they had the experience of choice, with a whole spectrum of feelings and emotions that went along with that choice.

Souls are also broken to gain access to previous life experiences covering all lifetimes. They are broken to bring up past trauma to begin the process of scrutinizing and understanding why the trauma happened, how best to deal with it, what can be done to make amends and prevent it from happening again, and how to heal and be redeemed. This is also done to skew a soul to the side of ego to accept it. Much of a lifetime is spent in ego, as it is also the fuel of the fire for conscious awareness, transformation, wisdom, and insight in spiritual growth. If there was no ego, there would be no experience of enlightenment.

The nature of illusions is to confuse and exhaust the conscious mind so it gives up easily in trying to understand itself, which limits its experience to illusion. God uses illusion to bring comfort or release pain. Carrying out unconscious spiritual intentions in physical actions is evil and based in illusion and the ego. Understanding evil, feeling without discernment, is what brokenness is based upon. Humanness is the internal erection of the ego, including behavior. Unconsciousness is the layer of thinking and feeling that keeps brokenness and humanness from being discovered and keeps one unconscious in illusion. The unchecked ego, indulging itself without consciousness or awareness, is sin, and sinning for the sake of sinning is evil. The key is discerning a feeling, acknowledging it with awareness, and then making a decision with free will as to what to do about it. Being completely present with feelings and awareness allows for a pause in the decision-making process to evaluate feelings. Feelings are, in fact, not evil, but what you do with them potentially is. Forgiveness is the only way out of them if they are dark and difficult, even if it doesn't feel that way. With revenge, you risk becoming trapped in the offender's hell inside, lost and in pain. People who commit inhumane crimes have lost the ability to discern feelings and have lost touch with reality. Their pain, based in illusion, has become real for them and has become their perception or primary reality. When this happens, persons no longer have free will to choose, let alone choose wisely, and thus, it is difficult, if not impossible, to hold them accountable, because they are not aware of what they are doing. To understand this completely is to be in their shoes and experience what they went through when the act was committed. Allowing yourself to have dark and difficult feelings is not evil or sinful if you have awareness and discernment to responsibly navigate them and choose forgiveness. Choosing forgiveness includes forgiving God, your parents, yourself, and the world, which covers everyone and everything that is a potential trespasser.

Jesus Christ went beyond sin into unconsciousness, humanness, and brokenness on the cross. The unholy trinity of unconsciousness, humanness, and brokenness is located in chakras one, two, and three. Humanness is in the third chakra and represents limbo. Unconsciousness is in the second chakra and represents purgatory. Brokenness is in the first chakra and represents hell. Unconsciousness corresponds to the soul, humanness to the mind, and brokenness to the heart. Psychospiritual emotional pain experienced with the ego has three components. The first is being broken, which corresponds to the first chakra and is a dynamic of the interphase of the soul and heart. The second is not being able to be who you are, which corresponds to the second chakra and the soul. The third is the ego's not getting its own way, which corresponds to the third chakra and is related to the mind. Together unconsciousness, humanness, and brokenness make up the ego, and it competes with the holy Trinity of Father, Son, and Holy Spirit.

Jesus's falling down three times while carrying His cross symbolized these three aspects of the ego that He was entering on His journey. As His soul began its descent, He came into contact with sin first, then humanness, then unconsciousness, and then brokenness before His soul merged with His heart. He had to go through everything that all of humanity had already been through or would go through, including everybody ever created or to be created. He brought awareness and discernment to every level of human experience while maintaining Himself and who He really is. He encountered and felt every feeling there is, until He uttered from the cross, "Father, why have You forsaken Me?" These words were spoken by Lilith as she was being broken and have been spoken by every broken heart and lost soul since. Jesus Christ's integration, incarnation, and spiritual work, including the work He did on the cross, were examples for us regarding how, when our time comes, to integrate and incarnate so we don't get stuck and become evil.

The ego's purpose is to defend and protect brokenness or the wound. To accept the wound is difficult to endure to its fruition of growth. The ego is constantly avoiding discovery of brokenness, because it does not like pain of any kind. At the same time, the ego seeks to project itself to alleviate itself of the pain it is carrying and protecting. During formation of the wound or brokenness, the ego perceives the fragmentation process of the heart, and if severe enough, it will include fragmentation of the soul and tell itself a story that is only half true. The story or perception is not seen through the soul's eyes of truth but, rather, is based in brokenness and, in particular, the fragmentation process. The perception then becomes the lens through which the ego views while constantly comparing its burden of brokenness to itself and others in the hope of finding a cure. This sets in place the error of perception that is based in brokenness. The ego desperately seeks wholeness, searching everywhere but where it needs to go: in and through the brokenness and the wound. The journey into wholeness begins with awakening the soul and then journeying through the ego to the heart. After the awakening and a sufficient amount of time for learning and remembering have taken place, the soul will enter the heart to face its contents and eventually become whole. When the soul encounters the wounded brokenness, it will also have to face the ego.

The layers of the ego have two main pillars, to which all else is fastened: fear and anger. Healing is not linear; it is eternal, with linkages to time and space that can speed up or slow down the process. Healing may come in any order—top to bottom, bottom to top, side to side—but always in reverse order of how the ego was formed and always inside out. The ego uses the emotions of fear and anger to barricade and protect brokenness or the wound. These two emotions the soul must face to get to and free the defense mechanisms of the ego; then the underlying unresolved feelings; and, finally, the illusion of the perception of brokenness, upon which all is built.

Any illusion, perception, or brokenness will not stand in the face of pure awareness or Christ consciousness. The fear to be faced is fear itself, and it cannot and will not be controlled in any way by anything. When the soul endures fear, it is like wind blowing in your face. The fear encounters the soul but cannot touch it and goes around it and not through it. The soul, on the other hand, goes through the fear, experiencing it fully and completely to know it fully. All its ways are exposed for what they are: not true. Anger will also be encountered. Anger is the insane rage of a broken heart or brokenness. The anger is the accumulation of all past lives and the current lifetime, experienced all at once. You must experience it fully to realize the pain is not real but based upon brokenness. The soul fully experiences and realizes the ego for what it is: a primitive coping mechanism for brokenness-based reality that has yet to experience wholeness from God, which releases the soul from brokenness. Once fear and anger are experienced fully, then the ego starts to implode. Defense mechanisms buckle and collapse, and underlying unresolved feelings are exposed. Unresolved issues begin to unravel, and the light and love of truth face the illusion at the bottom of it all, revealing all of it to be incomplete without the light and love of God. With God's light and love, the truth is realized, and the psyche is flooded with Christ's light, or Christ consciousness. The light eclipses the darkness of the wounds, brokenness, and the ego to reveal wisdom, insight, and intuition not previously experienced, which is possible only through the process of growth and healing. Once this process starts, it uses free will to continue to choose love and truth over fear and judgment. Fear and judgment are part of the default setting of brokenness and the ego. Growth is slow at best, if present at all. Growth through love and truth is exponential in leaps and bounds and makes up for lost time. The soul endures the process of going through brokenness into wholeness with the help of Christ's light, or Christ consciousness, which is the new default setting in love and truth. Once the epiphany has taken place, any strongholds present will be next in line to enter the light of truth to be converted from fear to love. This is part of personal psychospiritual growth work, which is necessary to maintain the new connection to God through Christ consciousness. Grief work may be necessary as well, along with simply maintaining connection to God and anything that tries to come in between the soul, God, and the heart.

When the light of Christ comes in and eclipses the wound, brokenness, and the ego, it obliterates the illusion and error as well as the ego so that only light remains.

Any part of this process may be experienced at any time and in any order, depending upon God's will and individual configuration. After all the growth work is done, daily maintenance remains, with a new default setting of peace, love, joy, and eternal bliss. What was contained in the shadow will be revealed with the light and make sense to the body (heart), mind, and soul with the complete story of how things were when the wound was created and the ego was formed; where it is in relation to the present moment; and what is needed to be reconciled, whole, and complete. Most importantly, it answers the question of "Why?" and others, fulfilling the soul's, mind's, and body's (heart's) natural curiosity and interest in such things, so the individual can learn, evolve, let go, and be at peace. The only emotion that needs to be processed is hatred, which is the active form of fear-based anger in and from the ego. All others are derivatives of anger and fear devised by the ego.

Tuning into the heart and heart-related activity leads to the development of intuition in the most profound sense from the illumined soul. The development of this faculty leads to balance of heart, mind, and soul. Thinking is counterintuitive and keeps one searching always outward for answers, whereas intuition comes through your heart from your soul, divinely directed to help you navigate and live life. For a person to understand how to function in its environment, it breaks down its environmental stimuli through the five senses and the faculties of intellect, logic, and reason. Left-brain-independent individuals break down data and information into categories and then compartmentalizes the information into files that are separate from one another and stored to be used in isolation from one another in an operating system based upon ego to learn and grow. The *either-or* paradigm or question, when applied to learning, doesn't allow for the opposite or competing theory or construct in consideration; therefore, it does not allow a *both-and* outcome. Christ consciousness connects heart, mind, and soul in design with God and the divine. It removes thinking and replaces it with intuition in a network that connects all three. Instead of left-brain-independent constructs running themselves in dysfunctional ways at best, Christ consciousness removes the boundaries separating all the files in oneself. When the process starts, the soul awakens and becomes aware of itself and begins to learn and grow as much as it can, until it eventually encounters the heart. The left brain and intellect become subordinate to the right brain and mind. Balance becomes primary, based upon the soul's connection to God and the heart's capacity to learn. When this happens, a person doesn't think anymore. Thoughts arrive from God, and persons become aware of where they come from. Life opens up, and Christ consciousness is the source of being, instead of left-brain doing. This is the kingdom of God as it was intended to be lived by human beings while they're alive in bodies on earth. This process connects people to their divine purpose and lets them know that God is in control and that there is a plan for their lives.

Feelings are neither right nor wrong; they simply are. They need attention, focus, and awareness to be successfully navigated. *Awareness* is simply another way of saying *soul*. Becoming aware, or embodying your soul, is a joyous time, though not without its challenges. Navigating feelings alone from the heart is next to impossible and difficult at best. In the midst of a feeling, shift focus to your soul, or awareness. If you're only in your heart, pray to become aware of the process of becoming a human being and how to navigate difficult feelings. When a feeling comes up, choose God, and ask Him to keep you secure in your perspective of successfully navigating through the feeling. Sometimes the feeling is so strong or intense that people can't remain in the heart, because of the pain, nature, and quality of the feeling, but they can find refuge with God in their soul. Sometimes Jesus Christ Himself is needed to release difficult feelings. With awareness of your soul present, let the feeling become temporarily part of your consciousness instead of who you are. This helps because it allows the feeling and its pain to be experienced without being judged or rejected, which is the case when it's experienced from the heart only. It is important to choose forgiveness every step of the way so as not to add to the entanglement of the feeling that is seeking acknowledgment and release. Faith—simply believing in God and His peace—will quickly release a person from a tapestry of feelings, especially if it is overwhelming and entangled. If it is important, it will come up again, or maybe the purpose of it is to maintain clarity during and after it processes. Staying with the feeling for as long as you can helps you to more fully experience it, and release is cleaner. When forgiving, forgive God, yourself, your parents, and the world; say no to revenge; and leave justice to God, who keeps track of everything that happens in heaven and on earth. By surrendering justice to God, you free yourself from suffering needlessly. You would suffer if you were to try to hold on to hurt or seek to hold someone accountable for something he or she did. Let go, and let God.

Feelings are important, but they are not everything. They are helpful and can lead to truth as well as other things, but they are not as important as well-being. We are, after all, human beings, not human feelings, although feeling is a component of being a human being.

Both introverts and extroverts need to achieve balance. That means for optimal integration, introverts need to be extroverted, and extroverts need to be introverted. Feelings arise all the time about different things. Some get more attention than others, but they all need to be addressed. The ones that get more attention are in response to something that is important to us. Oftentimes, feelings are a source of argument or fighting. A lot of the time, arguments and fights go unresolved, with the participants feeling displaced. Choosing how to respond or not respond can lead to a more fruitful outcome for all involved. We should let our feelings have their say without retaliating with them. Oftentimes, letting our feelings play out internally will lead to a more satisfying conclusion than fighting with someone else with them. Honoring our feelings this way will allow God to hear our hearts and souls regarding whatever we feel so strongly about and will honor the dimensionality of our hearts and souls to resolve conflict through nonviolent, peaceful means. We should be listening to our feelings and giving them to God, not stuffing our feelings, letting them play in perfection. If we were to verbalize our feelings every time, they would lead to senseless fighting, abuse, and suffering. Oftentimes, the desired outcome we would like to see come about will come about if we choose not to fight about it and, at the same time, honor our feelings and listen to them, knowing God hears them loud and clear, sometimes without a word being verbally spoken. There are different types of feelings internally. There are the feelings of ego not getting its own way; there are feelings of unconsciousness, humanness, and brokenness, which the ego avoids; and there are divine feelings, which the ego tries to take credit for.

Intelligence shifts from worldly, ego-based, secular data and information to divine intelligence that is all-inclusive and pertains not only to what is external but also, more importantly, to what is internal and unifying. Emotional intelligence shifts from surviving (ego) to interpreting emotions of others as well as identifying emotions and feelings as something positive instead of negative. Spiritual intelligence, a component of Christ consciousness, contextualizes and transforms experiences and searches for the deepest, most meaningful explanations of phenomena and experiences. The mind, heart, and soul, under the new configuration of consciousness and awareness, use the faculties of the ego, which are intellect, logic, and reason, to convince the ego and others to go all the way to God and show the ego that following its own desires will lead to its eventual undoing and demise. The ego is taught through consciousness to yield through its own experience, hand over control to the soul, and either be an observer or go into the light.

Soul is awareness, heart is intuition, mind is God, and intelligence is Christ consciousness. If knowing is based upon believing without experience, then an illusion is being created by the ego. From God come Christ and light. From Christ comes awareness. From awareness comes discernment. From discernment comes realization. From realization comes experience. From experience comes knowing. From knowing comes believing. From believing comes faith. From faith comes relationship. From relationship comes integration. From integration comes oneness. From oneness comes God.

The ego, consisting of the feelings of unconsciousness, humanness, and brokenness, blocks or obscures the light of God's presence within. The light of God's presence still shines, but one experiences whatever the light shines on in the darkness within. As with a film strip and movie projector, images are projected internally onto the screen of the subconscious mind. Simultaneously, they are also projected into the outer environment. The pictures and narrative are directed and edited to make sense to the ego, which is trying to learn and interpret itself through its own limiting system. The ego, because of its compartmental tendencies, divides and categorizes data and information into subdivisions, using its determining mechanism of thinking consisting of *either-or* discrimination. This process looks only at data and information the ego deems relevant, and anything that doesn't fit or comply with it is arbitrarily discarded with prejudice.

This is the operating mode of the ego, which functions in a beta brain-wave state—like the autonomic sympathetic nervous system when stimulated to fight, flight, or freeze—and because the subconscious has not yet become conscious of itself, it is subject to the influence and programming of ego. Karma is part of the ego configuration of a given lifetime and must be faced and accounted for.

Charlene Proctor, in her book *The Oneness Gospel*, describes a Vedic theory of healing called samskara, which refers to dysfunctional patterns or imprints left on the energy fields of an individual.

Samskaras are deep impressions or seed habits that are at the root of all karma acquired in previous lifetimes or from the present. The word *samskara* is Sanskrit and refers to the impressions of past actions contained in the nervous system, or the subtle energy body. They are a driving force behind karma. *Shuddhi* means "cleansing." Samskara shuddi, then, is a process that deeply cleanses a person of fears, conflicts, or limitations carried over from earlier experiences from the current lifetime or others. It corrects negative life patterns, clears deep pain, and invites levels of forgiveness.

In the process of samskara shuddi, a person is put into a deeply relaxed state called *yoga nidra*, neither wakefulness nor sleep, but a state of conscious deep sleep. This is said to be a mystical state wherein a person comes in touch with the divine spirit within. The body and mind are comfortable and tranquil, and the brain is in a state of nonarousal. Brain waves are well beyond the alpha and theta states. They are in delta, the brain-wave state of dreamless sleep. In a deep state of conscious stillness, one remains awake while focusing the mind. Emotions, sensations, thoughts, and images are allowed to arise and flow, and can lead a person to supreme insight and personal transformation. By witnessing the samskaras in the state of yoga nidra, a person slowly empties the contents of the mind. It is an exercise in nonattachment, in which no attention is given to the physical body or the breath. We neutrally observe our thoughts as they arise. It is a total and complete submersion inward, in which a person can objectively see old behavior or incidents and be aware of them. In this process, the samskaras' intensity and impact are softened, and people can transcend them by shedding their attachment to thoughts or emotional charges. They do not control a person's mental or emotional processes any longer and have no effect on his or her present-day reality; hence, a healing is experienced (Proctor 194–95).

What Proctor offers here is an effective, thorough cleansing and healing release for emptying the mind, heart, and soul. It also works with the integrated process. Simultaneously, soul, heart, and mind all get worked on and processed together. The order is subject to how they were disassembled in regard to ego dysfunction. In truth, in the world or physical plane, earthly life is but a mixture of shadows. Science, as it currently exists, is an attempt to classify and understand shadows rather than to search more directly into the light source or life itself. Few of today's scientists are exceptions to this. The few exceptions are God-motivated from within themselves to discover the ultimate first cause (Masters). What Dr. Masters is referring to here is the difference between ego-based science and soul-based science. Ego-based science seeks to prove its illusions and beliefs, which are also illusions through experimenter bias. Science by enlightened people seeks the truth of phenomena and the explanations for those phenomena. Science performed by unenlightened individuals only reflects their subconscious bias inwardly and its political influence outwardly. Therefore, their science is predetermined in its outcome and becomes a self-fulfilling prophecy to their predetermination, not focusing on true phenomena to be discovered but supposedly proving deep down what they already believe they know. Science, to these people, involves manipulating outcomes and people to serve the purpose of guaranteeing their egos survive and stay in control at the expense of the truth and their souls. All their so-called data will reflect this, and all other possibilities and explanations will therefore be automatically omitted from their experiments in consciousness, leaving them with no intelligent conclusion but an assumption that what they are trying to prove is indeed correct, based not on science but on the flimsy mindset of the insecure, uncertain ego, which is susceptible to negative outside and inside political and cultural influences. The ego competes with others to prove to itself that it has a right to survive and not change and that there is no justification to change, as reflected in its ego-biased pseudoscience. Science was created to prove to the ego and explain God, not deny God, so the ego can understand God and God's methods to relinquish control of its demanding ways so that it can surrender appropriately to them when presented with moments of truth as they arise or are needed, providing hope in seemingly hopeless circumstances to maintain or evolve the human condition to beingness from humanness.

In this paper, we have studied the process of integration and the journey from beginning to end, though it only begins again. The psychopathology of the ego, including spiritual bypass, is at the heart of all miscommunication and conflict between self and others. Currently, conflict is prevalent between contemporary Christians and lesbian, gay, bisexual, transgender, and queer groups of people. Both groups have a political agenda to change the world outwardly, avoid inner growth, and not be who they were created to be. Both groups are creating a spiritual bypass, using their faith or spirituality to change the world outwardly instead of facing themselves inwardly and their egos. The premise of changing the outer reality or world to avoid growth is a form of negative, dysfunctional projection. Both groups lack the awareness and discernment to overcome this dilemma. They are both drawing conclusions on incomplete data or experience. Their feelings of who they really are are based upon the elation of the ego in not having to face anything internally that will make them uncomfortable with the brokenness, the lost reality, and the subsequent apathy of the ego to face itself and challenge internal entities or demons that may or not be evil. Only Satan stifles dialogue and debate, using hatred to demonize opposition, calling it tolerance, without giving truth its voice to be heard. Politically, the LGBTQ community uses this tactic of Satan, using hatred to silence any and all opposition to its theology and rhetoric, including inquiry as to how such a complex psychopathology involving ego is formed and why it exists. This exposes it for what it is: a dysfunction no unenlightened person has found an explanation for yet and a positionality of ego, not a valid civil rights issue. This positionality does not provide conversation, discourse, or dialogue between the two sides to try to understand each other. Anyone or anything that questions its veracity is demonized as a hate-monger. Such positionality of ego does not allow communication to take place, and fear, anger, and judgment prevail. Both gays and contemporary Christians are prejudiced because of their egos and, therefore, prejudiced against God (both project against each other). They only can see the imperfections in each other and are blind to the divinity in each other.

Nobody should be discriminated against; however, it also should not be encouraged to keep people from being who God created them to be. Assumptions and conclusions are drawn on a lack of scientific evidence, excluding wholeness, and taken as fact. But this is not whole, complete, or truly scientific. The ego, as a last-ditch attempt, will use past or future lives to identify with to live out potential scenarios to keep itself intact. This involves prolonging its existence and delaying oneness or unification with God. It is a delay tactic and a form of spiritual bypass to eventually put off facing the inevitable remainder and final constructs and feelings of brokenness within it. It is the end of the ego psychologically, psychospiritually, and psychophysically.

Dr. Masters comments on this finalization of the ego in his *Mystical Insights*:

> There comes a time in the life of every soul that an emptying out of the personal ego takes place, with the subsequent replacement by universal God Presence Consciousness. The intention is to bring the energy field of the soul's human manifestation into greater harmony, balance or alignment with manifesting Universal Energy or Universal God Consciousness/Spirit. In this way, it is universal consciousness or God entering into the awakening person's surface frontal consciousness that creates the prayer, visualization, affirmation, or other spiritual practice and the personal ego is less and less involved.(86)

Dr. Masters's comments on the basis of society and how it is created to support the ego are also insightful: "The basis of identity as viewed by clinical psychology and psychiatry is that the self, one's identity, is that of a personal ego identity. ... The flaw in all this is that a society comprised of personal ego identities is still a society of persons isolated from each other by virtue of believing themselves to be separate, isolated entities"(133-134).

The psychopathology of being indoctrinated into illusion illustrates the plight of a heart and soul being broken and becoming human, unconscious, isolated, and separate by illusion from God. Worst of all, the illusion of it all becomes true to the individual, while the reality of God is obscured. This is the psychospiritual perception of illusion, which is not based in love or truth and coerces all to comply with it to accept the world and be of it by Satan and the powers and principalities that God allows to run it. God has the final say on everything. Every person coming into the world goes through this process, and some don't recover from it, which is why the world is as it is today. This process has continued and has been in place since the beginning of human history. Satan solicited God to argue that humans would not truly be human unless they were conformed and made in such a way that they had a real alternative in which their free will could choose between God and being human. God allowed this so His created could choose Him, using free will, but they would have to acknowledge their feelings in order to grow and choose to become human beings instead of just being human. Adherence to this new covenant or law created by illusion demands strict compliance. One must not break it, or severe punishment will follow. One cannot follow it and be saved at the same time.

Jesus Christ said, "You cannot get to the kingdom of heaven by following this law." This is the same law He speaks of. Only through Christ can it be obtained. It is a psychospiritual event and process; it has nothing to do with the intellectual formality of accepting Jesus as your Lord and Savior, which is, for many, an illusion to cover over illusion and keep following the law. Spiritual bypass is the reason Christians think that everything has been done for them as far as spiritual growth is concerned, which is also an illusion. Christians make an assumption, which is a conclusion based upon incomplete experience. They believe there is nothing for them to do, because spiritual bypass is preventing a complete experience upon which to appropriately realize, contemplate, and conclude correctly in wisdom, love, and truth.

Dr. Masters, in his *Mystical Insights*, quotes Psalm 139 and his insight about it: "When the psalmist praised God, proclaiming himself fearfully and wonderfully made, he alluded to the mysteries of our being-ness that mystics through the ages have discovered that the reality of who and what we are is complex. Indeed every human being is a microcosm of the macrocosmic universe" (37). It is important to know that before David had this revelation, his ego caused him to sin, after which he became unconscious about it and denied it. Seeing holes in reality is a precursor to detecting illusion in one's reality. The holes are pieces or fragments of the concealment of the ego breaking down because the internal pressure caused by feelings of unconsciousness, humanness, and brokenness has reached its limit in conclusion of what they have to teach, and they have nowhere left to go except to meet their divine destiny, being dissolved in the pure awareness of Christ consciousness. The holes formed by this process begin to multiply, and as consciousness grows with the aid of awareness, connections and realizations simultaneously occur, creating an expansive network based upon the universe and its underlying creative consciousness as the macrocosm and in the central nervous system as neurons make new connections in a microcosm. These connections continue to form, creating a state of presence, becoming more aware, until achievement of a state of self-aware beingness. Once self-awareness is achieved, it continues to grow until it is whole enough to break the confines of its imprisonment to be born and travel from its previous destination to its present-day destiny to merge and integrate with the body being truly born again. Being born again of light and spirit into beingness is part of the destiny of the soul in its expression of pure awareness. This is a metaphysical, mystical, supernatural process that fulfills not only scripture but also the person who is open to God and willing to grow. For every hole formed in the ego, a piece or fragment of the soul is recovered and brought back to integrate after it has been healed to create wholeness from trauma incurred from brokenness.

Once the soul has embodied, it is understood that at some point in the future, it will integrate the ego, and the predominant consciousness is soul-based consciousness, leading to reconciliation of both ego into soul and soul into God's mind. During the process, before its culmination and conclusion, the ego and the soul are equally predominant, and a person must use free will to choose which one will be the prevailing consciousness to follow in the process eventually leading to mystical union with God. During the reconciliation process, both the ego and the soul are present. The ego, with its illusions and unbelief, and the soul, with its love and truth, coexist. A person uses free will to choose which one to follow, learning wisdom in the process and also obtaining knowledge to learn, discern, and become fulfilled. Predominant soul-based consciousness begins with the soul's awakening, which may happen with or without embodiment accompanying the experience. Choosing to follow the soul leads to eventual mystical union with God, while choosing the ego leads away from God.

If, at any time during this process, the ego is chosen and consequences ensue that lead to a negative outcome, then corrective measures can be expected in the form of negative karma, judgment, disease, impairment, and even death to persuade the ego to relent, repent, and choose God or the soul to continue the journey toward God in mystical union with God. Mercy is offered at each interval in the process to mitigate negative consequences of the ego and will be experienced accordingly when the choice of the soul or God is made for the purpose of growth and soul evolution to eventual oneness with God in mystical union with God. Jesus Christ is both merciful and a just judge and rules accordingly according to love, truth, and wisdom to instruct and teach every life-form and soul the most efficient and direct way to mystical union with God. With mercy, there is no judgment, but it does require the feelings in question to be evaluated and, with awareness, to be discerned, processed, and released in forgiveness. It is important to note that the veil between ego and soul will re-form if one is not consistent and persistent in processing feelings leading to eventual embodiment and oneness with God. This is evident in the Bible, portrayed by the temple's cyclically being destroyed and rebuilt again and again until Jesus Christ's crucifixion (integration), resurrection, and ascension, which completed the process of total integration of being—that is, the process of becoming a human being from being just human.

In the ego and the collective unconscious, negativity, darkness, and Satan are encountered. One must take every thought and feeling captive while fighting the evil forces that try to defeat one's self. This is a trial that every soul must go through at some point in its evolution back to God. For many, it takes place in the union of marriage. Jesus Christ, on the cross, fought Satan internally, exchanging blows in spirit, until he freed Himself from the negativity, the collective unconscious, and His unfinished business from His ego. Once this is completed, the kundalini rises, maintaining the organism, and then the Alpha and Omega of Revelation returns feelings to be processed and reveals true heart contrasted with the ego while all along maintaining divinity and soul consciousness. At this point, the powers and principalities return feelings that were taken at breaking, healing the wound after defeating Satan and exiting the collective unconscious. Satan is defeated in spirit from ego and from his ego to his soul but also through love and compassion through light (his revenge). This is the goal of two people in a marriage: to reach this point of oneness and wholeness with God. The main reason divorce happens is because it is so difficult to go through for one or both people in the marriage. At this point, Satan is bound and defeated and is no longer a threat or a problem for souls as long as they use their free will to keep choosing God, love, and truth to navigate their lives and maintain and nurture their connection with God. One must be like Jesus Christ in this manner to be successful when it comes time for his or her trial. The purpose of the trial is to strengthen weaknesses; build endurance; purify the heart; exhaust the negative energy of the ego accumulated over the life span of the soul, which covers many lifetimes; and restore the divine heart, which is now whole and complete.

This leads to victory if sustained over a period of time sufficient to accomplish the task of total integration of being, wherein body (heart), soul, mind, and spirit are connected and integrated with one another, God, the infinite, and the eternal, or eternity, which are one. Awareness and discernment are the keys to not only distinguishing different feelings and where they come from but also maintaining one's self while growing and moving forward toward God and the guidance to become one with God through Christ consciousness. When one is processing a negative emotion or feeling, the location where it takes place is the head, in the frontal bone region of the forehead, and it temporarily occludes the forebrain area and prefrontal cortex, which correlates to the mystery of Golgotha (which means "Skull"), where Christ was crucified. You will experience pain in this area—a combination of egoic pain (emotional pain of being human) and spiritual pain (pain of not being who you are)—while processing it into being. After it concludes this process, it processes out of consciousness, leaving only the memory behind as a reminder of the path you have traveled to become who you are and were created to be. The wound has three levels—corresponding to the heart (body), soul, and mind—that must be retraced back to their source on the level of heart, soul, and mind so that there is complete integration and restoration of wholeness and well-being.

CONCLUSION

Total integration of being includes the emergence, convergence, and integration of the soul, mind, and body, or heart, free of ego constraints, configurations, and constructs that were obtained in the process of indoctrination into unconsciousness, humanness, brokenness, and what is known psychologically and spiritually as *ego*. Through the introduction, we learned from scripture and spiritual insight that there is a growth process for people to go through if they are willing to grow and have faith in the process and God. Jesus Christ's mission was and still is to show us the most efficient way to go through this process of total integration. We have also learned about the seemingly infinite but truly finite aspects of the ego, including its etiology, function, formation, and demise. We have learned about the fragmentation process of the soul, heart, and mind, which, in the ego, are all separate units unified by illusion to serve the ego. The illusion of separation corresponds to the mind. The illusion of perfection corresponds to the heart. The illusion of imperfection corresponds to the soul. In total integration of being, all three are liberated from illusion and ego and are integrated and unified with one another, the mind of God, and the universe. We have also learned about the reality of such an undertaking, which requires suffering, pain, and even illness. We have also learned that the process is guided divinely, with built-in mechanisms or promptings to cue the soul to awaken and begin the process. In addition, we have learned through the fragmentation process to deal with darkness, our shadow side, and evil. Furthermore, we have learned not only how to deal with our feelings that are divine (guidance and intuition) but also how to deal with feelings and energies that are lower in consciousness, and from scripture, we have learned what integration is and looks like when complete and whole. All of this is important because the fragmented, unconscious people in the world far outnumber those who are whole.

There is a lot of deception, along with misinformation, in the view of ego as the predominant consciousness on the planet. Being human is no longer viable or sustainable on this planet, but being a human being is. We need to help others when they are ready and willing to carry their cross and follow Christ consciousness. This seems like an overwhelming task, but it really isn't if we go through it first and then help them. We need to be the change we wish to see in the world. People hunger and thirst for the truth. The hunger and thirst stem from their brokenness or woundedness. Churches have been emptying out all over the world because what people seek—love and truth—is not found there. People's woundedness will lead their natural curiosity to metaphysical pursuits because those are what interest them. Their woundedness and curiosity will eventually lead them to love and truth, or God. If they persevere, endure, and accept the suffering that goes with it, they will find God and themselves, fulfilling the scripture "He who loses himself or herself for My sake will find themselves."

Wounded people usually need to spend some time and experience with their woundedness at its level of consciousness. This is necessary to get familiar with one's woundedness to study it and learn from it. Many people suffer psychic wounds, which are harsh and traumatic, and that's why there is such a fascination with that level. It is OK for people to get acquainted with it, but it is also important to move on from it when it is time to do so. This will go on until the previous realization is realized, and then it is time to go higher and deeper and, eventually, be born in God's heart of true spirit.

During this time of soul study and getting acquainted with one's woundedness, the soul contemplates its merging and penetration into and through the ego, which contains the feelings of humanness, unconsciousness, and brokenness, which obscure or block God's love, light, and presence. Spirit guides are really who we were in past lives. This helps us to learn and navigate the lessons we need to learn in order to progress and move forward. The ego, through questioning and experiencing itself through dissolution and sublimation, learns to release and let go of itself for a greater state of consciousness, yielding to the soul, as this process proceeds from start to finish. The ego is the gateway or gauntlet the soul must travel to reach the heart and merge with God. Jesus told the Pharisees "to clean the inside of the cup," referring to the fragmentation of the heart and subsequent formation of the ego. The heart must be free from the ego to integrate soul into heart, which then integrate into mind spirit, or God. This merging, along with continuing forward to enter ego, transforms it with and into light, cleansing the heart (or the inside of the cup), making it like new—like a new wineskin to accept divinity into the flesh. Jesus's miracle of turning water into wine signifies integrating divinity into flesh, and his doing so at a wedding signifies the true meaning of marriage.

Jesus Christ's baptism signifies the soul's awakening. His crucifixion signifies the soul's embodiment and integration into the heart through the ego. His resurrection signifies the heart integrating into the soul. His ascension signifies the heart and soul that have integrated with each other finally integrating and becoming one with God and fulfilling the holy Trinity. Insight, wisdom, and truth are important to share with others because they come from the source of God and creation itself. It is important also because it is a living creation that, when heard, read, or experienced, illuminates and transforms all it comes in contact with. The *nous*, as talked about by Leloup, allows past, present, and future experiences to be experienced for learning, using free will to choose. One goes to the deepest part of him- or herself to find the light of awareness, or the soul. One goes even deeper to find God.

Craniosacral therapy is a form of body work that releases the soul and awakens the soul to be integrated with the heart, or body. It activates the light body. Reconnective healing reconnects the heart and also the ego to be transformed and worked through to integrate heart (ego) into soul. It activates the astral body. Remote viewing activates the etheric body, which converts the mental faculties from ego to soul. The University of Metaphysics and the University of Sedona reconnect both integrated soul and heart with the spirit and mind of God. This activates the spiritual body. These four healing modalities all work with one another and provide for all that is needed to achieve total integration of being.

Jesus said, "Blessed are the meek for they shall inherit the earth." Eckhart Tolle explains who the meek are:

The meek are the egoless. They are those who have
awakened to their essential true nature as consciousness
and recognize that essence in all" others", all life forms.
They live in a surrendered state and so feel their oneness
with the whole and the source. They embody the
awakened consciousness that is changing all aspects of life
on our planet, including nature, because life on earth is
inseparable from the human consciousness that perceives
and interacts with it. (309)

After total integration of being, the created creates with creation
as creator, one with God. Humanness and mind of the third chakra
become "I am," or the creator. Unconsciousness and the soul of the second
chakra become creation. Brokenness (heart) of the first chakra becomes
the created. Heaven consists mostly of the upper chakras: chakra seven
is God's light, or Christ consciousness; chakra six is God's intelligence;
chakra five is God's Word; chakra four is God's spirit, love; chakra three
is the Great I Am, or Creator; chakra two is the creation; and chakra one
is the created.

Now that the lower three chakras have been transformed from ego
consciousness to God consciousness, heaven gets brought down to earth
and grounded in the reality of the experience of love and truth, allowing
one to be an agent of change in the world but not be of it. Father (God,
mind), Son (soul), and body (heart, Holy Spirit) are now fulfilled and
complete.

WORKS CITED

Clow, Barbara Hand. *Chiron: Rainbow Bridge between the Inner and Outer Planets*. Woodbury, MN: Llewellyn Publications, 2013.

Dale, Cyndi. *The Complete Book of Chakra Healing*. Woodbury, MN: Llewellyn Publications, 2012.

Dorland's Illustrated Medical Dictionary. 27th ed. 1988.

Foster, Jeff. *The Deepest Acceptance: Radical Awakening in Ordinary Life*. Boulder, CO: Sounds True, 2012.

Goleman, Daniel. *Emotional Intelligence*. New York, NY: Bantam Books, 1995.

Harvey, Andrew. *Son of Man: The Mystical Path to Christ*. New York, NY: Penguin Putnam, 1998.

Hawkins, David R. *Discovery of the Presence of God*. Sedona, AZ: Veritas Publishing, 2007.

———. *The Eye of the I: From Which Nothing Is Hidden*. Sedona, AZ: Veritas Publishing, 2001.

———. *Letting Go*. United States: Hay House, 2012.

———. *Transcending the Levels of Consciousness: The Stairway to Enlightenment*. W. Sedona, AZ: Veritas Publishing, 2006.

The Holy Bible: New King James Version. Thomas Nelson, 1984.

Leloup, Jean-Yves. *The Gospel of Mary Magdalene*: One Park Street, Rochester, Vermont: Inner Traditions International, 2002

———. *The Gospel of Thomas*. Rochester, VT: Inner Traditions, 2005.

Marion, Jim. *Putting on the Mind of Christ: The Inner Work of Christian Spirituality*. Charlottesville, VA: Hampton Roads Publishing Company, 2011.

Masters, Paul Leon. *Master's Degree Curriculum*. 2 vols. Burbank, CA: Printing, 2011.

Modi, Shakuntala. *Remarkable Healings*. Charlottesville, VA: Hampton Roads Publishing Company, 1997.

Proctor, Charlene M. *The Oneness Gospel*. Minneapolis, MN: Two Harbors Press, 2011.

Rachele, Sal. *Soul Integration*. Wentworth, NH: Living Awareness Publications, 2013.

Raheem, Aminah. *Soul Return*. Lower Lake, CA: Asland Publishing, 1987, 1991.

Tolle, Eckhart. *A New Earth*. New York, NY: Penguin Group, 2005.

Whitfield, Charles L. *Boundaries* and *Relationships: Knowing, Protecting, and Enjoying the Self*. Deerfield Beach, FL: Health Publication, 1993.

———. *Co-Dependence: Healing the Human Condition*. Deerfield Beach, FL: Health Communications, 1991.

———. *Healing the Child Within*. Deerfield Beach, FL: Health Communications, 1987.

———. *The Power of Humility: Choosing Peace over Conflict in Relationships*. Deerfield Beach, FL: Health Communications, 2006.

Zohar, Danah, and Ian Marshall. *SQ: Connecting with Our Spiritual Intelligence*. New York, NY: Bloomsbury Publishing, 2000.

3

The Science, Art, and Philosophy of Being

A Dissertation Submitted in Partial Fulfillment of
the Requirements for the Degree of Doctor of
Theocentric Psychology on Behalf of the Department
of Graduate Studies of the University of Sedona

RAMON LAZARUS
MAY 9, 2016

INTRODUCTION

The science, art, and philosophy of being are part of the continual renewal of mind, heart, and soul when oneness with God has been achieved, focusing on beingness; healing; and the relationship with God, self, and others for the purpose of coherence and harmony in love in the world and in the universe. Renewing of the mind takes place through transformation from finite to infinite. Oneness with God is the science of being. Renewing of the heart takes place through realization, and expression of that realization with self, others, and God through intuition is the art of being. The soul is renewed through beingness itself, and the experience of being in and one with the presence of God is the philosophy of being.

Mystical contact is the primary building block of spiritual experience that unifies mind, body (heart), and soul. With each experience, God builds His creation, a human being—a living, breathing manifestation of Himself in individualized form. Once the inner foundation is formed and the inner state of beingness is achieved, then progression to the outer world and its brokenness becomes the focus to heal and establish a relationship based upon beingness. This is what is meant by evangelizing or sharing the good news of God and His workmanship in and among people. Saint Paul said to be transformed by the renewing of your mind. Although Saint Paul was referring in scripture to a pre-total-integration-of-being state of consciousness, it continues on after total integration of being, in which mind, heart (body), and soul are one with God and free of the ego. Theocentric psychology is the science, art, and philosophy of being. It is interested in cocreatively being, healing, and sharing the Christ mind and Christ consciousness with self, others, and God. This unifying wholeness seeks to share itself with all life and life-forms so it and they may experience life in a full spectrum of consciousness to make choices and decisions and then learn and grow from the choices and decisions made. The Christ mind seeks to fulfill and establish love and truth in it encounters in mind, heart (body), and soul. Each person who obtains this level of consciousness and being becomes like an avatar to all those who come in contact with him or her. The job of an avatar is to balance, restore, and maintain harmony not only with oneself but also with a group of people, the planet, or the universe.

The science, art, and philosophy of being, or theocentric psychology, involve an ascended state of consciousness and being one with the Christ light and God. The transition from base mortal consciousness to the ascended state covers the full spectrum of human consciousness. Once ascended, a soul, or totally integrated being, may descend to earth or lower dimensions to resolve conflict and chaos among those less evolved and to bring light and love in the form of healing any suffering among or within individuals. At every level of consciousness, there is a representation of consciousness from having gone through each level that has been integrated into beingness, with all lessons learned, realized, understood, and assimilated. There is much variation in states of consciousness from the lowest base mortal consciousness to mystical union and oneness with God. Transitional states of being describe the relationship of hybrid states of consciousness between base mortal consciousness and spirit, or the ego and the soul.

From the stirring of the divine memory beginning the spiritual journey and beginning of the end of the ego to the remnant of the ego that marks the end of the ego and the culmination of the spiritual journey to mystical union, oneness with God in superconsciousness. The ego will try to persuade, manipulate, and control the soul through its feelings of humanness, unconsciousness, and brokenness to indulge in and fulfill its desire to spiritually bypass these same feelings and forgo oneness with God in favor of a lesser state of mind, forgoing becoming a human being and settling for just being human. The ego and the soul have animosity toward each other because of the soul's woundedness at the hands of the ego, which projects its pain onto it internally or externally through another.

The ego despises growing and facing its own feelings of brokenness, of which the soul reminds it.

The ego and soul are unconscious through becoming human, giving life experience that produces cause-and-effect experience. The ego is comprised of karma, personality, family-of-origin issues and feelings, and generational aspects of sin and ancestral lineage passed down from generation to generation. Past and future life lessons are carried over, including what has been learned, is resolved, has yet to be learned, and is unresolved. All aspects of both the ego and the soul are configured, patterned, and paired to correlate and correspond, giving a unique experience of each simultaneously, albeit unconsciously. In awakening, each becomes conscious, and the reconciliation process is worked through and completed, dissolving the ego into the light of God's presence.

The main reason for becoming human is to experience ego-based consciousness to contrast with soul-based consciousness, determine if it serves your highest purpose, and discern if that purpose truly meets your needs for growth and evolution of beingness. When the moment of truth arrives, one must either make a choice higher than one's karma or make a choice that leaves karma unresolved and, subsequently, continue on in life and future lives by indulging the ego or fulfilling the soul.

The Bible is an illustration of the relationship of the ego and the soul in varying stages of unconsciousness, awakening, development, integration, resurrection, ascension, and wholeness. From Revelation, as the first book of the Bible before Adam and Eve, to Moses and Pharaoh to the epoch of the prophets and kings to Jesus Christ and the New Testament, the Bible reveals the story and saga of this relationship. The heart (ego) and soul in the Old Testament are separate, distinct entities. The heart, whose core is the ego at this stage of development, is an outward manifestation representing a whole host of people who are leading lives apart from God. The soul is represented by those who make it through their trials and tribulations, no matter the obstacles they are facing, and by the prophets who advised kings to the New Testament of Jesus Christ and the apostles Peter and Paul. Through mystical experience, the mind, body (heart), and soul heal, transform, renew, realize, and release the consciousness of the ego to receive the consciousness and beingness of the soul, which leads to oneness with God's presence. Each step is just as important and significant as the one before it and after it, revealing love, truth, knowledge, wisdom, and insight. From the initial stage of stirring the divine memory to the remaining remnant of the ego, the spiritual journey is rich with soul-satisfying, fulfilling experience, leading to one's life purpose.

With this introduction and overview in mind, let us enter into the deepest level of beingness, realize that beingness, and share it with others in relationships through healing as mind, body (heart), and soul become one with God and others.

REVIEW OF LITERATURE

The beatitudes describe the life experience of an integrated soul, its destiny and destination, and what can be expected on a spiritual journey. The following quotes from the beatitudes are from the New King James Version of the Holy Bible, specifically from Matthew 5. Verse 3 says, "Blessed are the poor in spirit, for theirs is the Kingdom of Heaven." This describes the overall attitude of humility—an authentic and genuine one, not a false or pretending one. True humility comes from an awakened soul. Verse 4 says, "Blessed are those who mourn, for they shall be comforted." This describes the work that the soul not only will go through itself but also will help others with. Grieving one's own grief brings a depth of compassion and understanding for others' pain. Verse 5 says, "Blessed are the meek, for they shall inherit the earth." This is a reference to the egoless who have done their grief work and maintained themselves to be able to be of service to others and God. These souls will have at their disposal all of heaven and earth for their mission and purpose of helping others. Verse 6 says, "Blessed are those who hunger and thirst for righteousness." Here the indwelling light force of God itself yearns through love to heal every soul to be one with God and establish mercy and justice for all to live in peace, harmony, and love. Verse 7 says, "Blessed are the merciful, for they shall obtain mercy." The soul, through its connection to God, is all-merciful and seeks to have mercy on all others amid their struggles and suffering. Having mercy is a divine attribute of God in God's presence, showing the depth of God's love for His creations. Verse 8 says, "Blessed are the pure in heart, for they shall see God." This is a reference to those who go through the process of becoming egoless. At the end of the process, they are pure in heart and spirit and see the face of God as God really is. The inside of the cup that Jesus Christ referred to when talking to the Pharisees is indeed clean. Verse 9 says, "Blessed are the peace makers, for they shall be called sons of God." A whole, integrated soul will connect and fill in the gaps or blanks between others where a lack of harmony or understanding is evident. This is for the purpose of illuminating others above and beyond where they find themselves in dysfunctional relationships, disagreements, and conflicts to restore harmony and peace to a given situation or circumstance. Verse 10 says, "Blessed are those who are persecuted for righteousness' sake, for theirs is the kingdom of heaven." This is a reference to those who act on their dysfunction against those who are in their wholeness. This is the classic clash between unconscious ego and conscious soul. Those who are in ego consciousness will lash out at those who are free, because those who are in ego are not free. Verse 11 says, "Blessed are you when they revile and persecute you, and say all kinds of evil against you falsely for My sake." This further describes the lengths the ego will go to in its denial internally of its own divinity. An integrated soul must be able to withstand this kind of attack against itself and be loving and compassionate in return.

To fully appreciate a fully integrated soul's mission and purpose, a brief history of the creation of creation is necessary to understand how things are, where they have been, and where they are meant to go. Norman Paulsen, a twentieth-century mystic and author of *Christ Consciousness*, describes the beginning of creation as the mystical marriage between the divine masculine and divine feminine energies of consciousness, which gave birth to the Christ, the first creation of light, and all things in the world and universe.

> As they neared the point of convergence, the Spirit of God, Mother and Father, felt the approaching climax as a tremendous merging of energies ... on the divine center of the smallest of all places, where it all originally began, the two radiant spheres of pure consciousness and light masculine and feminine merged as one. This mystical union completed the image of the first creation of light, the androgynous, immaculate body of Christ. The cosmic

sea of life and energy had given birth to the Christ child
of pure consciousness and light. (286)

From this account of the beginning of creation, we now turn to an
excerpt from *Mystical Insights* by Dr. Masters, founder of the University of
Sedona and the University of Metaphysics:

> First, the manifestation of light is manifesting within
> the un-manifest. The light gives the illusion of dividing
> itself. All the divisions of light give further illusion of
> individual entities. Yet because the light is so active in
> these entities, they still know that they are part of God
> living in reality within God as God lives within them—
> they are individualized expressions of God's being-ness of
> love or absolute union. Expression at last: such expression
> from what can be described as the highest angelic realm.
> God expresses love to them and through them, while
> they express love back to God. God loves and is loved in
> return. In this flow of love God is acknowledged: God's
> presence can rightly declare to its creation "I am that I
> am." However, because of the illusion of separateness,
> dualistic concepts of time and space begin to occupy
> the consciousness of the angelic entities. Consciousness
> begins to yield to an illusion of divisions. Over a period
> of illusionary time, the divisions cause a dimming of the
> angelic oneness with God, even though, in truth they have
> never left God's presence. In truth they are God's presence.
> But some in the angelic realm begin to believe they are
> separate entities apart from God. The personal ego begins
> to cloud their consciousness. Illusion continues until they
> can no longer exist in dimensional consciousness just a
> light step away from the all-ness of God.

These two accounts of Paulsen and Dr. Masters together make up what
is known as the *divine memory* from the perspective of ego consciousness,
beginning the process of the spiritual journey. It is a fundamental step

in the process of beginning growth. It is devoid of spirit, but spirit uses the divine memory to communicate with the indwelling soul to impart wisdom so it can gain in strength to awaken fully to spirit and possess real mystical power. But until that happens, it is just a memory that reveals knowledge or knowing on an intellectual level of ego. Dr. Masters comments on the intellectual knowing of the ego in an excerpt from his *Mystical Insights*: "Knowing and accepting something on an intellectual level is knowing and accepting something by your false personal ego identity—by that illusionary part of yourself that is divided from the whole, the one life or God. The intellectual acceptance by the personal ego is a ploy or game that this false sense plays to pacify the soul into thinking it is progressing spiritually." The ego is not dependent upon the five senses. It is a completely independent entity separate from God within the body and mind. The soul is divine and is connected to God. Both ego and soul use the body or bodily senses to reinforce their contrasting experiences of life. To know about something is to reference intellect based upon past experience, memory, or thought, and it is associated with the ego. To know is to reference soul-based experience based upon the soul and be in the present moment of experience a state of becoming and being in which experience is direct beyond thought.

As far as human history is concerned, the story of Adam and his first wife, Lilith, begins the dysfunctional relationship of the ego and the functional soul in struggling for equality. Adam and Lilith were both created equally from the earth. Adam was predominantly ego-based consciousness, and Lilith was predominantly soul-based consciousness. Adam projected his dysfunction onto Lilith, which caused her to become Adam's illusion and transformed her into just being human like Adam. Lilith was the first to become human through the powers and principalities transforming her. Both Adam and Lilith had souls and egos to contend with, but Adam's behavior put his burden on Lilith, and it took many centuries to correct and heal from that with Christ's help. The powers and principalities break open a soul so it can become aware of its feelings of humanness, unconsciousness, and brokenness and can have an experience contrasting to the soul's divine experience. It then can use its free will to make a choice as to which is fulfilling and serving the highest purpose of the soul.

The wounding of the soul causes trauma and tension in the soul, mind, and body through the trauma itself and through feelings of humanness, unconsciousness, and brokenness. This is what makes healing from it vital. It is necessary to recover and function from it.

The primary disease due to being wounded and fragmented is codependence, a hallmark of ego-based activity and behavior. The cardinal characteristics of codependence are as follows, from Charles Whitfield's book *Codependence*:

> It is learned and acquired. It is developmental. It is outer focused. It is a disease of lost selfhood. It has personal boundary distortion. It is a feeling disorder, manifested especially by emptiness, low self-esteem and shame, fear, anger, confusion and numbness. It produces relationship difficulties with self and others. It is primary, chronic, progressive, malignant and treatable. (26)

As mentioned, boundary distortions come from one's own boundaries being violated spiritually as well as psychologically and emotionally in the wounding process. Charles Whitfield points out, in his book *Boundaries and Relationships*, what a healthy, functional boundary is: "It delineates where I and my physical and psychological space end and where you and yours begin. A boundary or limit is how far we can go with comfort in a relationship" (1). What gets wounded and has its boundary violated is our true self, or higher self, which Whitfield refers to as the *child within*. In his book *Healing the Child*, Whitfield gives a description of what our true self feels like: "Overall we tend to feel current, complete, finished, appropriate, real, whole and sane" (11). Healing is important because it restores wholeness, completeness, and function, establishing being. Trauma to the true self or soul permeates not only the soul but also the mind and body. This permeation forms tension in the mind and body and leads to disease. Aminah Raheem, PhD, comments on this tension and maintains that healing it is the way to freedom: "As Body armor softens a person can allow awareness to come closer to the inner child's original perceptions, hurts and fears. Once the numbness of armor has been penetrated, the pain of the original traumas will surface. Re-experiencing such pain, is difficult but is also the way through to freedom" (163). She uses body work to discharge negative energy from her clients' beings. Even though a soul, or true self, goes through such hardship and needs help in healing itself, it is still there, remaining within us. Danah Zohar, in her book *Connecting with Our Spiritual Intelligence*, comments on this: "The deep self is within us as our human birthright, and is always there bearing witness to our unfolding lives. It is there whenever we strive for and act on meaning" (191–92).

The left side of an individual represents the heart, which, when unhealed, contains the core of the ego. The right side of an individual represents the soul, heaven, and beingness. Healing brings these two opposites together, removing imbalances as they arise, and rebalances the system to beingness, eventually leading to full integration and wholeness. Zohar comments on this dynamic: "In many traditions, the right eye represents the sun's perception of the active and the future, the light of reason, whilst the left eye represents the moon's perception of the passive and the past, or the sight which comes from emotion. But there is also a 'third eye' which synthesizes the two and gives us wisdom" (208). Difficult feelings cause disease and illness when not processed and released from the soul, mind, and body. Healing alleviates the complexity of suffering and the layers of fear, anger, and hurt that, if left unattended, lead to more suffering and possibly projection, affecting others in a cascading, snowballing domino effect, causing pain and discomfort for others.

What does the healing? The vital life force of the soul, or prana or chi, from God's presence within the soul and spirit within the mind and body (heart). The heart of hearts is the soul. Paul Pearsall, PhD, in his book *The Heart's Code*, shares this insight: "It has been seen as what author James Hillman refers to as a sense of calling from within, what he calls a type of central, guiding force and what we know in our 'heart of hearts' we must do and be and why we are here in the first place" (41). Pearsall also embraces an energetic model of disease and healing: "For twenty-three centuries, one of the oldest forms of medicine has focused on the heart as the center of the spiritual energy that expresses our soul. ... Talking about and trying to measure life energy is not something modern western medicine is comfortable with, but Chinese medicine, like almost every other older form of medicine, has always emphasized an energetic approach to understanding disease and healing" (29).

Mitigating negative emotions is essential to restoring and maintaining well-being. Candace Pert, PhD, comments on this in her book *Molecules of Emotion*:

> To repress these emotions and not let them flow freely is to set up a disintegrity in the system, causing it to act at cross purposes rather than as a unified whole. The stress this creates, which takes the form of blockages and insufficient flow of peptide signals to maintain function at the cellular level, is what sets up the weakened conditions that can lead to disease. All honest emotions are positive emotions. (192–93)

Pert comments on this further in regard to illness via a virus: "Because the molecules of emotion (neuropeptides and their receptors that are found in the nervous system, organs and cells) are involved in the process of a virus entering the cell, it seems logical to assume that the state of our emotions will affect whether or not we succumb to viral infection" (190). Pert goes further, establishing scientific evidence of the body-mind link or connection: "Emotions are at the nexus between matter and mind, going back and forth between the two and influencing both" (189). Pert then includes the soul in her response to the public: "But the truth that I have learned through my own late twentieth century science is that the soul, mind, and emotions do play an important role in health" (304). Pert then concludes, "Perhaps this is the same thing that Eastern healers call the subtle energy, or prana—the circulation of emotional and spiritual information throughout the body mind" (307).

Valerie Hunt, a mystical consciousness researcher, says the following of the mind, body, and soul relationship regarding emotion: "Emotion is an energetic agitation or condition, first in the field, and then in the body and awareness. It has a source, a response, and an interpretation in the continuum of consciousness. If focused in the space time domain, the concern is with body and self. If out of time and in a mystical state, its concern is the soul" (172).

Metaphysicians are uniquely gifted to be able to work with the emotional, spiritual, physical, mental, and mystical components of being with self and others and have a lot to offer others as far as achieving wholeness for themselves. Hunt comments on the lack of training of clergy in dealing with these matters: ... "There is nothing in the training of priests, ministers or rabbis which prepares them to enter into and decode the mystical experiences of people" (168). Hunt comments on why this is the case for the Christian church: "Remember that many of the mystical passages in the Bible were removed by Christians at the Nicene Conference in Constantinople in the twelfth century" (168). Hunt continues her comments on healing by comparing spiritual healing to medical diagnosis: "Spiritual and psychic healers, on the other hand, place primary emphasis upon healing the soul when it gets off track" (244). Oftentimes, symptoms and pathologic states will correspond to the healing needed and involved and will completely resolve when addressed at all levels they're manifested at, with final resolution at the spiritual level.

Hunt continues her comments by defining *health*: "Health then, should be viewed as the perfection and maintenance of a dynamic energy field which is flowing, coherent, and strong, giving it the capacity to vibrationally interact" (245). This is a major difference from the medical model's interpretation of health, which views health as the absence of symptoms and pathology that can be measured. Hunt summarizes and comments on Pert's work with neuropeptides in the body as follows: "In other words, there is a communication system attached to each cell which is in touch with remote cells, not just by direct contact or regular circuits, but by almost simultaneous transmission through the energy field" (249). Hunt, like Pert, believes the communication system of the mind-body field and soul not only integrates the physical but also instructs the healing process as a whole. Like Pert, Hunt comments on repressed emotions and how they manifest in the body in regard to past lives or life-hoods. "Both repressed and conscious mind-field information from other life-hoods can directly create these life health problems. These are broad psychosomatic disturbances if emotions are repressed, or they are highly specific disturbances similar to what was experienced in prior traumatic episodes. The mind field has access to the soul's memory and delivers instructions to the body tissues" (256).

Hunt again addresses the unwillingness of the church to embrace the spiritual and spiritual aspects of beingness regarding mysticism and reincarnation: "But as early as 180 AD the Roman Church with all of its power branded Gnosticism as heresy" (210). The teaching of reincarnation was outlawed, which led to the Inquisition in Spain in the thirteenth century. Hunt mentions the laying on of hands as a healing catalyst that works not only within the mind field but also physically: "Touching and manipulating encourages the release of peptides locally. ... In other words, the neuropeptide is the receiver and the encoder, while the source of information can come slowly through the liquid system, it is rapid through the electromagnetic field" (251). Hunt sums up the science with her conclusion regarding consciousness: "To say it another way, when consciousness or awareness is cut off from an area, stagnation occurs, creating a functional health problem or when anti-coherency or lack of energy exists in areas of the body, pathology and degeneration occur" (257). Hunt addresses the transformative phenomenon of superconsciousness and how that affects individuals in two different ways. Sorokin, at the Harvard Research Center for Creative Altruism, became aware of two distinct patterns of creative growth in superconsciousness from a study of life histories of the greats. There were those who grew quietly and gracefully in altruism and creativity, accessing superconsciousness, and those who had catastrophic or sharp conversions with drastic rearrangement of ego, group affiliation, and values (165).

Superconsciousness is the fulfillment of Christ consciousness, unifying in mystical union with God. It is transformative and transcendent and unifies mind, body (heart), and soul. Pandit Usharbudh Arya, PhD, in his book *Superconscious Meditation*, comments on an individual who has reached and obtained this level of consciousness.

> Because he does not act from the subconscious, his superconscious flows directly into his conscious, without intervening layers of darkness of the subconscious. A Christ has no subconscious, therefore no dark little corners and niches full of cobwebs and dirt. He is transparent so that the superconscious flows through his conscious unhindered and its light is visible and clear, its joy is catching and infectious. (32)

Ayra adds that "a master, a liberated one, has no personality and this is so overpowering all personalities bow humbly in his presence and court his favor" (32).

Charlene Proctor, PhD, author of *The Oneness Gospel*, also comments on this state of consciousness: "To be a Christ is to reveal God through your own humanity" (326). Proctor elaborates on this further, stating that it is available to anyone: "When a spiritual master achieves Christ consciousness, or God realization, we can see and feel the presence in him or her because God consciousness is fully manifested. One who has achieved this level of mastery is recognized as a Christ. It is possible for anyone to attain this perfection, as we are all created in God's image, likeness *and* potentiality" (327).

David Hawkins, MD, PhD, an enlightened psychiatrist, in his book *The Eye of the I*, comments on the presence of God: "The presence of God is the quintessence of profound peace, stillness, and love. It is overwhelming in its profundity. It is totally enveloping, and the love is so powerful that it dissolves any remaining 'non-love' held by the residual ego" (202). Hawkins comments on what he refers to as the *last illusion* in his book *Discovery of the Presence of God*: "Thus arises the fear of absolute death or annihilation into nothingness and nonexistence forever. At this point, it is obvious that what is to be surrendered to God is the life of the self and its motive to continue to exist as the experiencer and seeming source and substrate of life (The Last Illusion)" (229). This marks a culmination point in the spiritual journey from a hybrid state of ego consciousness and spirit or soul consciousness to all spirit or soul consciousness. Hawkins, in his book *Transcending the Levels of Consciousness*, comments on the kundalini spiritual energy and its purpose: "This process is assisted and supported by the unimpeded inflow of spiritual kundalini energy to the higher etheric spiritual bodies above the crown chakra. The flow of the kundalini energy is a response to surrendering the personal will directly to the Divine Teacher, Avatar, Sage, or Divinity by what ever name is invoked" (300).

Cyndi Dale, in her book *Kundalini*, describes kundalini as a divine feminine phenomenon: "This connection easily leads to the idea of kundalini as the feminine principle of creation, the life giving properties within our physical bodies that lead to higher consciousness" (4). Dale further elaborates on kundalini thusly: "It's what gives us life and now sustains it, linking us with the fertile, emotional and prosperous sources of divine energy" (4).

These authors, most of whom are mystics, describe both the state of the ideal healer and the ideal state hoped to be reached in the patient. The states of consciousness achieved signify success in one's journey in the maintaining of that journey in relationship to God and others. Energetic healing is part of the restoration of wholeness; the other part is letting go. The part of the patient is to let feelings come up and out, feeling them if necessary and releasing them to God in forgiveness. David Hawkins comments, in his book *Letting Go*, on the real source of stress: "The real source of stress is actually internal; it is not external, as people would like to believe. The readiness to react with fear, for instance, depends on how much fear is already present within to be triggered by a stimulus" (15).

Richard Bartlet, DC, ND, author of *Matrix Energetics*, comments on healing with intention and consciousness. Healing occurs "…as long as the intended change is visualized clearly, the belief is strong, and the emotional force behind the intention is both focused and sustained" (x). What Bartlet describes here is working in the unseen realm of God, using belief, emotion, visualization, and intention to energetically catalyze healing, using and directing consciousness.

Bruce Lipton, PhD, a cell biologist researcher whose work became the basis for the new science of epigenetics, shares his discovery in his online course *The Biology of Belief*. He discovered through his experiments that environmental signals and the cell membrane determine cellular behavior and the awareness of the cell, not the genes of the cell. The genes involve correlation, not causation, as medical dogma has demonstrated for decades. He further elaborates that perception, by its physical definition, is the equivalent of awareness of the elements in the environment through physical sensation. He then surmises that belief from and through perception determines cell behavior, whether a cell expresses health or disease. Metaphysically, this can be expanded upon. Health and disease are determined not only by belief but also by emotions, feelings both positive and negative, thought forms, unbelief, illusion, memory, constructs, thinking, level of consciousness, dimensions, and spirit, all of which comprise the ego or soul and whether one or the other is the predominant consciousness. Soul expression is equated with health, healing, and vitality; and ego expression is equated with dying, death, and disease.

Jean-Yves Leloup, in his book *The Gospel of Philip*, talks about the place where sacred union takes place within us, between God and the soul, in the bridal chamber, the holy of holies, which is hidden from us until sacred union takes place: "The Bridal Chamber, where Union is realized, is hidden from us; it is the holy of holies" (167). Leloup elaborates as to the content one can experience about the holy of holies: "It is through fragile images and symbols that we penetrate into that which is worthy of reverence and filled with power" (169). Leloup goes on further to describe the bridal chamber and the holy of holies: "Realization makes a human being impalpable and invisible. If they were visible, people would enclose them within the bounds of the visible. To know the grace of true communion with Him one must be clothed in clear light" (135). "It is right to say that the inner and the outer are one" (99).

Danielle Van Dijk, in her book *Christ Consciousness*, describes the heart of the holy of holies at its core: "The spirit is breathed into the body by the 'Most Sublime' and was consequently referred to as the inner spark, eternal and filled with the same cosmic spirit as the Most Supreme" (158). The terms *Most Sublime* and *Most Supreme* refer to a cosmic Most High God. The inner spark is the basis of God and being, and from this divine inner spark come the symbols and imagery directly into the conscious mind, superconsciously utilizing spirits and archetypes to communicate with the indwelling soul; sending, through the life force, spirit, light, energy, and information to the nervous system and heart; and expressing itself and its superconscious contents positively with vibrant vitality full of life. Disease happens and presents itself when this process gets blocked or disrupted through the feelings of the ego, fragmenting and decomposing itself through its feelings, constructs, thought forms, emotions, and unconsciousness, which causes stasis of energy and awareness, leading to dysfunction and disease.

According to Swami Vivekananda in his book *Raja Yoga*, "The rousing of the kunda-lini is the only way to attaining Divine Wisdom, superconscious perception realization of the spirit" (28). ..."Samadhi is called the superconscious state" (38). Samadhi is perfect concentration beyond instinct and reason to go higher to superconsciousness. The Dalai

Lama, in his book *Dzogchen: Heart Essence of the Great Perfection*, defines the teaching of the title of his book as the fundamental innate mind of clear light and that alone, which is practiced and laid bare in all its nakedness: "Dzogchen in fact is uniquely the practice of clear light or naked rigpa (which is the innermost nature of mind), alone" (127). What Swami Vivekananda and the Dalai Lama call *samadhi*, or superconsciousness, and the fundamental innate mind of clear light are both experienced at the same time upon fulfillment of each with mystical union with God, which is a direct result of the activation and fulfillment of the kundalini's rising to clear the soul, mind, and body (heart) of the feelings of humanness, unconsciousness, and brokenness, or the ego.

In *The Nag Hammadi Scriptures* edited by Marvin Meyer, there is a passage found under "The Acts of Peter and the Twelve Apostles" that mentions Jesus Christ instructing apostle Peter on healing people: "So, first heal bodies, that through the real powers of healing their bodies, with no medicine of this world, that they may come to believe in you, that you also have the power to heal sicknesses of the heart" (365). In the dialogue of "The Savior" in *The Nag Hammadi Scriptures*, Jesus Christ comments on a spiritual state of health: "The lamp of the body is the mind. As long as what is within you is kept in order that is,[the soul] your bodies are enlightened" (303). The mind is the convergence point of integration and unification of mystical union with God. The state of superconsciousness, or samadhi, and Dzogchen, or the fundamental innate mind of clear light and rigpa, once attained, becomes the source of all health and vitality in the body, mind, soul, and spirit and universal life; and the mind of God establishes divinity and divine wisdom, from which the nature of God and divine natural healing abilities occur for one who has reached and obtained this level of beingness for healing self and others. Healing the body is important because the body, along with the mind and soul, translates disease or healing. The body is the reference point as far as a stimulus to prompt an organism to seek remedy or healing for its perceived discomfort or pain, prompting growth. Superconsciousness, or samadhi, and Dzogchen (the fundamental innate mind of clear light and rigpa) are complementary aspects of a purified state of beingness in which the ego has been completely dissolved and discarded. *The Gospel of Philip* references the *clear light*, which is a reference to samadhi and Dzogchen. They are essentially the same. Samadhi is the state of beingness (soul), Dzogchen is the state of the mind (the clear light), and purified spirit (heart) is the purified state of consciousness achieved in mystical union with God.

According to Greg Braden, author of *Resilience from the Heart*, there is now evidence, science of the anatomy and physiology of the heart, that supports ancient wisdom and the communication of consciousness from the soul to the heart and body mind. Sensory neurites are tiny projections of axons and dendrites, which are part of the neurons. Found in the heart, they form an intricate network of... "neurotransmitters, proteins and support cells similar to those found in the brain proper" (12). The heart acts as a monitoring system, monitoring hormones and other chemicals and then communicating those changes to the brain, translating the chemistry of the body into the electrical language of the nervous system so that it makes sense to the brain. This description of physiology is analogous to the realization process of conscious awareness in the soul, body (heart), and mind relationship. Braden adds that the heart functions also provide "heart intelligence or wisdom, intentional states of deep intuition and allowing for intentional precognitive abilities" (13). He is actually referring to the soul integrated and incarnated in the heart or body mind—similar to the discoveries of two-way communication between mind and body in Pert's and Lipton's case and of consciousness in the soul, mind, and body in Pert's and Hunt's case. Together the science supports awareness-based consciousness research leading to the existence of God, not the absence of God, leading to the mystery of life itself. It is imperative for enlightenment-based science to continue on this path of discovery, providing unlimited potential and creative solutions for our problems today and challenges of tomorrow. The answers are there; we just need to tune into them, discover them, and share them with others.

Ego-based science and the Newtonian three-dimensional mechanistic model of health are outdated and antiquated. Even so, that model still has a purpose, but it should not be the standard-bearer for health, because its main function is to detect absence of disease. Well-being is not the absence of symptoms but the full expression of the spirit through the mind and body, with the soul illuminating and animating the life-form with vitality and vibrancy to shine like a star in the night sky and like the sun during the day, brilliant and perfect in its beingness, expressing optimal health and feeling whole and complete.

Enlightened, spirit-based consciousness approaches to treating disease and restoring and maintaining health, along with traditional medicine when needed, will keep more people alive and restore wholeness to them so they can live their lives, discover their purpose, and fulfill God's will for them, filling the world with peace, love, and joy; making the world a better place for all who are here now; and preparing it for those to come in the future.

So far, we have learned about creation and the link to the lower energies and lower creations from the higher in the mystical marriage. We have learned about the individual who embodies theocentric psychology and the science, art, and philosophy of being from the beatitudes. We have learned the origin of the ego-and-soul conflict, and as a result of the process of becoming human, we've learned that the powers and principalities make us aware of our feelings of humanness, unconsciousness, and brokenness and that these feelings require healing in order to be released, along with the cooperation of the person to be healed or the patient. We also have touched on the level of consciousness required for such healing and the eventual role of the patient.

The remainder of this review of the literature will not focus on which people can be helped—anyone with a spiritual intention to truly heal can be—or on those who would understand, for they are not a problem and, therefore, are coherent with spirit and what they can learn from it. Our focus is on those who present an obstacle to spiritual reform and those who are ego-based or an ego-based hybrid, which will be discussed in the "Discussion" section of this paper.

Jim Marion, a contemporary mystic and author of *Putting On the Mind of Christ*, elaborates in his book on the developmental level of consciousness from infancy to adulthood to spiritual maturity in Christ consciousness and the kingdom of heaven. For the purposes of this paper, I will focus on what he calls the *mythic level of consciousness*, ages seven through twelve, when ego begins to emerge to an outer expression through projection to impose its way of thinking on others outwardly. It is a shift from inward selfishness to the outward culture but is still egocentric. This is a mindset in which the child wants to please others in his or her immediate environment and God and sees the world as it is through dysfunctional eyes. The child therefore sees rules and roles taught by authority figures, such as parents, teachers, and ministers, as the only way to please the one true Christian God. "The child assumes that everything in its immediate cultural environment is the only true way to do things and the only true way to think" (44). This thinking continues, as Marion explains:

> For the adult Christian whose consciousness has not progressed beyond the mythic level of consciousness, it is important to convert the whole world to the one true Christian religion (and to make sure governments enact laws that agree with what the believer has been taught are Christian morals) because, in the end this is the only real way the mythic believer can safely secure his own righteousness. This requires the elimination by conversion or otherwise, of all "others" because all such "others" are seen as threatening the mythic believer's eternally defined sense of worth. A mythic Christian cannot rest until the whole world thinks and does as he or she has been schooled as a child to think and do. (44)

This level of ego causes all conflict in the world and the universe. David Hawkins, in his book *Dissolving the Ego, Realizing the Self,* comments on the ego: "Although the human mind likes to believe that it is "of course" dedicated to truth, in reality, what it seeks is confirmation of what it already believes. The ego is innately prideful and does not welcome the revelation that much of its beliefs are merely perceptual illusions" (47). Hawkins also adds this insight: "The ego presumes and is convinced that its perceptions and interpretations of life experiences are the "real" thing and therefore" true". It also believes by projection that other people see, think, and feel the same way—if they do not, they are mistaken and therefore wrong. Thus, perception reinforces its hold by reification and presumptions" (46). Hawkins comments specifically on ego and spirit: "Historically, man paradoxically fears his own projections and confuses Divinity with the repressed dark side of his own nature" (28).

Andrew Newberg, MD, found the following in his research for his book *How God Changes Your Brain*: "Those engaged in eastern spiritual practices were more accepting of outer religious beliefs than those adhered to Western mono-theistic traditions" (81).

It is clear that spirituality is universal and more accepting of others' differences and that religion is more focused on egoic behavior and immaturity. Spirituality is more mature.

DISCUSSION

I alluded, in the closing remarks of the review of literature, to the introduction of hybrids. A hybrid is a composite or composition of ego and soul. There are ego-based hybrids who are predominantly ego-based but have the memory of the soul and its origin intact. This is known as the divine memory, which includes the complete story of creation to mortal consciousness. There are also soul-based hybrids. This means the soul has awakened but may still need to embody and has yet to process and integrate the last remnant of the ego to achieve mystical union with God. The other two possible configurations of ego and soul are pure ego and pure soul. The majority of people on the planet are hybrids of consciousness. It is important to point out that until mystical union with God is achieved, a hybrid may awaken, and the spiritual development is conceptual, not experiential, at this point. In other words, the word has not yet become flesh or real.

After embodiment of the soul, which leads to processing and integrating the ego when dealing with feelings internally, one must guard against others' internal projections as well as negative thoughts and feelings, in addition to outer projections. The dynamic of the ego is such that at the inception point in the mind (where the ego and soul originate, because they occupy the same internal space, only not at the same time, unless in the reconciliation process), the powers and principalities pass through humans' minds and hearts, committing the acts and potential acts of evil in spirit and in the world. It is part of being human to experience and express this, and it usually involves others. For those who have not awakened, this is the case, and souls who still have not worked through their remaining ego and woundedness are intimidated by doing God's will, until they mystically, spiritually become one in union with God. The soul is working with memory of being and not being itself until union with God is achieved. The soul yearns to fulfill its divine feelings, while the ego desires to deny its feelings of humanness, unconsciousness, and brokenness. With stirring of the divine memory come hope and the memory of God, but because the soul has not yet awakened, the ego occupies the heart, occluding, through illusion, God's presence and reserving space for the powers and principalities to enter the heart and commit evil acts toward self and others. Jesus washed His disciples' feet because the disciples' self-righteousness was escalating to the level of judgment. Thus, Jesus washed their feet, cleansing their understanding, to disengage their egos and empower their souls through humility.

Working out a solution with others' feelings internally in each encounter will begin or move further along the process of awakening or growth in others. When working on oneself and the feelings involved, one has to mitigate one's own feelings of ego, which switches to mitigating interaction with others. Generational sin consists of unconscious, unresolved feelings passed down from generation to generation. Once resolved appropriately, they transform into blessings. Chakra three is volitional sin. Chakra two is the sin of omission. Chakra one is generational sin.

Ego the illusion of being. When confronted with truth, the ego will have a split-second delay from spiritually bypassing but will choose, because of its default setting, illusion. It chooses illusion not by choice but by its programming and habit. When spiritually bypassing, the ego will create an illusion complete with a narrative of an explanation that brings it comfort and maintains its illusionary nature. The ego tells itself what it wants to hear that correlates to the voice of illusion (the broken Lilith) and its default setting of separation from God and nature. This is known as the error to justify its existence to itself to keep the illusion of being intact.

When one is operating out of the ego, the ego generates confusion. Confusion exists because of the ego itself and as a result of double-mindedness, which is indicative of a hybrid state. This confusion is based upon predominant ego consciousness as the controlling mechanism of the organism. Confusion is present because the ego competes with and tries to control anything or anyone who contradicts it, especially the consciousness of God. Within an individual, thoughts and thought forms of the ego compete directly with God's communications through the divine memory or the soul, giving one the experience of a split-second gap or pause between thoughts. The ego constantly tries to conceal the gap or pause. This back-and-forth dynamic goes on until one gives up trying, exhausted. Fatigue leads to one's giving up in defeat to the ego. The soul is divine and is an individualized, living creation of awareness and God consciousness that has all the attributes of God. It has permanent staying power; it is eternal. It vanquishes and sublimates the ego, eliminating it and the confusion that goes along with it, leaving love, truth, and peace within instead of doubt, uncertainty, anger, and fear.

The book of Revelation precedes Genesis from a chronological and spiritual perspective. It marked the beginning, not the end, of humanity and organized the details of creation from the highest to the lowest on the consciousness scale. It depicted and laid out the gauntlet or path one must travel to earth from heaven and from earth to heaven. John's vision in Revelation illustrates the struggle the soul is to go through and is the first coming of Christ. Jesus's incarnation and embodiment are experiences of the soul in the body and represent the second coming of Christ. John's other vision on Patmos Island was a vision of peace, an experience of Christ through the mind, and is the third coming of Christ. The mystical knowledge of the book of Revelation was given to start the creation of humanity, not finish it. The positioning of the book of Revelation at the end of the Bible should be questioned, given the church's history of omitting and changing the Bible and its teaching over time.

The kings of the Bible, specifically in the Old Testament, led complex lives. Kings, such as Solomon and David, had concubines,,who had a spiritual purpose and related to power. Because Jesus Christ's second coming in the flesh had not happened yet, spiritually, life was different back then than it was after Jesus Christ's incarnation. The kings took concubines to stabilize their souls when it came time to incarnate. Incarnating back then almost assuredly led to the possibility that one would become evil, because internally, the pathway had not yet been established in the body by Jesus Christ. Each concubine represented a different facet or past life that was played out externally in physical reality with both blessings and curses. This was done because intuitively, the kings, with the guidance of the prophets, knew the marriage of Adam and Eve represented illusion and led away from God. The kings had to deal not only with their egos but also with the anguish of their souls. Astrology was and is an art and science for navigating the ego, karma, and the feelings the soul goes through. This is why the wise men visited the birth of Christ—because it would help souls to lead simpler, less complex lives.

Adam and Eve and Jesus and Lilith

Before Eve, there was Lilith. Both Adam and Lilith were created out of the earth. Adam, being predominantly ego, and Lilith, being predominantly soul, disagreed over who would be in control and whether feelings would be acknowledged or denied. They fought over it, and neither would submit to the other. Original sin is the original disagreement between Adam and Lilith. As a result, Lilith took the blame (took on Adam's negative projection) for the incompatibility and was banished to hell or earth. She had to go on the journey alone, and along the way, she encountered Satan, who was there for her when she could not go on anymore under her own power. Lilith didn't fully realize what she was taking on, until it was too late, and after the process had started, she didn't know at the time how to stop it. It continued and broke her. It made her human.

She became aware of evil, and the feelings she experienced were indiscernible from divine feelings, which she previously had known. It all happened so fast and in a way that she felt as if she didn't have a chance or a choice as to what happened to her. Her choices became limited, and soon she only saw one way of doing things. She became angry and resentful as a result of her journey and destination and feared she would become forever lost from God. As a result of her brokenness, unconsciousness, and humanness, her negative emotions vowed revenge on all souls who journeyed to earth, as a way to get back at Adam and God for her brokenness and her transformation.

Meanwhile, God tried again to create another woman for Adam who would get along with him. Adam was put into a deep sleep, and God took a piece of Adam, his rib, and made Eve from it. When Adam awoke, he was pleased with Eve. God created Eve from Adam, but they were not equal.

The rib signifies Adam's heart and the positive virtues that go along with it. Because God took the rib from Adam to make Eve, the light of his soul shone outward as a reflection on her. Because of these two aspects of his heart and soul, Adam was satisfied.

Lilith and Satan devised a plan to make others become like them, brokenhearted and lost. They were the first ones to succumb to humanness, unconsciousness, and brokenness and, as a result, took over earth with their power and desired control of heaven also. Lilith transformed into a serpent and visited Eve in the Garden of Eden to inform her of God's plan to atone for blame she had taken from Adam. She convinced Eve of God's plan for Jesus Christ to rescue her and all of humanity from her sin that she put all of humanity in after her transformation. God had mercy on Lilith and allowed her soul to awaken, but she would not be free until after Christ's crucifixion, resurrection, and ascension. He gave her a chance to totally and completely redeem herself with Jesus Christ's help. Adam and Eve fell into brokenness, unconsciousness, humanness, and, eventually, sin. Lilith had gotten her revenge on all souls who made the journey from heaven to earth. Lilith was the one who took the blame for her and Adam's not getting along, and God allowed her revenge so Adam would begin to understand what the disagreement really had been about between himself and Lilith.

Adam refused to look at the brokenness, unconsciousness, humanness, and loss of becoming human. They argued about who would be the first to go through the process. By default and Adam's projection, Lilith became the first to become human, brokenhearted, and lost. Lilith went through the process of being deceived by feelings that were not based in love and truth. Lilith became the feelings that refused to be ignored and had to be dealt with maturely and resolved with love. Lilith became all negative feelings and emotions, with no outlet of expression except for evil, until God allowed her soul to awaken. Jesus Christ's job was and is to guarantee all souls are able to choose good or evil, using their free will consciously and with awareness. Christ's integration and incarnation into wholeness on the cross by the resurrection allow all souls to have free will to choose love or fear. Christ's light and love allowed Adam and Eve to work through their difficult feelings associated with brokenness and loss and do spiritual growth work to realize the truth of their relationship. Eve represented

Adam's heart and soul, which Adam had to accept responsibility for, as reflected to him in Eve. Eve represented virtue in his heart and love in his soul. As Adam realized this, his rib returned to him, and Eve disappeared, for Eve was an illusion created for the sole purpose of helping Adam to realize what was truly important. Eve disappeared, and Lilith returned. Adam, through Christ's help, was integrated and incarnated and whole, and he became the reflection of Lilith. With Adam's and Christ's help, she worked through the difficult negative feelings to become integrated, incarnated, and whole again. She was no longer lost or broken and remembered her divinity. At that point, Adam transformed into Jesus Christ, and he and Lilith returned to the garden and had access to the Tree of Life, living in the light of the resurrection, integrated, individuated, incarnated, and whole.

While Adam was with Eve, because she represented the reflection of the virtues of his heart and his soul, he spent a lot of time in his head, learning about the faculties of logic, reason, intellect, and thought. Eve, because she was created from Adam, felt controlled and longed for her turn in the relationship to grow and experience life being. He lived from his soul, expressing his heart, and learned wisdom and discernment as to the different aspects of the heart, being, ego expression, soul expression, brokenness, and virtue. Adam became perfect, meaning he was a living, breathing human being, living from his soul and expressing the virtue of his heart, which was now whole, while taking responsibility for his negative feelings of brokenness, unconsciousness, and humanness and not blaming or projecting them onto Eve or Lilith. Jesus and Lilith returned to heaven in the glory of the angels in God's presence, fulfilling the scripture in the resurrection. There was no marriage, but the individuals were like the angels.

The apostle Peter denied Jesus Christ three times, which symbolizes the chakras the feelings of brokenness, unconsciousness, and humanness occupy, respectively. This is evidence that Peter was a hybrid. He was spiritually awakened but not yet embodied or integrated and incarnated. He had not yet become whole. Jesus, after the resurrection, asked him to feed His lambs three times, giving further evidence that Peter had not yet completed the journey set out before him. Jesus chose Peter to be the rock upon which the church was to be built. The rock symbolizes mystical experience, because the storms of life will not knock it down or wash it away. The remnant of the ego is the last stronghold within before mystical union with God. Jesus Christ was the stone rejected by the builder because the collective ego didn't accept him, but the same can be said of Peter as well. The last remnant of the ego inside Peter was what Jesus was referring to when He chose Peter to establish and lead the church. The rock of mystical experience, by giving up the last remnant of his ego, was imperfect and rejected by him. By integrating it into himself, he would become the rock and the church Jesus Christ envisioned.

Strongholds are places and pieces of brokenness we give up in the breaking process God uses to test our loyalty to Him. Once they are worked through and processed, they are integrated and contribute to wholeness. Whenever there is a remnant of the ego or a stronghold present, a spiritual bypass is actively blocking connection to God's presence and preventing a complete or more complete realization and understanding of a perceptual or apparent division or conflict of ideas, thoughts, or feelings among self, others, and God. Awareness and discernment are needed to identify the source and origin of the illusion-based construct perceptually believed to be real during the breaking process.

Healing comes from God, and for a cocreator being one with God, it is OK to allow oneself, through the soul, heart, mind, and spirit, to be part of the process. It is understandable why one would want to be careful about claiming credit for healing. After all, such a self-conscious realization about oneself would indicate one is aware of a remnant of the ego or stronghold still left as a potential source of ego elation or ego inflation diverting one's self from God. However, to hold such a notion as to not allow one's self to become part of the process and share in the experience not only is a subtle form of denial of one's divinity but also prevents one's self from further healing what remains left to heal. The ego protects the remnant, which gives the ego a purpose to remain. After all, once we become one with God, we share in God's attributes and become God in the flesh, just as Jesus Christ did and modeled for us millennia ago. If there is a remnant of the ego unaccounted for, it will prevent full expression of God's presence, prevent healing, and not allow acceptance of God's gift of total wholeness and the abundant life God promises for us when we finally reach that point in our relationship with Him where total oneness is achieved.

There is a reluctance to give up the final remnant or stronghold of the ego, because of the fear of death. One of the many experiences a soul goes through is learning from the past and future how it relates to the present moment. Processing a traumatic death or passing is difficult for the soul to endure, and it takes another lifetime at least to process and integrate it into one's self. There is a fear that a future death may occur similar to the previous one, especially if one was following God's will. Using awareness and discernment, one must process the voice of illusion in the offender's consciousness to free not only one's own soul but also the difficult entanglement of the offender's. Both need to be forgiven and freed for harmony. Both need to be reestablished so a higher choice can be made regarding the interaction or stimulation of both in any further activity between the two.

Oftentimes, there is a response threshold for internal or external stimuli that will be low regarding tolerance of dysfunctional behavior. In the midst of dealing with and processing these difficult feelings, a person may be agitated easily, be quick-tempered, or be a hothead. This is when the cross or load gets heavy and is difficult to carry. This is a temporary, transitional soul-based state of consciousness that lessens as one moves through it. When a formerly offending behavior or consciousness is no longer discerned to be intolerable, then the event has been successfully processed, and a new beginning begins. The work of the soul evolves over many lifetimes, until it reaches the lifetime where all is reconciled in not only the soul but also the heart and mind. Then all parts and all lifetimes are integrated and totally whole, and the wisdom, truth, knowledge, insight, love, and understanding are of God Himself, resolving any and all conflict before it begins with the living Word of God. One can use the lessons of the past and the future yet be in the present moment and make enlightened, intelligent choices by considering all possibilities and outcomes simultaneously for the benefit of one and all. The repression mechanism of the psyche relaxes once this has been achieved.

Jesus Christ, after His baptism (awakening), was a student as well as a teacher for others and God. When Jesus was presented with the woman caught in adultery and had to decide what to do with her, he paused and wrote in the sand, turning inward and tuning into God. This act of writing in the sand set a boundary internally to determine for the woman to bring awareness to her feelings and to consider them before they were acted upon and became sin. Jesus knew what the problem was, but He didn't know how each encounter with others would go or how He was to deal and interact with them. Jesus had faith. In the case of the woman, He affirmed what He already knew: she was doing the best she could with where she was. But He didn't know yet specifically what needed to be done for her. Jesus awakened her soul to at least be aware of her internal process, discern the different types of feelings that were her experiences, and begin using her free will, giving her a sense of positive self-esteem and well-being.

At the same time, Jesus knew it wasn't her fault but also knew she had to take responsibility for her actions. Therefore, He forgave her trespass of the law, raised her up to fulfillment of the law, and left the rest up to her as far as where her life would go next. He told her to go and sin no more. The penalty for her actions would not have helped her to learn and evolve. Mercy and forgiveness, Jesus knew, lead to life and love. Penalty and punishment add insult to injury for someone experiencing sin and death. The woman was spiritually dead, not conscious or aware of what she was doing and how it was affecting herself and others. Jesus brought the woman's experience outside herself by telling the angry mob, "He who is without sin may cast the first stone." This act brought her inner experience outward to her new reality, which persuaded the crowd to also stop and consider their feelings leading to their actions. The woman was transformed and given another chance with awareness and discernment to make a higher choice to follow love and truth, or God.

The angry crowd also learned the same lesson, as Christ's divinity used that incident to teach everyone involved, including Jesus. It was a stepping-stone in redeeming the inner lives of people back to God and making inner reality one with the outer reality in a positive and loving expression, with love and truth showing God's mercy and forgiveness, instead of a negative expression of sin and death. Jesus Christ left the woman with the affirmation to go and sin no more, affirming her experience and allowing her to realize that from that point forward, she now had a choice and was equipped to make it.

When Jesus Christ asked Peter, "Who do you say I am?" and Peter responded, "The Christ," Jesus said it was God who revealed this to him. Jesus was ascertaining if and how His teaching and influence were being received internally within the collective unconscious and where He was in His mission to integrate (through crucifixion), incarnate (through resurrection), and ascend back to heaven, fulfilling His journey. Jesus's soul knew of His impending future, but He didn't realize it until His time in the garden of Gethsemane. Jesus's realization continued all through the last twelve hours of His life and through His death, resurrection, and ascension. At that moment, all was realized. The purpose of His beingness was in fulfilling God's will, and His soul's purpose was in helping others to obtain for themselves what He obtained with His life in the physical and the spiritual.

Each piece of the ego that is sublimated has an attachment to every soul fragment in the psyche. The soul is concerned with love, truth, meaning, and purpose. The ego is preoccupied with escaping reality through illusion, spiritual bypass (bypassing lower, painful, or difficult feelings), and living a fear-based consciousness that is only interested in survival of itself, in which any means justify the ends, regardless of others. Every piece of the soul that is integrated and healed restores wholeness and unity with love for God, others, and self. Every piece of the ego that is surrendered releases selfishness, dysfunction, and the attraction of grandiose illusions of ego elation associated with personality traits and the status of who a person was in a past life, versus a life-hood, which is interested in the meaning and purpose of a past life and how that past life relates to and is significant to the present moment. Each piece of the ego has with it a pattern and program for a potential future life based upon past existences. Each one culminated similar to the soul's fragments, with a cumulative summation of consciousness as to what has been learned, what has been resolved, and what remains to be learned and done as far as experience, leading to realization and appropriate resolution.

Each piece of ego contains a configuration of some negative process that needs to be experienced and explored from the viewpoint of being separate from God so it can have a believable reality as to its experience. In this way, it has something to compare to when the soul awakens, so it can begin to determine if the life experience it experienced is sufficient for the purpose involved. Does the purpose involved have meaning? Does the experience lead to God and onement? Or does it lead away from God? That is the question asked at the moment of truth if it can be determined when this point arrives. Does it satisfy the soul? Or does it indulge the ego? Does it give the illusion of satisfying both? God does not judge or condemn. God only asks if we accomplished what we set out to learn and experience and if we have enough information and experience to make the choices necessary to grow and evolve.

Has the purpose of oneness with God been achieved, or is there more to do to get there? Once the soul realizes and determines with the heart that future lives for the purpose of ego gratification are not fulfilling, then onement and harmony can be achieved with God. Then onement and the present moment become real, as do the soul, heart, and mind, integrated as one. One has the realization that the learning the ego provided was just enough and sufficient for the soul, heart, and mind to be able to realize and determine love and truth from its experience of illusion, spiritual bypass, and fear. The decision for future lives comes from the soul, based upon its capacity for learning and the realization that more life experience is required for the soul to be satisfied to obtain oneness with God. Until it is realized and determined that the soul, not the ego, is the one that makes the choices for its growth and evolution and that the soul, not the ego, is in control of the life-form, there will be confusion present when these feelings and issues arise in the life-form, and the process will come to a stop until successfully resolved. God is not the author of confusion, and confusion is not of God. Confusion comes from the ego thinking, in its illusion bypass state, that it is God and in control and can make choices that entrap the soul as an attempt to avoid itself and avoid facing its pain to grow, heal, release, and relinquish control to the soul.

Because of how closely tied the ego is to the soul through the voice of illusion, when the moment of truth comes, there is confusion, because the basis for the ego and the basis for the soul occupy the same space internally at the inception point, or the back door of the mind, through which the powers and principalities pass through in the mind. The voice of illusion competes with the living Word of God, and because illusion has been the predominant consciousness for so long, when it comes up to be evaluated, it is rejected by the indwelling life-forms because deep down, they know they have erroneously chosen unbelief in God and belief in illusion, but they don't know how to rectify it, because of how the ego was configured to begin with. They cannot answer God, because their minds won't let them amid the confusion of the voice of illusion competing with the voice of the living Word of God. This predicament is resolved only through healing or awakening through healing or meditation, and whether it is through one's own internal consciousness or involves another soul from a current, past, or future life, incarnating will be premature and lead to an unfulfilled life. God grants transitional states of consciousness in expression because the soul may need more life experience to make a choice based upon realization, discernment, and determination to evolve and move forward in its evolution toward onement with God and because the ego may simply not be ready to surrender control to the soul. This prolongs the transitional state so it may experience both the soul and the ego in transition to arrive at the inception point of both the ego and the soul's origin to understand the etiology and origin of both, using awareness and discernment to determine if its learning and life experience are sufficient to make the choice to go through the last remnant of the ego in the final transition from being human to being a human being.

While experiencing a transitional state, a person may continue to accrue important life experience, but there will be an overall sense of unfulfillment and emptiness from the remainder of the ego. Sometimes the ego will need to exhaust all its illusions and escapes to finally arrive at the point where the soul's longing and yearning for union and onement with God become stronger than the ego's need to fantasize and escape. This stage of transition and development is critical because the ego is finally ready to surrender itself, learning that its own desires will eventually lead to its own demise and undoing and that it is better off surrendering on its own terms versus ending up a failure and prolonging potential misery for another lifetime or longer. When this is realized, the ego surrenders to the soul, and evolution happens and progresses forward to reveal what the ego had hoped for in its surrender: the true expression of the heart through the soul and integration also of the mind to become the person one was meant to be. Our beingness, after going through this transition, matches the creation created in the mind of God. We are now like God, and God is like us. Life is lived from this fully integrated higher perspective. The soul navigates life with intuition and God's guidance in harmony and is at peace because it is allowed to be, and the ego rests in peace because it has successfully lived out and fulfilled its purpose.

The transitional states of expression are both part of who we really are (soul) and not who we really are (ego) at the same time. The potential problem with this state of transition is that a person may draw a conclusion based upon this state and be fooled by the ego and its desire to be stronger than the soul's yearning to evolve and be. This, accompanied by the elation of the ego over not having to face its contents and feelings of pain, is a more desirable state overall to the ego, and people will think this composite construct of mind is who they are supposed to be. Thus, they inadvertently stop the process and progress of soul evolution and who they really are and are meant to be, in favor of a lesser state of being. In this lesser state, the ego is still in control and has not reached the moment of truth and the inception point of both for the ego to surrender and for the soul to use its free will to choose to become a human being instead of being just human.

The accumulated summation of all past lives at this point, and their stages of learning and development, will be reconciled, determining if a future life (or lives) is (or are) needed or if the learning is sufficient to become a human being and enter the present moment with past, present, and future as one. Dysfunction results when the internal state, transitional or otherwise, other than God, is manifested in behavior being negatively projected outwardly by the person onto his- or herself or others. If it is projected onto oneself or others, it causes harm to self or others in the form of emotional or spiritual abuse or both. This will lead to conflict within oneself or others, causing dissonance within the collective consciousness and the collective unconscious, as well as disharmony within oneself and the others it affects.

A projection is a disowned construct or fragment that is part of a thought or feeling that is rejected because of the pain it causes to the inhabitant, who displaces it onto his or her soul inwardly or projects it onto another outwardly. In either case, the disowned construct being rejected is subconsciously judged to be wrong by default (caused by the associated illusion and spiritual bypass) and, therefore, unacceptable and undesirable to the inhabitant, so it is projected onto the soul within the inhabitant, onto others, or both. The conflict it creates must be appropriately dealt with to achieve agreement between the one projecting and the one being projected upon. The one coming from higher consciousness through the living Word of God will be given the wisdom, knowledge, truth, love, understanding, and discernment to isolate and reveal the source of the conflict so that others on the receiving end of the projection are unburdened by it, atoning for the projector or offender and offering counsel through a spirit-discerned observation. This will allow offenders a reflective pause to reconsider their behavior, actions, and internal status; be honest with themselves; and evaluate where they are compared to the truth they encounter.

The consternation and strife caused by the incident must be appropriately resolved so harmony and peace are restored; the projector may make another, hopefully higher, choice; and those projected on may forgive and remain free. A spirit-discerned observation points out character flaws or shortcomings of the ego that are capable of being changed by the person it inhabits.

The goal of Christianity is to eliminate the ego within oneself. It was never meant to be a way for the ego to have God on its terms, which is what it has been since Christ and before. Jesus Christ's life and events, along with what the living Word of God proclaimed and spoke through Him, illustrate the growth process from start to finish regarding how to eliminate the ego so one is not double-minded as a state of mind, continually being human (with exception of being a hybrid in a transitional state of consciousness with the goal of union with God), and how to appropriately become a creation of God in being a human being. According to the *Gospel of Philip*, the goal of Christianity is for one to become a Christ. The Word of God uses economy and efficiency in how to accomplish this with every soul ever created.

The feelings of humanness, unconsciousness, and brokenness impose themselves on your soul to create the illusion they are who you are supposed to be by the nature of experiencing them. The imposition they impose is a cumulative effect of many feelings at once, experienced one at a time, with each one building upon the one previously experienced, until eventually, the intellect constructs an identity and narrative based upon the data and limited information of the feelings of humanness, unconsciousness, and brokenness. It fully compartmentalizes all inquiry into them back into themselves, enclosing the entire creation back into itself to create an individualized ego connected to the source of the feelings and the collective ego as well. This process of ego formation is based upon shadows and illusion, with traits, characteristics, and constructs that mirror the soul as its opposite, overcompensating for its limited lack of divinity by imposing how the ego feels and how it was created onto other life-forms, trying to create another in its own image based upon its own creation through negative, dysfunctional projection, not taking responsibility for its own feelings of humanness, unconsciousness, and brokenness.

Unbelief is the point at which the soul gives in to illusion during the process of being broken and configured with an ego. This is why many Christians believe Satan and ego over God and have such a difficult time with sin and their faith. It causes not only unbelief in God but also unbelief that they are capable of becoming evil.

Choices that are ego-based compound negative feelings expressed in the mind, body (heart), and soul. These lower energies cause tension in the soul, body (heart), and mind and alter, distort, and contract the natural homeostasis of the soul, mind, and body. The tension of lower energy causes higher energies to pool and become isolated, walled off, and compartmentalized in the soul, mind, and body, which is a reflection of the internal state of the individual, with the ego expressing through the mind, body, and soul and its state of humanness, unconsciousness, and brokenness. This dynamic, which is static, is based upon the soul's journey into brokenness, unconsciousness, and humanness. Feelings that are based in brokenness are separate from God and the soul and cause fragmentation, based upon the ego's own morphology and physiology, which is isolated, constricted, and contracted. This activity and part of the condition of the soul, mind, and body disrupt the natural healing intelligence, which is interrupted by the feelings of lower, unconscious energies surfacing into the subconscious or conscious mind, becoming dysfunctional to the surface level of the conscious mind and changing the function, structure, and morphology of the soul, mind, and body.

Physically, the cells of the body, morphologically speaking, become distorted, causing a disruption in cellular exchange of depolarization of the cell membrane; thus, nutrients cannot enter, nor can waste products exit the cells. This causes stasis, or a condition that causes temporary cell dysfunction and can lead to cell death. It causes natural physiological processes to stagnate and build up pressure within the body. This feeds back into the mind and the soul, compounding the pain or discomfort of the feelings of brokenness and leaving the person experiencing this in misery, with all the faculties of the soul, mind, and body at a standstill. The person remains focused on the misery that will not let up, until the person seeks a remedy to counteract the pathology of unending suffering and subsequent cell death absent vitality and life force, or prana. The energy that gets cut off in the soul, mind, and body needs to be reconnected as part of the life force and healed to unify the overall energies and consciousness of the soul, mind, and body. The feelings themselves need to be released, as well as any other entities or energies that are part of the composite structure of the pathology originating in and with the ego. Healing restores balance and equilibrium and removes disruption and interference with God. Through the breaking process, the soul is broken, as are the mind and body, by lower energies.

There is an internal environment and an external environment. They are separate from each other, although they interface and interact with each other until mystical union oneness with God is achieved. Then the inner and outer environments are one. The internal environment is the predominant or governing mechanism of the mind, body (heart), and soul. Physically, the awareness of the cells—through their receptors for environmental signals that indicate emotional, spiritual, mental, and physical interpretation and behavioral expression as either health or disease of the mind, body (heart), or soul—is dependent upon expression of either the ego, with its feelings of humanness, unconsciousness, and brokenness, or the soul, with its divine feelings of love and truth and attributes of God. This determines whether disease (ego) or health (soul) is expressed and experienced through the cell membrane.

The powers and principalities release the contents of the soul's subconscious, complete with personality, karma, and all life lessons of every incarnation, to predispose the soul to favoring the ego, not only to become one with the ego but also to live with it and accept it as a normal state of alternative consciousness to the soul. With this comes the aforementioned process of a complicated feedback mechanism to attempt to bring awareness to the inner brokenness and pathology in the hope that free will is chosen and used to begin the process of healing and integrating one negative feeling at a time to become whole. The transfer mechanism and manifestation mechanism of consciousness referenced by Pert, Hunt, Braden, and Lipton in this paper give evidence of the physical manifestation of disease. That same mechanism is used to bring about healing. The soul, mind, and body, in disease and dysfunction as well as healing, operate as a unit. In dysfunction and disease, they operate as separate, distinct entities, reflecting the fragmentation of the soul as expressed by the ego. Contrastingly, the unified, integrated whole is evident in healing, leading to well-being and wholeness.

At the soul level, the breaking process by the powers and principalities causes fragmentation of the soul into pieces enveloped by negative feelings of humanness, unconsciousness, and brokenness. This, at the level of mind, causes thought forms and constructs that cause blockages in the mind body. These blockages occur in consciousness and affect the soul, mind, and body. Healing reverses this process, restoring wholeness and well-being by removing blockages until the ego is eventually consumed into light. Then this process no longer continues, and the complete history of the ego from all lifetimes is resolved.

The ego is a false facsimile separate from God, based upon illusion of spirit, for the purpose of experiencing itself as a separate, distinct entity not associated with God. It creates an experience that is less dimensional than divinity to have as its source to rely on, with only a memory of its former heritage at its disposal to learn from. It navigates life from a limited perspective, seeking fulfillment outside itself and never achieving it, spiritually bypassing its inner contents and chasing illusions to fulfill itself. Its etiology and morphology are closely fabricated with the soul to create a similar but opposite viewpoint that is incomplete, with an insecure, uncertain outlook and a personality that competes directly with the soul for control and dominance over itself to maintain itself for the purpose of illusion-based experience.

The ego will use scripture to try to justify itself and its positionalities, establishing itself through religion or religious insinuation to pit itself against others as the one and only true religion or source of God, making itself right according to itself, making all others wrong, and justifying discrimination as God's will for its life and the lives of others.

Faith is the trusting that takes place in God between intervals of experience. It is knowing that each succeeding step will lead to union with God.

Belief is the construct used by the ego when it has no conscious knowledge to base its experience on. Thus, an illusion is created to fill the void or gap left by lack of experience.

Illusion is something untrue conceived by the ego to bring comfort to itself.

Believing is the mechanism used by the soul to transcend from one level of consciousness to another, appropriately adjudicating feelings of humanness, unconsciousness, and brokenness.

The soul believes. The ego creates illusions. The soul transcends. The ego thinks it knows, based upon its illusions. The soul believes in God because it knows God. The ego creates illusion to compensate for not knowing God. The ego thinks it believes but is fooling itself with illusions, which are false beliefs. The soul knows Christ because it is Christ and has Christ consciousness. The ego has illusions, doesn't know Christ, and is unconscious.

So when Christians say, quoting from the Bible, that whoever believes in Jesus Christ will not perish but have eternal life, they are creating an illusion, because the ego does not believe; only the soul does. There's also the illusion that Jesus Christ has done their spiritual growth work for them, which is a spiritual bypass bypassing necessary growth. Because of the illusions the ego makes regarding scripture, the ego assumes its own created illusions are true and fools itself by its own thinking. It thinks it knows what believing and Jesus Christ are all about. It concludes according to its own thinking, judging itself as correct by its own illusion-created thinking. It knows its illusions well and, therefore, also concludes they are correct, according to its self-created illusion. The ego thinks its illusions are true and rejoices in them and feels elated. It incorrectly interprets the elation as the Holy Spirit and God, but it is actually ego elation. This ego elation will produce false joy, love, humility, and piousness. Therefore, it becomes loving toward others and wants to share this dynamic with others. These individuals think they are free because their illusions are free of feelings that were created by the intellect, and their egos are based in illusion.

The soul, and the experience of spirituality, will use scripture to convey wisdom, unifying divisions among different people and expressing truth that is inclusive of all and has a message of love and truth for all to empower and make whole all who come in contact with it. Modern-day religion promises all kinds of things to its members if they pledge their allegiance to it. Most religions try to repackage themselves and distance themselves from religion because religion itself is viewed negatively. Religion through the ego promises a relationship with God that doesn't deliver because it is based upon the ego, and a memory of one's former past as a child of God is relegated to just that: a memory. A real relationship with God is a living, breathing, full manifestation of spirit, not rah-rah religion or a pep rally once a week on Sunday. It is a real, living thing that is sustainable without the need of others, a church, or a pastor as a go-between to connect the self to God. Religion and churches dominated by ego consciousness use control, power, guilt, and manipulation to retain members and keep them coming back and seek to change the world by converting more people to this mindset in ego. Such institutions keep the true source of God within the soul, and a real relationship with God is held captive in favor of a dysfunctional, codependent relationship with the ego and others in the name of God to perpetuate the ego and make it feel good about itself. But ultimately, this leaves one feeling empty inside. The person will try to fill that void with a whole host of dysfunction instead of what will really satisfy him or her: being in the light of God's presence, This is found only in the soul with mystical experience of God. God's light presence is the only real relationship there is. It is meant to be spread and shared with others. This is true beingness based in love and truth, with realization of oneself in a state of beingness instead of ego based in doubt, dysfunction, and uncertainty. Religion tells the ego what it wants to hear, not what it needs to hear, as far as what people can do for themselves to get to heaven by taking emotional and spiritual responsibility for themselves.

What goes on in most mainstream Christian churches on Sunday is a display of dysfunction and abuse. The current trend is offering the congregation a relationship with God through Jesus Christ. Most pastors' idea of challenging you to grow is offering you a negative, dysfunctional projection; seeing if you agree with it; judging you for it if you do; and getting you to take it on so they can feel useful. Such a pastor then can preach and counsel you out of it into his illusion that he uses to justify his ego-based salvation (ego elation), which is not based in love or truth. He wants you to be like him, and if you don't agree with that, then in the pastor's opinion, you are not following God. The negative, dysfunctional projection of the pastor is usually given through anger and contempt of the pastor's own self-righteous indignation. His own wounding travels out from him to the congregation. The pastor's own hurt comes out through his preaching, and it wounds or abuses those who receive it as if it is true and is the Word of God, which it is not. Emotionally and spiritually, it abuses those who listen and absorb it, and they're traumatized by the event. Pastors, in most cases, are not aware they are doing this, and the congregation thinks that a loud, boisterous, bombastic, obnoxious, and pompous person preaching is just filled with the anger and spirit of God. Along with not being aware of being abused in the process, both the pastor and the congregation are blind to each other's dysfunction, and according to scripture, both shall fall into a ditch. It is the blind leading the blind. This dynamic is not about spreading the Word of God; it is about perpetuating ego and ego consciousness.

This occurs because both the pastors' and the congregations' ego-based consciousness or default setting was established when they were wounded and broken. Through ego elation, which is a trick of the mind established by Satan himself to deceive one's self, an illusion or false sense of salvation is created. However, the pastor and congregation think it is real. In real salvation through the soul, one works with God directly with the help of Christ and the Holy Spirit. The dysfunctional, illusion-based dynamic between the pastor and the congregation is the message they wish to share with others to convert the world and is what comes across when they present themselves to and interact with others and the world.

Common sense is spirit-based, and nonbelievers (those who do not share their dysfunction) see the dysfunction for what it is, quickly surmise and discern the double-mindedness, and see it as hypocrisy and conflict within the person presenting as a Christian. The Christians are not alive in the Spirit, for if they were, none of the negative dysfunction being talked about here would exist. They would have realized through awareness of the soul and Christ consciousness and effectively and appropriately worked through dealing with and eliminating their double-mindedness by dissolving their ego into the light of God's presence, experiencing directly their salvation and being secure in it. If they did this, then the pastor and the congregation would be taken seriously and not come across as walking contradictions of memory of spirit and ego-based dysfunction.

Because of double-mindedness in the church and the world, the church struggles with its assigned mission to help others. The people at the top and at the bottom are equally double-minded and dysfunctional, and nobody has a solution that will truly work, with few exceptions. The pastor and his congregation, other than offering basic spiritual common sense of loving others and forgiveness, don't have much to offer others to really help them to know God the way God wants them to know Him. If the pastor and the congregation really want to make a difference in the world and the lives of others, they must awaken their souls and Christ consciousness within, work through the negative dysfunction of their egos, and dissolve them in the light of God's presence. This is not achieved by intellectually proclaiming that Christ is your Lord and Savior, and it is not achieved by baptism, a mere formality and absent ritual not containing real mystical power. It is found within oneself, not outside oneself, through healing and meditation. Jesus Christ proclaimed that the kingdom of heaven is within you, and it is here and now. *Now* means in the present moment in your present lifetime, while you are still alive, not after you are dead. It is the ego that worries about death and dying. The soul and the spirit are concerned with life and living. God can work through anyone and anything, including the worst kind of unconscious, negative dysfunction there is. The pastor and congregation could do much more with God if they were open to it, but instead, because of their double-mindedness and egos, they will have to settle for a small, limited role in how they can help others. God waits patiently for them to take emotional and spiritual responsibility for themselves to become whole, balanced people who then would become effective agents of change in the world but not of it.

God says, "It is not them; it is you." This means taking responsibility for one's feelings and not blaming. The ego says, "It is them, not you," and projects its feelings onto others. The pastor and the congregation need to be the change they wish to see in the world. They are the ones who need to change to be wholly used by God and not pontificate platitudes of piousness. "Do not turn to the left or the right. Do not go forward. Turn around, and follow me" is God's admonition to go within and begin the process of becoming a real spiritual being with a real relationship with God. Once this is established, then one can see exactly what one is to do by living the soul's purpose, not only being part of God's plan for the world but also being a citizen and resident of heaven.

The practice of mainstream Christianity is based upon attending church weekly, attending Bible study, being in a small group, and volunteering in your church. If you do all these things and believe Jesus Christ died for your sins and absolved you of all responsibility emotionally and spiritually, your state of consciousness is rooted in false belief and wishful thinking. A false belief is a belief based upon illusion and wishful thinking that the illusion will come true. The ego elation that accompanies the practice of mainstream Christianity is based upon placating and keeping the ego happy by indulging in illusion versus real, authentic joy from God in beingness. The practice of mainstream Christianity is about outer busyness and doing, almost as though one is trying to get to heaven by how many good deeds one can do or how many activities one can be involved in. It is true God is busy being God and busy all the time, but a true sense of serving others comes from a state of being and wholeness found in the soul and God's presence. Trying to help others from a state of negative, dysfunctional consciousness will eventually lead to burnout, and one's health and circumstances will be affected negatively.

Helping others because it is your soul's purpose leads to fulfillment, meaning, health, longevity, and the blessing of others' lives as well as your own. The practice of mainstream Christianity may be helpful when the time comes for the soul to awaken, but the practice of it based upon ego will not get one to heaven, nor will it lead to eternal life. Mainstream Christianity, like most mainstream religions, is a holding cell for souls to spend time in until they are ready to take responsibility for themselves and become who God created them to, becoming human beings instead of just being human.

What many Christians think is their heart is actually their ego. This is because when they search or reference what they know where their heart is supposed to be, they find their ego there. When they encounter it, it tells them what to think and feel based upon its own programming. The ego is based upon itself, with its own God created to compete with the real God. However, in the ego, what it thinks is God is illusion, and through blame and projection of brokenness, it thinks the real God is the devil. It is backward from reality. The only relationship these individuals have is with themselves and is dysfunctional, operating out of the ego and a distant memory of God and heaven.

The ego occupies the space where the soul would normally be, so when people access that part of themselves, they encounter the ego and are deceived by it. They do not know the difference, because they lack the awareness of the soul that should be there to inform them of their dilemma and the truth of the matter as well as what is needed to heal from it and change accordingly to be truly transformed and be right with God. This does not make Christians or others who are in this predicament with ego wrong (unless they are hurting others or themselves through their intentions, acts, or behaviors); they are just incomplete. Their divinity is not active in their state of consciousness to their soul and God's presence. This leaves them with a limited experience. They try to interpret themselves and their world from a consciousness that is also limited to what it thinks and believes it knows, based upon its own experience through its own perception, lacking the living connection of infinite spirit and the unlimited contact of God.

All people have gifts and talents within themselves that are part of who they are. These are to be used as expressions of doing God's will, fulfilling the soul's purpose. However, if you don't pursue God inwardly, they will not be revealed or discovered. There is immense joy when the soul awakens, and there is even greater joy when the soul experiences its gifts. Fulfillment comes when one is utilizing them for the purpose for which they are given: to help and serve others in a unique way that expresses the love of God in practical, meaningful ways to those who need assistance and attention. Through the laying on of hands and meditation, healing is activated in the mind, body, soul, and spirit. This healing activation is God reversing the process of ego configuration and formation from being just human to being a human being. It is a process that can happen instantly or take time. Once mystical union with God is achieved, then the kundalini energy maintains life.

It is both journey and destination and a continuing journey with many destinations once liberated from the ego. Gifts and talents are discovered or revealed by God according to the maturity of the soul. Some are revealed out of need, and some are revealed as part of growth to gain wisdom, obtain knowledge, learn truth, experience love, receive insight, and explain the mysteries of the universe and God. One becomes a teacher and student of God, instructing others directly and indirectly, ascertaining through discernment what exactly is needed at the right time to bring love and truth to any given situation or circumstance that comes into your life. Your soul will respond with the dignity and grace of God to bring restoration and wholeness to whatever or whoever needs it, alleviating suffering and establishing tranquility and peace. Before such intercession, such attributes of God were perceived as absent or obscured by illusion.

The stirring of the divine memory provides momentary, transitory, intermittent relief from the ego. It can present as being born again, as Christians claim, but what actually occurs is this: the divine memory temporarily penetrates the ego but is obscured again because the ego is still the dominant consciousness. When the divine memory is obscured by the ego, the psychological phenomenon triggers ego elation, which overrides the divine memory, creating an illusion that there is no more to the process of growth of the experience of God. Therefore, the individuals experiencing this think that they are free and that there is no more for them to go through. God, at this point, is reduced to an idea or concept that fits within the parameters of the illusion-based ego mind. All kinds of illusions about God are created to compete with the memory of the real God. This is illustrated with Pharaoh and Moses in the Bible. God has yet to be experienced for the omnipotent, omnipresent, and omniscient being He is. The divine memory, although based in love and truth, is just that: a memory. It lacks the real mystical power of a living spirit through mystical experience of oneness with God. God works through the divine memory to invite, communicate, and guide the individual to a deeper, more intimate, more comprehensive, and more complete experience of God and oneself as God in mystical union, or onement with God. The ego, by its very nature, works hard to cause doubt and chaos through its dysfunctional feelings and its illusionary nature to keep the indwelling soul held captive from the deeper mystical relationship that God yearns for and wants with every life-form and soul.

Conversion by intellectual admittance or the empty ritual of baptism, which are void of real mystical power of the presence of God, is limited in what it can offer those seeking an authentic relationship with God. It is a basic beginning step, but it can help to change a person's life. It is a fundamental step, hence the labeling of people who do not got beyond it as fundamentalists. The different degrees and variations of religions in the world serve a purpose to those in various stages of their growth or lack thereof. The less evolved are more ego-based and believe theirs is the only true religion, whereas the highly evolved are soul-based and recognize that all religions, through mystical experience and expression, can lead to oneness of God. It is likely souls will go through the full spectrum of experience mentioned here in one lifetime if they are highly evolved or advanced.

Less-evolved souls may take many or several lifetimes. Less-evolved souls have yet to awaken fully and learn how to master illusion instead of being snared in it. The illusion of spiritual growth is a creation perpetuated by the dysfunctional projection mechanism expressed by the ego. God uses the divine memory to bring unresolved feelings and issues to the surface mind to be worked out and through and resolved appropriately according to God's will through God's guidance and presence. The ego then tries to take credit for and compete with this dynamic and negatively projects the unresolved issues and feelings within onto others because it doesn't like the way it feels. The ego, according to its own way of thinking, believes the feelings were resolved or dealt with, when in fact, they haven't been dealt with at all and still linger and fester within the individual in which they reside. The perpetually revolving, circular self-containing mechanism of the ego is symbolically and literally linked to the wheel of karma: nothing changes, and people keep going in circles indefinitely until they try something different that is above and beyond where their ego is.

When confronted with love and truth, the ego has a split-second delay before spiritually bypassing. During that split second, the living Word of God, a photon of light, aligns the tumblers (ego) in the lock (infinity) with the key of creation. They line up along the divine memory occluded by the ego-formation complex, return to God's mind and presence inside the receiver, and sublimate ego, revealing a revelation, leading to realization of truth and love with a yearning to learn and discover more, inspiring hope to continue the invitation to the journey for more experience, and leading to eventual mystical union with God. As the living Word of God passes through the psyche, it stirs the divine memory, passes by the soul level of mind, and makes a connection at the soul level before reaching the mind and presence of God, fulfilling the scripture that God's Word does not return empty or void. The connection made leaves those who receive it more whole than before it was received. Each time the living Word of God is received, it connects pieces of the fragmented soul and heart. At the same time, the ego that remains works to occlude and obscure the soul and God's presence, which is why free will must be used to continue to move forward toward God—because the default setting of predominant consciousness from being broken is ego consciousness, which was incurred and experienced at the beginning of one's life in the physical realm of earth to experience being human to compare with being and becoming a human being later in life. This back-and-forth dynamic goes on until the soul is strong enough and the ego is ready to surrender. Until that happens, the illusion of failure is experienced and believed, until a time when truth prevails. However, a yearning of wonder remains from the fruitful Word God for more.

It is important to note that the source of the living Word of God is God's presence and mind. From the soul, it is expressed from a whole, connected, spiritually aware, integrated, individuated human being and not an ego-based or hybrid being. For the latter, a negative, dysfunctional projection is the message being given, not the Word of God. To give the living Word of God, one has to be perfect, as your heavenly Father is perfect, orientated and expressing and communicating from the soul. Otherwise, an ego-based message is given, or at best, a mixed message of ego and divine memory is given, and one needs discernment to filter it or will be contaminated by the ego-based portion of the message. This culminates in confusion, spiritual and emotional abuse, and bewilderment instead of a state of being based in empowerment. The living Word of God speaks itself into being in consciousness, birthing itself as spirit and the light of awareness from itself, being the presence of God. Creation is infused with the light, and the continuum of this process is called life. Intelligence is based upon Christ consciousness, which organizes and carries out the process of creation and oversees integration and development, culminating in self-realization of the soul (awareness), mind (God), body (heart), and spirit (pure consciousness). Through the realization component of being, each is fulfilled independently, and then all are unified and integrated into one another, establishing beingness and one's place in the universe and in the world. This is known as the mystical fulfillment of being.

CONCLUSION

Theocentric psychology is a psychospiritual perspective of applied practical mysticism. In a modern and timeless, eternal Christed being, the full faculties of God are individualized into a fully integrated, individuated, and incarnated life-form, a human being, for the purpose of expressing love and truth and healing to all other life-forms to help them become aware, realize their divinity, and recover from their brokenness. This culminates in mystical-union oneness with God.

The science, art, and philosophy of being are an internal, eternal state of beingness of the fully integrated, incarnated, individuated, whole soul, body (heart), and mind, wherein the inner spiritual journey merges with the outer world. One is prepared to live life through the spiritual growth the soul, body (heart), and mind have completed and achieved. Dr. Masters comments on this wholeness and completeness in his doctor of theocentric psychology degree program: "Wholeness gives meaning because when you feel a synthesis or oneness between your body, mind and spirit it is as if God's consciousness, filled with meaning and your consciousness share parts of what is meaningful in life" (55:25).

The living Word of God, from God's presence and God's mind within and through the soul to the heart, stimulates creation to act and bear fruit through the creative process.

The living Word is constantly sending out signals or messages to enliven and enlighten all it comes in contact with. The living Word is both lock and key. It's the key to higher states of consciousness and being. The lock is symbolized by infinity (∞). Infinity represents the infinite God and universe. The key is symbolized by the symbol for pi (π), equating to the ratio of the circumference to the diameter of a circle, with a never-ending numeric value representing the ever-growing, never-ending process of creation: creating as creator and also being created. Infinity and creation (∞ and π) together unlock superconsciousness, which is one with both infinity and creation as well as individualized as an expression of the infinite and creation. The living Word of God gives life to the mind, body (heart), and soul. Part of its purpose is to awaken the consciousness of life-forms to higher states of being. It also instructs or teaches, through wisdom and intuition, how to be the highest expression and representation of life: being one with God. Wisdom of the soul is realized as a state of beingness, and as part of that beingness, divine feelings reveal love, truth, wisdom, and knowledge. Wisdom of the heart is revealed and realized not to indulge in negative feelings but to let the divine ones in to be realized in the current lifetime. Wisdom of the mind is experienced by decisions made by God, and there is no longer an ego to get in the way of God. Wisdom of spirit is realized as having access to all who ever lived or will live, including all souls, life-forms, and spirits in all dimensions and the universe, thereby exceeding and succeeding where they left off, fulfilling Jesus Christ's words "You shall do greater things than I." The heart is the child. The soul is the adult. The mind is God. The expression of the cosmic mystical marriage in the review of the literature is experienced as the union of Jesus and Lilith, both archetypally and spiritually. Together the essence of infinity and creation itself through the cosmos and universe finally has its expression in human form within the individual who has obtained this level of beingness in relationship internally and now externally.

When the mind is empty of all feelings of humanness, unconsciousness, and brokenness, then oneness, or integration with God oneness of spirit in superconsciousness, is experienced. God takes the final step, bringing the soul and heart that have been integrated into each other into God's mind, heart, soul, and spirit in the upper room of consciousness, the holy of holies. In becoming one with God in mystical union in the clear and gold light, a purified spirit is completely transformed from being human to being a human being, uniting heaven and earth, the inside with the outside, and the masculine with the feminine. As above is now as below. Now God is experienced everywhere inside and out. Real life begins from this moment on. Soul, body (heart), and mind become true, purified spirit, fully integrated, embodied, incarnated, individuated, whole, and complete.

WORKS CITED

Arya, Pandit Usharbudh. *Superconscious Meditation*. Honesdale, PA: Himalayan International Institute, 1978.

Bartlett, D. C., and N. D., Richard. *Matrix Energetics: The Science and Art of Transformation*. USA: First Atria Books/Beyond Words, 2007.

Braden, Greg. *Resilience from the Heart: The Power to Thrive in Life's Extremes*. USA: Hay House, 2014–2015.

Dalai Lama. *Dzogchen: Heart Essence of the Great Perfection*. Boulder, CO: Snow Lion, 2004.

Dale, Cyndi. *Kundalini: Divine Energy, Divine Life*. 3rd ed. Woodbury, MN: Llewellyn Publications, 2013.

Hawkins, David. *Discovery of the Presence of God*. Sedona, AZ: Veritas Publishing, 2007.

———. *Dissolving the Ego: Realizing the Self*. United States: Hay House, 2011.

———. *The Eye of the I: From Which Nothing Is Hidden*. Sedona, AZ: Veritas Publishing, 2001.

———. *Letting Go*. United States: Hay House, 2012.

———. *Transcending the Levels of Consciousness: The Stairway to Enlightenment*. W. Sedona, AZ: Veritas Publishing, 2006.

The Holy Bible. New King James Version. Thomas Nelson, 1984.

Hunt, Valerie V. *Infinite Mind: Science of the Human Vibrations of Consciousness.* Malibu, CA: Malibu Publishing Company, 1996.

Leloup, Jean-Yves. *The Gospel of Philip.* Rochester, VT: Inner Traditions, 2003.

Lipton, Bruce. *The Biology of Belief.* USA: Hay House, 2016.

Marion, Jim. *Putting On the Mind of Christ: The Inner Work of Christian Spirituality.* Charlottesville, VA: Hampton Roads Publishing Company, 2011.

Masters, Paul Leon. *Master's Degree Curriculum.* 2 vols. Burbank, CA: Printing, 2011.

Meyer, Marvin. *The Nag Hammadi Scriptures.* New York, NY: Harper Collins Publishers, 2007.

Newberg, Andrew, and Mark Robert Waldran. *How God Changes Your Brain: Breakthrough Findings from a Leading Neuroscientist.* USA: Ballantine Books, 2009.

Paulsen, Norman. *Christ Consciousness: The Emergence of the Pure Self Within.* Buellton, CA: Solar Logos Foundation, 2002.

Pearsall, Paul. *The Heart's Code.* New York, NY: Broadway Books, 1998.

Pert, Candice B. *Molecules of Emotion.* New York, NY: Scribner, 1997.

Proctor, Charlene M. *The Oneness Gospel.* Minneapolis, MN: Two Harbors Press, 2011.

Raheem, Aminah. *Soul Return.* Lower Lake, CA: Asland Publishing, 1987, 1991.

Swami, Vivekananda. *Raja Yoga.*

Van Dijk, Danielle. *Christ Consciousness.* East Sussex: Temple Lodge Publishing, 2010.

Whitfield, Charles L. *Boundaries and Relationships: Knowing, Protecting, and Enjoying the Self.* Deerfield Beach, FL: Health Publications, 1993.

———. *Codependence: Healing the Human Condition.* Deerfield Beach, FL: Health Communications, 1991.

———. *Healing the Child Within.* Deerfield, FL: Health Communications, 1987.

Zohar, Danah, and Ian Marshall. *SQ: Connecting with Our Spiritual Intelligence.* New York, NY: Bloomsbury Publishing, 2000.

4

The Mysticism of Mysticism Being Mystical

A Dissertation Submitted in Fulfillment of the Requirements
for the Degree of Doctor of Philosophy, Specializing
in Mystical Research, on Behalf of the Department
of Graduate Studies of the University of Sedona

RAMON LAZARUS
NOVEMBER 5, 2018

INTRODUCTION

The mysticism of mysticism being mystical is the process of God with and as creation, creating beingness from inception to full realization and culmination of that process of creation and beingness. Contemplating oneself as the created, one creates with creation as creator how God creates: with God, in God, as God, and being God with infinity in God's mind.

Mysticism, according to Dr. Masters, has several qualities that are not limited to the following: "Discovering one's ultimate self-reality Ie. The relationship of man, woman, mind and the universe. Discovering if there is a supreme universal intelligence or God that resides in the deeper levels of the human mind. Making direct contact with this supreme universal mind of God experiencing it, and knowing that it exists" (2).

God and Dr. Masters take mysticism further, applying it to the improvement of one's life, creating a better or best representation of oneself that is God-guided and God-centered, being God in the process of creation, and creating with the created as the creator or God. Once this process is achieved, it then becomes a mechanism of continual self-improvement for not only oneself but also all other life-forms that come in contact with it. The process of mysticism in becoming who you really are and were created to be parallels creation itself, as it is also a mystical process how the physical universe came to be through the creative process. Mysticism means union with God, and through the mystical process, the human being is created from being just human. Everything, from its spiritual essence (infinity) to the physical, is created, maintained, and improved, culminating in who you really are and were created to be. The mystical process of creation consists of the presence of God (the radiant white light). From that comes the living Word of God (etheric body), from that comes unmanifest spirit (spiritual body), from that comes the infinite of God's mind, and from that comes the Christ light (the light body from the presence of God). Then comes creation, and with creation comes darkness (the astral body). Then comes manifest spirit, and from that comes archetypes. Finally, from those come life-forms, including human beings.

In this paper, I will briefly look at this process of mystical creation in becoming human and also look at it as the process is reversed in becoming a human being and in being who you really are and were created to be. We will examine the mystical traditions of Vedanta Hinduism, kabbalah from Judaism, and the Christian mystical traditions in regard to this process. Collectively, this process is called the *inception of creation*, and with it, mysticism, through meditation, reverses the process of ego formation, leading to eventual mystical union with God on all levels. Once this is obtained, the process of meditation as functionally creating a human being ends. Mysticism remains, and life begins with a new process, now only a realized divinity: the Word made flesh in being a human being. I will include a practical application for this process, using scriptures from the King James Version of the Holy Bible, as well as the mystical perspective of the process, as seen from the third eye of the soul, taking into account all the levels as set forth in this paper.

REVIEW OF LITERATURE

Mysticism and spirituality go hand in hand and become intertwined and interdependent on the spiritual path. Spirituality is the study, contemplation, and practice of cultivating consciousness with the goal of its fulfillment. Mysticism is the culmination of spirituality in purified spirit and what is truly spiritual in mystical union with God. Christ consciousness is the divine intelligence, or the Word, that governs the state and process of spirituality and mysticism. *Mysticism* refers to experiencing God as God is in the infinite expression of God's love for life and evolution of life through all its stages, from inception of divine genesis to physical form to mystical union with God and returning back to energy and spirit.

All growth in consciousness is a process of inner realization. The inner realization is a result of some kind of meditative experience, with either meditation or laying-on-of-hands healing producing the effect. As a person goes through this process, he or she becomes less self-centered and less attached to physical matter and worldly things. Along with realization comes an equally significant event: validation. Michael J. Tamura, in his book *You Are the Answer*, explains what validation means from a spiritual perspective: "To validate means 'to ascertain the truth or authenticity of something' ... 'to discover with certainty, as through examination or experimentation' ... 'the quality or condition of having true authorship or being from the true source'" (83). So to validate experience, we must discover with certainty the true source, become aware of it, appreciate it, and communicate it to ourselves and others as spiritual beings. Validation can come from mystical experience, realization, or both at the same time. Validation, like realization, lets us know we have learned something about pertinent matters regarding our beingness and also allows us to let go of what was troubling us and move forward. This is important because it allows us to know where we are, where we've been, and where to go next as far as the mystical journey. As far as spiritual growth is concerned, the previous level of consciousness (mortal) is transcended with the light body, or soul, to bring awareness and discernment to the ego construct of humanness (etheric body), unconsciousness (light body), and brokenness (astral body) to determine what is useful to keep and what can be discarded for growth purposes. Then understanding of the spiritual body compares the truth it contains to the in-process construct of the ego, and as a result, understanding is gleaned. The construct presented now is reduced to the feeling that created it, which is transformed, resulting in realization and validation, which not only takes place at this level but also may happen at every level prior to it. Caroline Myss, in her book *Entering the Castle*, gives insight into the relevance of revelation of realization and validation: "Your comprehension is instantaneous, as if you are transferred from a state of not knowing to one of complete knowing at the speed of light. The message does not fade from your memory, ever, whereas we forget, sometimes in minutes, other things we hear. Authentic words are burned into your memory and soul" (313).

Realizations and validations can be clairvoyant, clairaudient, and clairsentient or seen, heard, and felt, as well as experienced mentally in thoughts and emotionally in emotions and feelings. Mysticism is the process of reducing constructs from creation into their constituent parts of feeling, thought, and emotion in ego consciousness to transform them into spiritual energy and beingness. After the transformation, mysticism remains a creative process free of the ego.

We will now look at three mystical traditions: the Christian mystical tradition, Vedanta Hinduism, and Kabbalah from Judaism. You'll see similarities in them for growth and transformation to become who you really are and who you were created to be.

In his book *Putting On the Mind of Christ*, Jim Marion quotes two Christian mystics, Saint Theresa of Avila and Saint John of the Cross, as far as counting or numbering the stages involved in the mystical growth process: The sixteenth century's Saint Theresa of Avila, in her masterpiece *The Interior Castle*, divided the path into seven stages of consciousness, or mansions. Her friend and contemporary Saint John of the Cross divided the path into five stages: the beginning contemplative, the dark night of the senses, an intervening period of progressive spiritual illuminations, the dark night of the soul, and union with God (26).

In Christian mysticism, the left side of the body is the heart, as represented by the ego portion of the astral body, and represents darkness until purified into pure spirit. The right side of the body represents heaven and the light body from God's presence, representing light. In Vedanta Hinduism, there are seven stages, or chakras, that must be transformed from ego to soul and involve the aspects of the light and aspects of the dark. In his online course *Awakening Your Kundalini* from the Shift Network, Raja Choudhury explains that there are seven chakras of the subtle body in consciousness to transcend and that "the right side of the body is made up of light or Shakti and that the left side of the body is made up of darkness or Shiva."

Ambika Wauters goes on to explain and label, in her book *Chakras and Their Archetypes*, the positive and negative archetype associated with each level or chakra. Chakra one (muladhara) is "Positive archetype Mother, Negative archetype Victim" (Wauters 28). Chakra two (svadhishtana) is "Positive archetype The Empress/Emperor, Negative archetype The Martyr" (Wauters 51). Chakra three (manipura) is "Positive archetype The Warrior, Negative archetype The Servant"(70). Chakra four (anahata) is "Positive archetype The Lover, Negative archetype The Actor/Actress" (90). Chakra five (vishuddha) is "Positive archetype The Communicator, Negative archetype The Silent Child" (108). Chakra six (ajna) is "Positive archetype The Intuitive, Negative archetype The Intellectual" (127). Chakra seven (sahasara) is "Positive archetype The Guru, Negative archetype The Egoist" (146). Wauters adds that "they are non-anatomical vortices of energy which exist just outside and within the physical body at what is called the etheric level of the aura; this lies outside of and interpenetrates our physical body" (21). The purposes of the chakras are to supply and filter energy throughout the system of the mind and body and to distribute vitality to the individual's life from the cosmos and the earth. If one or more of them gets blocked, it will disrupt this process, causing stasis or stagnation.

A physical problem can ensue in the area related to it or with the organ or gland associated with it. Each chakra needs to be purified of the corresponding ego construct's negative archetype through spiritual growth. As illusions and constructs are transcended and transformed, the negative archetypes are shed, and the positive ones remain as a reflection of the transformation that has taken place. The chakras correspond to different forms of consciousness, with the lower ones associated with mortal consciousness. The top is where God, or cosmic consciousness, exists. The colors from bottom to top are red, orange, yellow, green, blue, violet, and white.

The following information on kabbalah will be presented from *The Way of Kabbalah*, an online course from the Shift Network by Rabbi David Ingber. The basic tenets consists of four worlds: Atzulit (unmanifest spirit, closeness; spiritual body), Beriyah (creation; light body), Yetzirah (formation; etheric body), and Asiyah (making; astral body). It also includes the ten, or sometimes eleven, sephirot, or divine emanations of the divine body: Keter, Hokmah, and Binah make up the top of the tree of life with this triad. Hesed, Gevurah, and Tif'eret make up the second triad. The next triad consists of Netzah, Hod, and Yesod. Below Yesod is Malkhut, and connecting the first triad with the second is Da'at. I will briefly list the qualities and characteristics associated with each.

- Keter: crown, head, auric body, suprarational, beyond comprehension, formless, transcendent, identical with God Head, crown chakra
- Hokmah: wisdom, intention, father, spark of insight, unbounded consciousness, right side of the brain, etheric body, blue, Yah
- Binah: understanding mother, thought, language, gestation, left hemisphere of the brain, emotional (astral body), green, Elohim
- Hesed: expansion, unconditional love, grace, right arm, white, Most High God
- Gevurah: judgment, constriction, containing, reserved, left arm, red, Elohim
- Tif'eret: beauty, harmony, compassion, holy one, balance, heart chakra, purple, Yhuh
- Netzah: eternity, perseverance, action, power, proactive, right leg, light pink

- Hod: splendor, elegance, softening, inactive, left leg, dark pink
- Yesod: foundation, communication, right action, sexuality, phallus, breasts, orange
- Malkhut: sovereignty, ground, feminine divine presence, manifestation, feet, mouth, physical body, black, and blue
- Da'at: integrated knowledge from experience

In addition to the four worlds and eleven sephirot are the concepts of *ein sof* (infinite) and *tzim tzum* (divine contraction as it relates to the creative process). "Ein Sof (The Infinite) withdrew itself into its essence, from itself, to itself, within itself. It left an empty space within its essence in which it could emanate and create" (Ingber module 4).

The kabbalah has thirty-two paths of spiritual growth from the eleven sephirot and the twenty-two letters of the Hebrew alphabet. The lower five sephirot and the left and right sides of the body need to be integrated and balanced, similarly to Christian mysticism and Vedanta Hinduism, through spiritual growth.

Reconciling the left side of the body with the right side of the body, the masculine with the feminine, the stages of growth and transformation, and the seven chakras and eleven sephirot leads to the mystical marriage of creation, as described by Norman Paulsen in his book *Christ Consciousness*: "The two radiant offspring of pure consciousness and light, the twin stars, were, by magnetic attraction, drawn toward each other. They moved toward the divine center of consciousness, the smallest of all places, the womb of creation" (285). "This mystical union completed the image of the first creation of light, the androgynous, immaculate body of Christ. The cosmic sea of life and energy had given birth to the Christ Child of pure consciousness and light" (Paulsen 286). This mystical marriage takes place at the divine genesis of creation and through the spiritual growth process. The offspring of the mystical marriage, the Christ light, comes from God's presence and the spirit of God, or infinity. The spiritual growth process is the revealing of one's true nature as God's presence (radiant light of creation) and God's mind (infinity), which, up until that time, is occluded by the ego-formation complex. The Christ light is the light of awareness with discernment and is part of the enlightenment process. The other is mystical union with God as one's soul becomes unmanifest and manifest spirit, one with the great I Am in God's mind in infinity. The growth process is both a revealing of the creative process and a returning to the creative process. As the cycle of life becomes complete, it retraces the steps back to and through to God's presence, where God's living Word returns to its source.

Awareness of the Christ light can be described as the awareness of awareness being aware. Eckhart Tolle comments on this awareness in his book *A New Earth*: "Awareness is conscious connection with universal intelligence. Another word for it is Presence: consciousness without thought" (259).

David Hawkins, an enlightened psychiatrist, comments on conscious awareness and the presence of God in his book *Discovery of the Presence of God*: "All is intrinsically worshipful as a consequence of the conscious awareness of the Presence of God as creation in its minute details. All is holy and sacred, as evidenced by its splendor as Existence itself" (Hawkins 230). Hawkins, in his book *The Eye of the I*, also comments on the awareness of awareness being aware: "The awareness is self-awareness that stems from the knowingness of actually being all that is; therefore there is nothing to know 'about'" (211). Hawkins, in his book *Transcending the Levels of Consciousness*, comments on a pitfall of Buddhism on the journey and path of oneness with the presence of God, known as the void: "The limitation (incompleteness) of the void is reached as a consequence of intense dedication to the pathway of negation; however, missing is the realization that love is a primary quality of divinity and is also nonlinear and that spiritual love is not an attachment" (302). The void is an illusion of the broken, transformed illusion of spirit of Lilith, Adam's first wife from Genesis in the Bible. It represents the end of the subconscious mind entering into the enlightenment of God's presence.

Another factor to consider while going through spiritual growth is resistance while in the collective unconscious. Charles Whitfield, MD, in his book *The Power of Humility*, comments on this: "Hindrances from the ego such as fear of losing one's self leads to pressure from other souls in the collective unconscious" (130). David Hawkins, in his book *The Eye of the I*, comments on the experience of enlightenment: "The strength to sustain and survive enlightenment experience itself is provided by the holy-spirit as a powerful energy that sustains the remainder of destined life. It is by means of the holy-spirit that there is a return to function of the faculties necessary, but they have been transformed forever" (209).

As we have seen, there is much evidence supporting enlightenment with God's presence (creation). We will now examine another aspect of enlightenment: oneness with God's mind, or the infinite. Ernest Holmes comments on the infinite spirit of God in his book *This Thing Called You*: "Your creative power comes from the originating spirit itself, which knows no limit, is conditioned by no circumstance and is governed by no law outside itself" (109).

God's mind of infinite spirit is merged with the soul in mystical union with God. It is a clear, purified state of mind. Pandit Usharbudh Arya, PhD, comments on this purified state of mind: "A pure mind is a clear mind, so all intuition and Godly knowledge can flow through it" (33). Arya also comments on the kundalini from the presence of God: "The Kundalini is a force of the divine light and superconscious sound" (130). It is clear from his book *Superconscious Meditation* that the kundalini has two components to it and superconsciousness. One is mystical union with God, the purified state of mind and oneness with God's presence, the white radiant light that produces the superconscious sound of creation. Swami Prabhavananda, in his book *The Sermon on the Mount according to Vedanta*, comments on the process of enlightenment from the existence of the last remnant of the ego to unification with God consciousness: "There is still a slight sense of ego left, and the aspirant longs to break-down that last barrier of separation from God. When the spiritual energy bursts into the highest center in the brain, the realization dawns that 'I and the Father are One' and perfect divine union is attained" (119). The kundalini rises through the sushuma up the spine, enlightening as it travels through the chakras and sephirot, using the spiritual, etheric, light, and astral bodies accordingly until union with God is attained on all four levels based upon the four metaphysical bodies. *The Gospel of Philip* by Jean-Yves Leloup finds reference to the clear light of superconsciousness: "To know the grace of true communion with him, one must be clothed in clear light. ... In this light we can see His light" (135).

In *The Nag Hammadi Scriptures* edited by Marvin Meyer, the book *The Wisdom of Jesus Christ* quotes Jesus Christ commenting on what the infinite is like: "He is all mind; he is thought, consideration, reflection, reason, and power and all are equally powerful. These are the sources of all that is, and the entire generation, from first to last was in the fore knowledge of the Infinite unconcerned Father" (289).

Jim Marion references mystical union with God in his book *Putting On the Mind of Christ*: "There is no annihilation of the individuated soul. Rather the soul is taken up into the Father so that the entire universe enters into the soul. The ocean enters the drop of water" (209). Marion also mentions that it is an ascension phenomenon or experience: "So completely are we raised up that, for example we see the entirety of creation as our own body. Because of this radical raising up the passage from the causal level to the non-dual level is sometimes called The Ascension Initiation. ... By this ascension we enter into the Kingdom of Heaven in our bodies while on earth" (209). Marion quotes Bernadette Roberts, a Christian mystic, as she explains the realization she had at this level of consciousness:

> The ultimate realization of no self is not its identity with Father or Holy Spirit—the omniscient un-manifested father or the omnipotent manifesting spirit—rather, it is the realization of our true nature, our true identity as the manifested aspect of the Trinity- Christ. In this Breakthrough, we also realize the oneness of Christ, Father and Spirit, the three distinct non-interchangeable aspects of the God head. (205)

As one can see from this review of literature, the process and experience of enlightenment and mysticism have been around for a long time. The process is transcendent and transformative, and the creativity of creation follows forward and backward with creation and the infinite, completing the cycle of life. There are many levels to enlightenment, but it can be quantified and qualified by the awakening of the spiritual, etheric, light, and astral bodies as far as charting or marking progress through it is concerned. Enlightenment's mystical union with God has four levels that correspond to the four metaphysical bodies mentioned in this paper. I will review the review of literature from an enlightened perspective and mystical-union-with-God perspective through the viewpoint of what it is like to have accomplished completion of all levels in the discussion section of this paper.

DISCUSSION

Validation comes from direct experience, realizations, or both. There are several realizations an individual may have while going through the spiritual growth process. The realizations of the heart free the ego, allowing it to submerge itself in the light of God's presence with no regrets. The realizations of the soul let the soul realize itself in all its glory as to its awareness, freedom, and gifts. The realizations of the mind realize infinity and creation in all their vastness in a pristine state of continual, changeless change. The realizations of the spirit allow spirit to realize its eternal wonder and life beyond the physical appearance of existence. A realization of being realizes that the spiritual body, the etheric body, the light body, and the astral body are one with one another and God. A God realization takes place with mystical union with God and takes place on all levels of being and beyond. It is creation with infinity and can be seen, heard, and communicated in consciousness and beyond consciousness. The wisdom and knowledge received from these realizations are transcendent, transformative, immanent, and ineffable, and they permanently leave their impression upon the soul in the heart through the mind and spirit of the life-form.

In Christian mysticism, we discovered a five-stage or seven-stage process to go through to reach enlightenment and mystical union with God. In Vedanta Hinduism, there are seven chakras to be transformed, and in kabbalah, the lower five sephirot need to be transformed as well. Spiritual growth is guided by Christ consciousness directly from God's presence through the divine memory, which is the conduit in the psyche left over from creation that God uses to communicate with His creation and life-forms once creation has created God's creation. Once activated by the life-form, it takes over the growth, transformation, and healing process, using the etheric, light, and astral bodies to eventually awaken them with an enlightening experience eventually leading to mystical union with God. As far as the seven chakras go, the upper four are transformed once the illusion of perfection is transcended, clearing the chakras of ego constructs and negative archetypes. The lower four chakras are transformed once the illusion of imperfection is transcended. Chakras one through seven are transformed once the illusion of separation is transcended. These changes take place with awakening (enlightenment) and embodiment. Integration leads to eventual mystical union with God, where spiritual growth of the densest parts of spirit are transformed into divinity. The densest parts of spirit are the feelings of humanness and are associated with chakra three, the etheric body, and the mind. Unconsciousness is associated with chakra two and the light body. Brokenness is associated with chakra one and the astral body. Together from the bottom up, the process presents the feeling, thought, and emotion of the constructs created by the ego before spiritual growth reverses that process, leading to enlightenment and mystical union with God on all levels.

The lower five sephirot are similar as far as growth and transformation are concerned. According to kabbalah, problems arise when there are imbalances in the eleven sephirot or the tree of life. To remove any hint of imbalance is to transform and grow, purifying, which culminates in mystical union with God. The lower five sephirot are transformed once the illusion of imperfection is transcended. The upper four sephirot below Keter are transformed once the illusion of perfection is transcended, and all below Keter are transformed once the illusion of separation is transcended. These changes take place with awakening, embodiment, and enlightenment. The sephirot are not only portals of emanation of God but also portals of transcendence, transformation, and growth, leading to mystical union with God. Binah transforms from the astral to spiritual body. Hokmah transforms from the etheric to light body. Tif'eret, the bottom of the second triad, is associated with the light body (soul) and unconsciousness upon integration. Netzah, the sephirot of the next triad below Tif'eret on the right, is associated with the etheric body (mind) and humanness. Hod, the sephirot on the left before reaching Yesod, is associated with the astral body (heart) and brokenness. Yesod, at the bottom of the triad with Hod and Netzah, is associated with the light body (soul) and unconsciousness. Malkhut is the bottom or base of the tree of life and is associated with the astral body and brokenness. In Christian mysticism, Vedanta Hinduism, and kabbalah, there is also integration of the left side of the body with the right side of the body, with the left side representing darkness and the right side representing light. In Christian mysticism, it is the ego on the left side and the soul on the right. In Vedanta, intellect (buddhi) is on the left, and mind (manas) is on the right. In Hinduism, Shiva is on the left side of the body, and Shakti is on the right. On the tree of life, the emotional or astral body is on the left, with the etheric body on the right, along with the formless of the spiritual with the light body or soul on the left and right, respectively, after growth.

Enlightenment brings liberation, awakening, and embodiment of the four metaphysical bodies: spiritual, etheric, light, and astral. The spiritual body connects the etheric, light, and astral bodies to God and divine awareness. The etheric body connects the subconscious mind to the conscious mind. The light body brings awareness and discernment to the subconscious mind. The astral body accesses feelings and connects the spiritual, etheric, and light bodies to the physical body. This process works with and corresponds to mystical systems of beingness and philosophies thereof.

Mysticism, culminating in mystical union with God, integrates all four liberated, awakened, embodied bodies back into the light of creation in God's presence and the infinite of God's mind. The experience of becoming one with the infinite of God is transcendent, immanent, and ineffable. The soul begins its ascension, first encountering the liquid-like substance of akasha in the uniform field of unmanifest spirit. It ascends through this and continues higher, exiting the sea of unmanifest spirit. As it continues to ascend, it realizes it is now manifest spirit going through the divine contraction, tzim tzum and ein sof, so God in God, with God, as God, being God, can create and emanate a creation. Simultaneously, the manifest spirit continues to ascend, reaching the heart of God, the Great I Am of God, in the Godhead, where ascension stops and mystical union with God as infinity takes place. God places the manifest spirit into God's heart with the realization "I Am in God, and God is in God," formerly manifest spirit. There is no *I-thou* relationship, only oneness. Then a large arm and hand stretched out straight begins to bend toward the manifest spirit in God's heart and God's heart, which are now one, and its pointed index finger writes the word *success* upon God's heart. After a moment, the realization is made that heaven and earth are one; the above is as the below; the inner and outer are one; and all this has taken place in the upper room of consciousness, the holy of holies, in the gold and clear light within consciousness and beyond. All of this experience is initiated by God when the time is right and after all feelings of humanness, unconsciousness, and brokenness have been released. The enlightened spiritual body returns to God.

This experience of mystical union with God represents part of the kundalini experience, which is the clear light of pure mind and consciousness, God, and the infinite. The other part of the kundalini is mystical union with the Christ light of creation, or God's presence. The masculine and feminine of the ida and pingula extend below the base of the spine to the soles of the feet. When this experience happens, the presence of God, when meditated upon or in a meditative state, will be activated, starting at the feet and traveling upward through the legs, torso, and head and out of the body to oneness with creation and God's presence in superconsciousness, with the superconscious sound of creation as the astral-body portion of the ego left to merge with God at a later time. Superconsciousness involves becoming one with the infinite mind of God and becoming one with God's presence or creation. The light body returns to God. The astral body, carrying the last remnant of the ego, must now face its destiny or fate in the collective unconscious inside the collective ego, where it will face its moment of truth to become who it was created to be—or not. If the temptation presented is not acted upon, revealing the flaw of one's being as represented by the ego, then the realization of error will take place, and with it, the choice to keep following love and truth removes error and brings love and light to the inception point of the ego, sublimating unbelief. This results in total freedom of being and total completeness of being, and most importantly, the Word becomes flesh, or the higher self embodies the physical body.

Heart integrates into soul and God's presence, and the process of retracing the origin of source completes with the Word returning to the sea of feeling that is the reservoir of infinite potential within and beyond God. It recreates and expresses that infinite potential, now one with it in mind, body (heart), soul, and spirit, integrated into the mind of God and the universe in superconsciousness.

This means the heart's journey to wholeness has completed, and the ego is completely gone, with no ties to it whatsoever. The heart, with its desires, is integrated and balanced with soul, and both are integrated into God's mind, superconsciousness, and spirit. A new expression of it will now come about as a result of it in something new. It will contain components of what it already is but with a newness to it, aligned with purpose and meaning of the overall creation of creation (etheric) creating (spiritual) with the created (astral) as creator (light), being who you really are and were created to be.

The heart is the connection to particulate matter of the earth and the universe. It integrates and fuses with the soul to bring life and energy to itself so it can experience the dimensionality of spirit and pure creativity with the expression of the essence of infinity and assign meaning and purpose to the process of life to grow and evolve to learn how to love at every stage and phase of the process until it becomes love in mystical union with God. Meditation as a process of growth and attainment ends. The goal of achieving superconsciousness is attained and has been achieved. Mysticism remains because God has no ending or beginning but is eternal. Mysticism remains as the underlying translation of God's communications within itself and is shared with life-forms who can comprehend and understand the workings and nature of God as creator and as infinite within God's mind. They work together as one as the origin of life itself, making it known to those who are ready and able to receive such grace as the love of God itself. The process of creation moves forward upon enlightenment and backward, retracing its steps, with mystical union with God, corresponding with each of the four metaphysical bodies. Danielle Van Dijk, in her book *Christ Consciousness*, comments on the phenomena and metaphysical being, the higher self.

> That part of oneself that is the highest self, of one's most profound self, which one has developed in reality in one's past life... can ascend to the spiritual world and live and

learn amongst kindred spirits and spiritual beings. After
a fusion with the complete higher self of the human being
in question takes place, so that all lessons that were learnt
in various lives on earth can be integrated. (161)

This quote from Danielle Van Dijk not only references enlightenment
and mystical union with God but also references what Dr. Masters and I
call the Alpha and Omega of revelation, where all lifetimes past, present,
and future are reconciled to God and the present moment, having gone
through the necessary spiritual growth outlined in this paper. It represents
the beginning of the end of the ego, the end of the beginning of the ego,
and the beginning of life with the soul without the ego. It has no beginning
and no ending; it's eternal. It also marks the realization that people will not
be able to get to this place on their own if they are trapped in their ego,
not realizing they have a choice to do so. It is the responsibility of those
who have gone through the growth outlined in this paper to communicate
their experience to others so they may discover enlightenment and mystical
union with God for themselves. Once this realization is realized, both
Adam and Lilith are freed from hell within the collective unconscious.
Both become transformed and are now able to go through the process
for themselves and help others. Both, with their feelings of humanness,
unconsciousness, and brokenness, can take responsibility for their souls
and do the necessary growth work required to reach and obtain the level
of growth needed for redemption. Redemption is the opportunity hoped
for to atone for all the lost or missed opportunities to share and express
love for self and others while in the ego. Once the last remnant of the ego
is sublimated in the collective ego within the collective unconscious and
processed, leading to the reversal of unbelief, the pathway to heaven from
such a place is now open and established for oneself and others.

Inner and outer experiences in the ego are one in dysfunction and
disease process. Ego is ignorant to process experiences of disease as coming
outside itself (germ theory). In contrast, in enlightened consciousness
of the soul, the inner and outer experience is one; the inner is the
predominant consciousness, and the dysfunction is eliminated or coming
from within oneself. Awareness and discernment intercede at the level of
dysfunction and delineate feelings. Causing dysfunction brings awareness

to it, identifying dissonance as cause and reestablishing equilibrium, or a healing system rebalances. Well-being returns (tissue resistance).

Faculty of mind-Level-Metaphysical Body---Component of being---Ego
Divine Clarity-Spiritual----Spiritual Body----Divine Memory--------Ego
Intellect----Mental---Etheric Body------Mind----------Humanness
Reason-----Emotional---Light Body-------Soul------Unconsciousness
Logic-----Physical----Astral Body----Body (Heart)-----Brokenness >
   DNA---------Cell Structure--------Brain Wave------- Lie of Satan
   Thymine--------DNA-----------Delta----------No Body Is Perfect
   Adenine----Cell Membrane-------Theta--------Your Only Human
   Guanine-----Nucleus-----Alpha-----I'm incapable of becoming evil
   Cytosine----Cytoplasm--------Beta/ Gamma------I have not lived
   another life than this one

Thy will, not *mine*, be done. *Thy* and *mine* represent thymine spiritual DNA.

The above chart shows the organizational structure of the psyche from the spiritual to the physical and how it translates into the physical or the Word made flesh, including the ego. For the realized divinity, the divine memory is replaced with the spirit; and the astral body portion of the ego, once sublimated, translates the spiritual into the physical, or the Word made flesh. The ego and lies of Satan then would disappear from the chart and placement in the psyche, with the component of being translating directly into the DNA and the rest of the chart.

Light body's awareness, since it is embodied, extends to the whole cell, including the cell membrane. It detects contents within the cell in the cytoplasm and nucleus and contents outside the cell through the cell membrane. From the base up, these contents inside and outside the cell determine the expression of the DNA for health or disease. If it is disease, mutations are activated; if it is health, spiritual DNA is activated, and the process of cell respiration follows accordingly. Left brain in ego creates constructs that lead to perceptions that create emotional blocks, which then create disease, and chromosomes are affected by the magnetic charge of emotion and construct to create disease. If this is negated, positive health results. Sin activates mutations and is not a punishment from God. Working on feelings of humanness, unconsciousness, and brokenness changes and releases this cause and effect when brokenness becomes humanness and humanness becomes sin. Genetic mutations are activated, which involves nonconscious choice to choose behavior to avoid difficult feelings and pain.

Ego construct, activated by the decision to avoid growth, triggers feelings of humanness, and emotional charge changes permeability of the cell membrane, causing by-products to stay within the cell and preventing nutrients from entering the cell. This creates free radicals that feed back into the nucleus, activating mutations through feelings of unconsciousness, which prevent detection of the pathological process taking place. The workings of the cytoplasm next become overwhelmed with the pathology (brokenness) and are broken down, destroying the cell and creating even more free radicals. The process repeats until awareness is reestablished, reversing this cascade of events, creating healthy new cells, and repairing damaged ones.

Each person who awakens empowers the soul and deducts emotional content from the ego individually and collectively. This, in turn, will lead to diminishing the collective pain of those who are overwhelmed by their feelings of brokenness, unconsciousness, and humanness, who are still, to a certain degree, double-minded and made pathological by acting out on their feelings. But this is also a transitional phase upon becoming a human being. Since the soul is awake and conscious but has yet to fully integrate the ego, God is behind the effort to evolve and supports the soul. However, if unresolved feelings of the ego, which are based in humanness, unconsciousness, and brokenness, overwhelm the soul, then the soul can be subject to those feelings and become confused and commit acts against others that are as violent as the feelings within. This gives people the illusion that they are justified in their actions to act out and harm others. These individuals are in pain and are sensitive to it because their souls are traveling in hell and haven't completed their journey upward and through it.

The unconsciousness of others in the world individually and collectively provokes people's souls in this predicament and gives a distorted purpose to those souls, causing them to act out and harm others. People who stand by and watch this drama play out in the world can do something about it and contribute to a positive, soul-based God-mind solution that will help to end the madness taking place on the face of the earth. Since the overwhelming population of the earth are unconscious, people need to awaken their souls through meditation and laying-on-of-hands healing. Doing this will stop their egos from projecting pain and unresolved feelings onto others through blame, which will take away the purpose of these souls acting out, who are struggling in hell to complete their journey from being human to being and becoming human beings. This will reduce their pain externally and internally enough to reduce their burden to the point where they can, if they are willing, confront and deal with their feelings, because they will be receiving love from those who before were projecting their pain. Their awareness has not fully penetrated the collective unconscious; therefore, their pain has not been healed, and purpose gets confused with blame and is projected in the direction of others' pain, thinking that by eradicating it, it will give them peace. But this is an illusion. This describes the state and condition of the collective unconscious, where hell is just below. This is where terror and fear come from and is a place that all must eventually pass through in becoming who they really are and were created to be. Each soul doing his or her part will help others on all levels to become this as well. Positiveness works exponentially for the good and will eventually put an end to terror and make hell a better place for all who pass through it. Fear and anger in action are hatred, and hatred projected is prejudice. Despair is the anticipation of experiencing the feeling and emotion of hatred.

The remainder of the discussion section of this paper will be devoted to the practical application of scripture taken primarily from the King James Version of the Holy Bible to outline the course to become who you really are and were created to be, including passages on enlightenment and mystical union with God.

John 1:1–3 says, "In the beginning was the word, and the word was with God, and the word was God. He was in the beginning with God. All things were made through Him, and without Him nothing was made that was made." Genesis1:1–3 says, "In the beginning God created the heavens and the earth. The earth was without form and void; and darkness was on the face of the deep. And the spirit of God was hovering over the waters. Then God said, 'Let there be light'; and there was light."

These passages from Genesis and John mark the beginning of creation and the manifestation of light. The Word of God, spoken through Jesus Christ and others, has its origin in the darkness, or the void of the womb of creation. The Word of God spoke everything into creation with wisdom, setting limits and boundaries for every created thing, including the animate and inanimate worlds and especially the worlds of matter and spirit. The Word, with the light from the presence of God, is constantly creating life with life by life to bring awareness and discernment to all life-forms and souls so they can learn to interpret their feelings and experiences and evaluate what has significance and meaning to stimulate free will to choose what brings fulfillment and purpose to the soul. Etheric and light bodies are created and awakened with enlightenment on their corresponding levels.

Matthew 3:16–17 says, "Then Jesus, when he had been baptized, came up immediately from the water; and behold, the heavens were opened to Him and He saw the spirit of God descend like a dove and a lighting upon Him. And suddenly a voice came from heaven saying 'This is My beloved Son in whom I am well pleased.'" Jesus's baptism signifies His soul's embodiment, along with embodiment of the etheric body as well, which is a psychospiritual, mystical experience. Baptism, over time, has lost its significance and become an empty ritual or, at most, an activation of the divine memory, which gives one a conduit to God but is not an eternal connection to God with and through the soul. The divine memory is a mechanism created by God to begin the process of reconciliation of the heart to God and eventually lead to soul awakening, where a true relationship with God begins and is established. This is an eternal, contemporaneous, conscious, aware state of beingness in being one with the presence of God and creation.

Romans 12:2, 4–8 says the following:

> And do not be conformed to this world, but be transformed by the renewing of your mind that you may prove what is that is good and acceptable and perfect will of God. ... For as we have many members in one body, but all the members do not have the same function, so we being many, are one body in Christ, and individually members of one another. Having then gifts differing according to the Grace that is given to us, let us use them; if prophecy let us prophecy in proportion of our faith; or ministry, let us use it in our ministering; he who teaches, in teaching; he

who exhorts, in exhortation; he who gives with liberality; he who leads, with diligence; he who shows mercy, with cheerfulness.

Once the soul awakens (nowadays through meditation and laying-on-of-hands healing), the awareness of the soul through God's presence differentiates truth from falsehood regarding all matters of significance to earthly as well as spiritual life, through discernment to use free will to make choices and to align the heart with God's will and fulfill its purpose. It constantly renews the mind, emptying it of its brokenness, making room for one's spirit to be born and reside in its place and become a member of the body of Christ complete with talents or gifts, which are universal and unique to each individual soul and spirit, to be used to eliminate suffering and bring healing and wholeness so others may join the body of Christ.

Acts 2:2–4 says, "And suddenly there came a sound from heaven, as of a rushing mighty wind, and it filled the whole house where they were sitting. Then there appeared to them divide tongues, as of fire, and one sat upon each of them and they were all filled with the Holy Spirit and begun to speak with other tongues, as the spirit gave them utterance."

This is the baptism of fire, which is a vortex of divine energy that descends from heaven and rests upon the head. It is the I Am That I Am of God. It supplies divine wisdom and attributes to the soul on which it rests. This phenomenon activates a deeper state of being, along with whatever gifts one has been given.

Luke 8:11–12 says, "The seed is the word of God. Those by the wayside are the ones who hear; then the devil comes and takes away The Word out of their hearts, lest they should believe and be saved." This verse represents a soul confused and disconnected because of ego. The devil, using negative feelings of unconsciousness, overcompensates and rejects the Word of God. Verse 13 says, "But the ones on the rock are those who, when they hear receive The Word with joy; and these have no root, who believe for a while and in time of temptation fall away." This verse represents an inaccessible heart that has built-up layers of feelings of brokenness that form a barrier around and in the heart, keeping the Word of God from taking root. Verse 14 says, "And the ones that fell among thorns are those who, when they have heard, go out and are choked with cares, riches and pleasures of life and bring no fruit to maturity." This verse represents mind a cluttered with feelings of humanness, which don't allow the Word of God to be cared for and nurtured. Verse 15 says, "But the ones that fell on good ground are those who, having heard the Word with a noble and good heart, keep it and bear fruit with patience." This verse represents total integration of being, wherein soul, heart, and mind are free from their ego constraints, configurations, and constructs, merged by Christ consciousness and God's living Word into unity and atonement with God.

Verses 16–18 further describe the person and soul who have achieved this total integration of being and its impact on one's life and on others in the world. Verse 16 says, "No one, when he has lit a lamp, covers it with a vessel or puts it under a bed, but sets it on a lamp stand, that those who enter may see the light." This verse describes the soul (an individuated expression of God's presence within) shining in the heart, illuminating the mind of itself and all others it may come in contact with. Verse 17 says, "For nothing is in secret that will not be revealed, nor anything hidden that will not be known and come to light." This verse describes the process of how God and God's living Word work within the individual soul who has obtained total integration of being. The light of the soul reveals a little at a time so it can be made aware and realize knowledge, love, and truth in a context that pertains to both the individual soul and others. Verse 18 says, "Therefore take heed how you hear. For whoever has, to him more will be given; and whoever does not have, even what he seems to have will be taken from him." This verse represents God's abundance. Those who act upon and live by it will be given more in abundance, whatever that abundance might be, whether it be wisdom, knowledge, or truth.

Matthew 22:14 says, "For many are called but few are chosen. Many are called to God but few Choose God when he calls." This verse is a wake-up call to choose God. Matthew 10:34 says, "Do not think I came to bring peace on earth. I did not come to bring peace but a sword." This verse represents the insecurities of the ego to keep peace in relationships at any price, particularly one's soul. The sword is the Word of God, which liberates the soul and cuts through the feelings of the ego, holding it captive in codependency. Verse 35 says, "For I have come to set a man against his father, a daughter against her mother and a daughter in law against her mother in law." This verse represents the purpose of Christ to dissolve and break the chains of codependency, which are an impediment to the soul and the Spirit. Parents and authority figures of the world conform children (and, once one grows up, the inner child) to the world. This conformity imprisons the soul in the ego, and Christ came to set it free. Verse 36 says, "And a man's foes will be those of his own household." When one is reconciling one's ego with God to prepare and accept one's divinity in embodying the soul, Satan will use those who have not yet gone through the process, and one will feel as if the world and one's family are against him or her. This is temporary as long as one is committed to God and the purity of one's soul, heart, and mind until the process is complete. Verse 37 says, "He who loves Father or Mother more than Me is not worthy of Me and he who loves son or daughter more than Me is not worthy of Me." It is important to point out that one must love and make God a priority above all things so that in the conversion process, all dysfunctional connections of the ego are severed and destroyed, because they are connections to dysfunction and the ego through codependency. Verse 38 says, "And he who does not take up his cross and follow after Me is not worthy of Me." The cross represents the convergence of matter and spirit and the suffering that is involved. The burden is the ego and all it represents that must be eliminated so the soul can occupy fully within the person, in the place the ego used to occupy, to make room for the soul and spirit, which become the new consciousness, which God can use to do His will, fulfilling the soul's purpose. Verse 39 tells us, "He who finds his life will lose it, and he who loses his life for my sake will find it. He who loses his ego will find his soul. He who finds his ego will lose his soul."

Matthew 27:51 says, "And behold, the veil of the temple was torn in two from top to bottom; and the earth quaked, and the rocks were split." This was when Jesus Christ's soul merged with his heart, destroying the ego, concluding the first part of incarnating. The second part includes resurrection and ascension. At that time, his soul was free, and Satan was finally defeated.

Romans 13:11 says, "And do this, knowing the time, that now it is high time to awake out of sleep; for now our salvation is nearer than when we first believed." This verse represents our soul's time of further awakening and serves notice of our long-awaited trial to freedom and life in the spirit and spiritual self-defense psychic protection. Romans 13:12 says, "The night is far spent, the day is at hand. Therefore let us cast off the works of the darkness, and let us put on the armor of light." This verse represents the transition of consciousness from ego to soul and the entering of the ego on the journey of incarnation, which leads to fulfillment of the holy Trinity: Father God (mind), Holy Spirit (heart and body), and Son (soul). This is where the astral body is created and begins its journey of destiny, activating the spiritual growth process. Enlightenment at this level shows what is to be learned in the darkness.

Let's look at Luke 9:22–35. Verse 22 says, "The son of man must suffer many things, and be rejected by the elders and chief priests and scribes and be killed, and be raised up on the third day." The suffering being spoken of here is the same that Saint Paul mentions in his epistles. We are to share in Christ's suffering in our own way, proportionate to our own humanness, to prepare for our souls to embody and inhabit our bodies to live our lives for God, doing His will and our soul's purpose. We will not be killed, because we have already gone through death. Jesus Christ's was more of a fully conscious realization of both His humanity and His divinity, dissolving His humanity of His ego into His soul.

Verse 23 says, "If anyone desires to come after Me let him deny himself, and take up his cross daily, and follow Me." Each soul is different, and getting through this process takes perseverance, dedication, determination, devotion, and persistence, all of which are attributes of God and the soul and the opposite of the ego. Verse 24 says, "For whoever desires to save his life will lose it, but whoever loses his life for my sake will save it." Clinging to the ego will lead to death. Losing the ego in exchange for the soul will lead to life. Verse 25 says, "For what advantage is it to a man if he gains the whole world, and is himself destroyed or Lost?" Satan will be relentless with temptations to manipulate the soul and pacify the ego, which is not true peace or lasting joy. Many who are in their ego think that keeping it happy means they are right with God.

Verse 26 says, "For whoever is ashamed of Me and My words of him the Son of Man will be ashamed when he comes in His own glory and in His Father's, and of the holy angels." The Word of God is not only the origin of life but also life itself. It is not limited to the Bible but extends to many sources of all peoples and religions. Most importantly, it is the source of who you are deep within and is eternal with life, love, and truth.

Verse 27 says, "But I tell you truly, there are some standing here who shall not taste death till they see the Kingdom of God. Jesus Christ said the Kingdom of Heaven is within you and it is here and now." The ego veils God and the kingdom from one's consciousness because of the experience of being human. However, being a human being is the opposite of being human, and death is really an unrealized manifestation of death of the spirit to become human. Unbelief is what makes death appear real. In actuality, death is the unrealized grief of experiencing being separate from God. But even this is an illusion. God makes it as painless as He possibly can for us so we don't suffer any more than we can handle or any more than is needed to free us from the ego.

Verses 28 and 29 say, "And it came to pass, about eight days after these sayings, that He took Peter, John and James and went up the mountain to pray. And as He prayed, the appearance of His face was altered and His robe became white and glistening." These verses represent an ascent to higher consciousness, with the white radiant light of God's presence being one with it. It marks mystical union with God and creation of both the light body and the etheric body. Verses 30 and 31 say, "Then behold, two men talked with Him who were Moses and Elijah, who appeared in Glory and spoke of his decease which he was about to accomplish at Jerusalem." These verses represent the superconsciousness of being one, with God's mind preparing for entry into the ego and the descent of divinity into the flesh to incarnate. Mystical union with the infinite is achieved. The spiritual body becomes one with God. This is purified spirit, pure mind. The last remnant of the ego is released after this to the astral body, following along in the collective unconscious, traveling toward the ego.

Psalm 23 says the following:

> The lord is my shepherd; I shall not want. He makes me to lie down in green pastures; He leads me beside the still waters. He restores my soul; He leads me in the paths of righteousness for his name's sake. Yea, though I walk through the valley of the shadow of death, I will fear no evil; For you are with me; Your rod and Your staff they comfort me. You prepare a table before me in the presence of my enemies; You anoint my head with oil; My cup runs over.

Surely goodness and mercy shall follow me All the days of my life; And I will dwell in the house of the Lord Forever.

This scripture is a narrative of David entering the ego, the collective unconscious, and hell. The soul is awakened and sustains David and allows him to alternate between transitions of the different consciousnesses, between the ego and the soul. The soul is nourished by the indwelling presence of God. Christ consciousness and the presence of God guide the soul through the contrasting landscapes of the mind. This is where evil is encountered on a psychospiritual level, and because the soul is awakened, the love of God and the soul are stronger than the ego, with its fear, so comfort is provided as the soul traverses through the inner terrain. Because David enters into this process willingly, he is not attacked by those who hold grievances with him but, instead, is anointed and reassured of the goodness and mercy he shall experience for going through this process.

The Aquarian Gospel of Jesus the Christ by Levi references Psalm 8 by David, including his descent into physical matter and his final ascent into an eternal oneness with God: "Unnumbered foes will stand before the man upon the plane of soul; there he must overcome, yea overcome them every one. ... Man cannot die; the spirit man is one with God, and while God lives man cannot die. ... And man will then attain unto the blessedness of perfectness and be at one with God" (13). Isaiah 54:17 says, "No weapon formed against you shall prosper, And every tongue which rises against you, you shall condemn." All of the forces of hell shall not triumph against you, and all who are not of God and allow themselves to be used for evil will be judged and condemned by you by the presence of God within you through your soul. This is God's promise of victory for the soul.

Second Timothy 1:7 says, "For God has not given us a spirit of fear but of power and of love and of a sound Mind." Fear is difficult to face, but the soul is equipped to penetrate it fully, realizing it for what it is: an illusion meant to stifle one's spirit. One can conquer it only by going directly through it. Philippians 4:13 says, "I can do all things through Christ who strengthens me." This represents a turning point and is a critical moment in reconciling the ego to God. It marks the point of realizing one's own potential for a sinful nature and when the struggle of carrying one's own cross is the greatest. It also marks the point when one's own unbelief began.

Jeremiah 29:11 says, "For I know the thoughts I think toward you, says the Lord, thoughts of peace and not of evil, to give you a future and a hope." This verse represents God's love toward a repentant soul who has labored hard and long through the reconciliation process and finally realized just how extensive the process is to become right with God. God shows His forgiveness after the realization has taken place to impart on the soul that its goodness and mercy will be honored and allowed to be after one's personal attachments to the ego are gone.

Matthew 22:37–39 says, "You shall love the Lord your God with all your heart, with all your soul and with all your mind. This is the first and greatest commandment. And the second is like it: you shall love your neighbor as yourself." A human being is made primarily of three components: God (mind), Holy Spirit (heart and body), and Son (soul). Mind, body, and soul make up a human being. Being human, on the other hand, means the mind, body, and soul are three separate entities connected in dysfunctional through the ego instead of integrated and whole in total integration of being. One must love his or her soul and its connection to God above all else. One must love his or her body and heart and allow divine feelings so he or she can experience God in the flesh until one becomes God through this process. Remember, the ego is evil, and now that is gone. The body and heart can now rejoice in authentic joy from God. One must love God with all his or her mind, because one's mind is now one with God in mystical union with God. Doing God's will and fulfilling the soul's purpose are now effortless and easy and no longer seen or experienced as impossible. Love your neighbor as yourself because now thy neighbor is thyself.

Matthew 27:46 says, "And about the ninth hour Jesus cried out with a loud voice, Eli, Eli, lama sabachtani? that is, My God, My God, why have you forsaken me?" These words Jesus uttered were the words of the first wife of Adam, whose name was Lilith and who was subject to Adam's negative feelings, which sent her to hell, where she became brokenhearted and lost and was the first to experience being human. This realization needs to happen for one to be at last truly free from Satan, dysfunction, and all negativity while one is still alive and on earth to begin to live the life God envisioned for His beloved.

John 20:27 says, "Then he said to Thomas, Reach your finger here, and look at My hands; and reach your hand here, and put it into My side.

Do not be unbelieving, but believing." This verse represents those whose egos' desire to escape is greater than their souls' yearning to be. Their unbelief has not been satisfied to the point where all possibilities have been narrowed down to one last possibility: the truth that they have been in denial about since their unbelief began, which their ego created. They can now rest in peace and stop running from the truth and finally face it. The ego portion of the astral body is sublimated in the collective ego, resulting in the reversal of unbelief.

Acts 26:16–18 says the following:

> But rise and stand on your feet; for I have appeared to you for this purpose, to make you a minister and a witness both of the things which you have seen and of the things which I will yet reveal to you. I will deliver you from the Jewish people, as well as from the Gentiles, to whom I now send you. To open their eyes and to turn them from darkness to light, and from the power of Satan to God, That they may receive forgiveness of sins and an inheritance among those who are sanctified by faith in Me.

As Jesus intervenes on Saul's behalf, He also intervenes on yours as well. The journey you have taken is not only what God wants for your life but also what you want now that you are truly one with Jesus in spirit and connected at all times to Him, unlike in the ego and divine memory in the beginning, when it seemed God was far from you. He is with you in all ways for eternity, everywhere, and in everything and everybody you will encounter. Jesus Christ will continue to minister to you so you may help others to realize what you are experiencing, so they may experience joy as well. With this, we become joint heirs with Jesus Christ.

The following scripture is taken from *The Living Bible*:

> O Lord You have examined my heart and know everything about me. You know when I sit or stand. When far away you know my every thought. You chart the path ahead of me, and tell me where to stop and rest. Every moment, you know where I am. You know what I am going to say

before I even say it. You both proceed and follow me, and place your hand of blessing upon my head. This is too glorious, too wonderful to believe! I can never be lost to your Spirit! I can never get away from my God! If I go down to the place of the dead, you are there. If I ride the morning winds to the farthest oceans even there your hand will guide me, your strength will support me. If I try to hide in the darkness, the night becomes light all around me. For even darkness cannot hide from God; to you the night shines as bright as the day. Darkness and light are both alike to you. You made all the delicate, inner parts of my body, and knit them together in my mother's womb. Thank you for making me so wonderfully complex! It is amazing to think about. Your workmanship is marvelous and how well I know it. You were there while I was being formed in utter seclusion! You saw me before I was born and scheduled each day of my life before I began to breathe. Every day was recorded in your Book! How precious it is, Lord to realize that you are thinking about me constantly! (Psalm 139:1–17 TLB)

This is the awakening of the divine heart, or the spirit. All realizations in this chapter are of the divine heart realizing its divinity. The promise of this psalm is for every soul going through this process to have the conscious realization of this process and David's life, except where he fell into sin. The psalm by itself, without David's sin, would mark the completion of this process.

In Matthew 5:3–10, this sermon of Jesus Christ and the beatitudes not only describe the soul now purified and integrated into God's mind of spirit with the body but also tell about how life will now be and what to expect in life after having gone through the process. Verse 3 says, "Blessed are the poor in spirit, for theirs is the kingdom of Heaven" (NKJV). This describes the overall attitude of humility—a true and genuine one, not a false or pretending one. Verse 4 says, "Blessed are those who mourn, for they shall be comforted." This describes the vocation that the soul will not only go through itself but also help others with. Sorrow of one's own grief brings with it a deeper compassion and understanding for others' pain. Verse 5 says, "Blessed are the meek, for they shall inherit the earth." This is a reference to those without an ego who have grieved and maintained themselves to be able to serve others and God. Verse 6 says, "Blessed are those who hunger and thirst for righteousness." Here the indwelling love of God yearns to heal every soul to be one with God and establish mercy and justice for all to live in peace. Verse 7 says, "Blessed are the merciful, for they shall obtain mercy." The soul, through its connection to God, is compassionate and seeks to have mercy on all others with their brokenness. Verse 8 says, "Blessed are the pure in heart, for they shall see God." This is a reference to those who go through the process of becoming without ego. At the end of the process, they are purified in spirit and see the face of God as God really is. The inside of the cup is now clean indeed. Verse 9 says, "Blessed are the peacemakers, for they shall be called sons of God." An integrated soul and spirit will bring together and fill in the gaps or blocks where there is a lack of harmony or understanding evident. Verse 10 says, "Blessed are those who are persecuted for righteousness sake, for theirs is the Kingdom of Heaven." This is a reference to those who are not free and who act out against those who are in their wholeness and to the circumstances involved to try to help them.

Revelation 22:12–14 says, "And behold, I am coming quickly, and my reward is with Me to give to everyone according to his work. I Am the Alpha and Omega, the beginning and the end, the first and the last. Blessed are those who do his commandments, that they may have the right to tree of life, and may enter through the gates into the city" (NKJV). This passage fulfills the hope given to each soul on its journey to wholeness. The Alpha and Omega connects the healed and restored heart with eternity, reconciling past, present, and future as one eternal moment of now in the present moment. It is the moment of coronation of the heart to receive its crown of glory, celebrating the end of the ego, binding Satan eternally, ending his reign, and beginning the reign of spirit. The soul exits the collective unconscious and hell and has lived out its purpose.

Matthew 5:48 says, "Therefore you shall be perfect, just as your father in Heaven is perfect" (NKJV). This verse is the self-fulfilling prophecy Jesus gave to Himself and all other souls.

The process of mysticism and spiritual growth produces a realized divinity, or a spirit person. It includes enlightenment of the spiritual, mental, emotional, and physical levels through the spiritual body, the etheric body, the light body, and the astral body. One progresses through the transition and process of each one accordingly. Mystical union with God marks the return of the individual bodies to oneness with God and their liberation from the ego. The final product of such divine endeavors produces who you really are and who you were created to be, revealing your purpose after you reach and obtain the Alpha and Omega mystical spiritual experience, as outlined in this paper. The ego is the stepping-stone to the soul, and the soul is the stepping-stone to the spirit.

CONCLUSION

The holy of holies is hidden from us to give the experience of the ego, with its unbelief, the illusion of being real. The holy of holies represents the truth of one's beingness and beyond. It is a place in consciousness and beyond. It is the mechanism God uses to reveal sacred truths when a life-form or soul is ready and has reached a certain level of spiritual maturity. In the holy of holies, beingness begins, and beingness ends with mystical union with God. It is where the light body is liberated and born into an angel of light created directly from God's presence and sent to the subconscious mind to illuminate it and bring awareness and discernment along with comfort and joy and return to God's presence, integrated and liberated in mystical union with God. It is where the etheric body is born in consciousness itself, connecting the conscious mind with the subconscious mind, revealing the Akashic records and the living Word of God. It returns to its source in mystical union with God. It is where the astral body is liberated and born to live out potential outcomes that may not be advisable in the body when serving the ego and translating divinity in the physical body when the Word becomes flesh. It is where the spiritual body is born and integrated in a sacred embrace and sacred union with God, unifying spirit, soul, and God in the infinite of God's mind in the clear and gold light. It is also where images, symbols, colors, life-forms, beings, spirits, and archetypes commune with beingness of the life-form within the holy of holies within the life-form. It is also where dimensions are experienced and explored. It also contains the spark of God, which is the living presence of Christ light merged and synthesized with the infinite mind of God.

As I close my eyes and look within, I see life-forms in the dark: Jesus

Christ and Lilith, representing the mystical marriage. They are both in their realized divinity form, or the Word made flesh. Off to the right, I see a black cross signifying that the lower nature and drive of desires have been appropriately conquered and settled. Jesus and Lilith are in a warm embrace, sometimes kissing each other and other times gazing into each other's eyes. I look deeper, and I see their light bodies as two souls in love. *The Gospel of Philip* comments on this union of opposites: "The name of Christian is welcomed with anointing, in the fullness and energy of the cross, which the apostles call the union of opposites; then one is not just Christian, one is the Christ" (Leloup 97). I look a little deeper, and I see the colors of the chakras and sephirot, accompanied by light penetrating the darkness, as well as images and symbols coming toward me. I look past this and discover the spark of God—radiant pure-white light—up close and personal, right there within my heart. From this spark of God, I see spirits, beings, and life-forms coming and going, communicating with me for whatever reason and purpose. The revealing of the spark of God is God's anointing when a being or soul is now part of God's plan for the universe and the world. As I look into the spark of God, it pulses and floods my consciousness with its light, cleansing any negativity. Then it dissipates, leaving the archetypes behind. Then the whole process starts over again if desired.

The kingdom of heaven resides within the spark of God. Having achieved enlightenment and mystical union with God on all levels, the spiritual, etheric, light, and astral bodies are represented in the holy of holies with the spark of God (an autonomous, self-sustaining cosmic ball of energy, a star), represented by the spiritual (infinity) and light body (God's presence); images, symbols, and colors (etheric body); and life-forms in their realized divinity form (the astral body). All together, it is God looking at God with God as God, being God, contemplating God, and the divine blueprint revealed that makes it all possible. That is the mysticism of mysticism being mystical.

Danah Zohar, in her book *Connecting with Our Spiritual Intelligence*, calls this the eye of the heart: "The heart of the spiritually intelligent self is, ultimately the quantum vacuum, the ground of being itself. It is a still and changing ground, and the heart knows it is the still and changing heart" (207). From Dr. Masters's book *Spiritual Mind Power Affirmations* comes this affirmation from *Seeing the Beyond Within*, which characterizes third-eye sight: "I Understand that the interior region of my forehead is open to view realities existing beyond physical life experiences" (123). From Dr. Masters's book *Mystical Insights* comes this quote, which sums up this paper: "The awareness of this intimacy of consciousness with the Supreme is the great gift to one's mind, peace to one's soul and love's ultimate Presence for one's spiritual heart of hearts" (188). Namaste. Shalom. Amen.

WORKS CITED

Arya, Pandit Usharbudh. *Superconscious Meditation*. Honesdales, PA: Himalayan International Institute, 1978.

Choudhury, Raja. *Awakening Your Kundalini*. Shift Network. Online course. 2018.

Hawkins, David. *Discovery of the Presence of God*. Sedona, AZ: Veritas Publishing, 2007.

———. *The Eye of the I: From Which Nothing Is Hidden*. Sedona, AZ: Veritas Publishing, 2001.

———. *Transcending the Levels of Consciousness: The Stairway of Enlightenment*. W. Sedona,

AZ: Veritas Publishing, 2006.

Holmes, Ernest. *This Thing Called You*. New York, NY: Penguin Group, 2004.

The Holy Bible. New King James Version. Thomas Nelson, 1984.

Ingber, Rabbi David. *The Way of Kabbalah*. Shift Network. Online course. 2018.

Leloup, Jean-Yves. *The Gospel of Philip*. Rochester, VT: Inner Traditions, 2003.

Levi. *The Aquarian Gospel of Jesus the Christ*. Marina del Rey, CA: Devorss and Company, 2001.

The Living Bible (The Way). Wheaton, IL: Tyndale Publishing, 1971.

Marion, Jim. *Putting On the Mind of Christ: The Inner Work of Christian Spirituality*. Charlottesville, VA: Hampton Roads Publishing Company, 2011.

Masters, Paul Leon. *Master's Degree Curriculum*. 2 vols. Burbank, CA: Printing, 2011.

Meyer, Marvin. *The Nag Hammadi Scriptures*. New York, NY: Harper Collins Publishers, 2007.

Myss, Caroline. *Entering the Castle: An Inner Path to God and Your Soul*. New York, NY: Free Press, 2007.

Paulsen, Norman. *Christ Consciousness: The Emergence of the Pure Self Within*. Buellton, CA: Solar Logos Foundation, 2002.

Swami, Prabavananda. *The Sermon on the Mount according to Vedanta*. New York, NY: New American Library, 1972.

Tamura, Michael. *You Are the Answer*. Parker, CO: Star of Peace Publishing, 2002.

Tolle, Eckhart. *A New Earth*. New York, NY: Penguin Group, 2005.

Van Dijk, Danielle. *Christ Consciousness*. East Sussex: Temple Lodge Publishing, 2010.

Wauters, Ambika. *Chakras and Their Archetypes*. Freedom, CA: Crossing Press, 1997.

Whitfield, Charles L. *The Power of Humility: Choosing Peace over Conflict in Relationships*. Deerfield Beach, FL: Health Communications, 2006.

Zohar, Danah, and Ian Marshall. *SQ: Connecting with Our Spiritual Intelligence*. New York, NY: Bloomsbury Publishing, 2000.

5

Becoming Who You Were Created to Be

A Thesis Submitted in Partial Fulfillment of the Requirements
for the Degree of Master in Business Administration,
Specializing in Metaphysics, on Behalf of the Department
of Graduate Studies of the University of Sedona
Ramon Lazarus
July 30, 2018

INTRODUCTION

Becoming who you were created to be is a process that is mystical in nature and involves who you really are, as spoken into being by the Word of God in God's mind from God's presence. It involves becoming a realized divinity in human form. The process involves many modalities or methods of healing, which are metaphysical in nature but outside the metaphysical field, though they work with what is in the metaphysical field. In this paper, I will explore this process and how it works, other modalities that should be included in the metaphysical field, and the costs involved in financial planning matters for a career as a complete metaphysical practitioner or healer.

In the ego, all five bodies related to being human and becoming a human being are compartmentalized and separate, not only from God but also from one another, inside the egoic mind of someone who is being human. Meditation and healing are necessary to heal from the ego and its human condition of selfishness and negativity, awaken individually each body, and begin the process of integration, which leads to wholeness. With each positive step forward, a better, more comprehensive, and more complete state of being emerges, leading eventually to your becoming who you really are and who you were created to be. This is a mystical process in which the divine, parapsychological, psychophysical, and psychological all connect and interface with one another, eventually merging and fusing together to become one with God in mystical union with God.

The five bodies consist of the physical body, the astral body, the light body, the etheric body, and the spiritual body. The etheric body is associated with the mental aspect of being human and beingness. The light body is associated with the emotional aspect of being human and beingness, including the psychic level. Both the etheric body and the light body are fashioned after the sacred androgyne and are universal bodies that have, when awakened, all the higher divine attributes of God respective to their function and purpose related to being. The astral body is associated with the physical body and lower nature when unconscious and, once sublimated, helps to translate divinity into the physical body. The spiritual body is associated with all that is spiritual and becomes one with God in mystical union with God. Both the astral and spiritual bodies take on the form of the current incarnation as patterned by the DNA of the organism and the sublimation of the astral body, and upon mystical union with God of the spiritual body, both become universal bodies within God's mind individuated. The astral, light, etheric, and spiritual bodies, which represent the physical, emotional, mental, and spiritual aspects of being, culminating in mystical union with God, lead eventually to your being completely free of the ego and becoming who you really are and were created to be.

With this overview in mind, we will explore the process of becoming who you really are and becoming the human being you were created to be and what is needed to accomplish this, including the healing modalities involved in and outside the metaphysical field, the cost involved for each, the process involved from both a practitioner's and a client's perspective, and what it takes to be a complete healer.

REVIEW OF LITERATURE

There are two primary healing professions considered outside the mainstream of society: chiropractic and massage therapy. Both have origins in the metaphysical realm, but as each evolved toward the mainstream, those metaphysical roots were lost in favor of a more acceptable secular existence. Also, there are many healing modalities leaning toward mainstream acceptance that are metaphysical in nature that should be included metaphysically to help legitimize the field of metaphysics and hold on to those tenets as they move into the mainstream for broader acceptance as far as what they have to offer.

There are two basic approaches to healing. The first is integrative healing, which involves addressing a client's or patient's issue with a remedy for that issue only and on an as-needed basis. This is done from a doctor's or technician's perspective. The second is healing as a form of emotional and spiritual growth, which not only addresses the patient's complaint but also offers wisdom and insight in love and truth in directing and advising the client on how to achieve a higher state of being and also, if the person decides, how to integrate, embody, and incarnate for mystical union with God. This is done from a healer's perspective or metaphysician's perspective. There are individuals in all healing professions who embrace the spiritual aspect of being, but it is not representative of the mainstream whole. For the purposes of this paper, I will focus on the professions of chiropractic and massage therapy and the modalities found among practitioners in in these fields, as well as some others that can be included in the metaphysical field to reaffirm their beginnings from which they originated.

Chiropractors today are trying to become more like medical doctors.

The profession is split down the middle between those who embrace the metaphysical and those who do not. Chiropractic philosophy states, as noted in Dr. Eric Pearl's book *The Reconnection*,

> Universal intelligence maintains the organization and balance of the universe; and that there's an extension of that intelligence, called innate intelligence, within each of us, keeping us alive, healthy and in balance. This innate intelligence, or life-force communicates with the rest of our physical being in large part via our brain, spinal cord and the rest of our nervous system, the controlling system of our body. As long as the communication between our brain and our body is open and flowing freely, we remain in our optimum potential state of health. (32)

What a chiropractor does, then, is remove interference (distortions of the nervous system caused by tension created by displaced vertebrae in the spine) by adjusting distorted vertebrae to reestablish communication with the nervous system, allowing the life force to take over again, bringing back a healthy state of balance. When one is out of balance when interference is present (through a lesion called a subluxation), disease may occur from the breakdown of the cells of the body, which makes resistance to disease low. Chiropractic adjustments remove the interference, allowing the life force to flow again and reestablishing balance and a state of health to the organism. This is the basic philosophy and premise of what chiropractic is and is about. As stated earlier, there are those who are more secular in the profession, who want to be like medical doctors and who practice from a strictly mechanical, biochemical perspective. They only see the physical signs and symptoms of a bone out of place and are only mediocre technicians or doctors. For those in the profession who embrace the chiropractic philosophy mentioned earlier, there are a number of modalities and techniques that qualify chiropractic as being included in metaphysics, where it rightfully belongs.

Applied kinesiology, founded by Dr. George Goodheart, DC, is an effective tool for accessing the nervous system of the body, using the following treatments: "adjustment of the spinal column and manipulation of the extra spinal articulations, nerve receptor treatment, balancing of the meridians and the cranial sacral primary respiratory system, and nutritional therapy" (Walther 3). Applied kinesiology also embraces, as part of its triad of health, the psyche, along with structural and chemical imbalances in the body. Its basic premise is determining how the nervous system controls a muscle with a strong or weak response in correlation with what is being tested as cause.

Total body modification, founded by Dr. Victor Frank, DC, is an offshoot of applied kinesiology that uses muscle testing as well as reflexes to determine imbalances. It is an expanded version of applied kinesiology.

Neuroemotional technique, founded by Dr. Scott Walker, DC, is an expansion of the emotional component of total body modification. It focuses on diagnosing neuroemotional components and their body memory and clearing them through specific adjustments and specific homeopathic remedies.

These three modalities will help people access with limited effectiveness the emotional, mental, and spiritual components of being and mark the line of how far a doctor or technician can go as far as helping clients or patients with activating and working with the physical body. To go further and get to the root cause of disease, a technician or doctor must become a healer or metaphysician.

Some modalities for going deeper to become a healer and metaphysician can be found in massage therapy. Reiki and bodywork—specifically, craniosacral therapy (CST) levels one and two, and its extension to SomatoEmotional Release one and two, and advanced classes leading to diplomate status—signify for the practitioner a transition from technician or doctor to healer and metaphysician and also signify a change from ego to soul as the predominant consciousness maintaining the organism. Craniosacral therapy, or CST for short, and SomatoEmotional Release, or SER, both created by Dr. John Upledger, DO, integrate consciousness with matter or mind with body. Contrastingly, in AK, TBM, and NET, they are separate entities but still function within that paradigm. Bodywork, such as CST and SER, begins the process of integration and embodiment of the light body (which brings awareness and discernment to the psyche) into the physical body, which is a mystical experience. Reiki is a modality that clears negative energies and supplies life-force energy to whichever part of a person's being needs it. Sometimes a person's life force needs to be reestablished after a disease, disconnection from spirit, or various feelings or emotions that are traumatic in nature, which can cause much pain. For someone who is deeply unconscious, Reiki can help to reestablish life-force energy to begin the process to transition from ego to soul or spirit.

What makes CST unique is the mind-body link, or the linkage in consciousness between mind and matter. In his book *Cranial Sacral Therapy*, Dr. John Upledger explains,

> The phenomena these scientists (Peter Phillips, John Hasted, Harold Putoff, Russell Targ and electrical engineers Robert Jahn and Arthur Ellison) and John Upledger are talking about represent in my estimation, different views of an energetic cosmos in which body, emotions and mind and spirit are all trans-formations or expressions of the same basic energy. ... Refer to spirit as the "subtlest form of matter." If however, you are not embarrassed by the word matter it can be thought of as the densest form of spirit. (xiii)

SER, like CST, is a modality of touch and consciousness. From *Somato Emotional Release and Beyond* by Dr. John Upledger, DO, we learn that SER is the expression of emotion that, for reasons deemed appropriate by some part of the patient's nonconscious, has been retained, suppressed, and isolated within the soma. We might think of the soma as the somatic psyche." Observations of SER in process suggest that independent retention of the energy or memory of both physical and emotional trauma is frequently accomplished by specific body parts, regions, and viscera" (3).

One modality that deserves its rightful place in metaphysics is reconnective healing and reconnection. According to Dr. Eric Pearl, reconnective healing is an activation of frequencies that transmit and translate light and information to one person from another, reconnecting their hearts to their souls, with the heart as the primary consciousness, bringing healing and wholeness from one individual to another. It is simple, and activation happens from the hands of Dr. Pearl to his students. It is not a technique but simply an evolved consciousness that is shared and experienced. It, like Reiki, can be used to heal over distances, as Dr. Eric Pearl explains in his book *The Reconnection*: "Richard Gerber, In his book *Vibrational Medicine*, discusses the Tiller-Einstein model of positive and negative space-time: physical matter existing in positive space-time; energies beyond the speed of light such as (etheric and astral frequencies) existing in negative space-time" (211).

Gerber writes,

> That positive space-time energy (and matter) are primarily electrical in nature, while negative space-time energy is primarily magnetic. Accordingly, positive space-time is also the realm of electromagnetic radiation, while negative space-time is the realm of magneto-electric radiation. Negative space-time energy aside from its primarily magnetic nature, has another fascinating characteristic: a tendency toward negative entropy. Entropy is a tendency toward disorder, disorganization disease. The higher the entropy, the higher the disorder. Negative entropy is the tendency toward order, organization ease. It is the tendency toward regeneration and healing. (147).

Reconnective healing and the reconnection activate the astral body.

Remote viewing, developed by Russell Targ and Harold Putoff, is a modality that activates the etheric body and allows for its participants to experience themselves beyond the bounds of time and space. It also activates the living Word of God within the individual, as target summaries are required for feedback purposes regarding target observations and impressions. It awakens and develops expansive, nonlocal, universal intuition, which can be used for applications other than the intent of the modality or user. Because of these aspects of the modality, it deserves its rightful place in metaphysics. It heightens and awakens mental faculties. It activates the etheric body.

The University of Metaphysics and the University of Sedona are valuable to the field of metaphysics because they activate the spiritual body and also activate the emersion of the spiritual body of the individual with the spiritual body of God in mystical union with God. This has enormous implications for applications used within metaphysics and outside metaphysics, such as counseling, healing, teaching, and more. This produces the peak experience of samadhi in the individual—enlightenment and eternal bliss. It heightens spiritual faculties and attributes of God. "It is called Nirvana by the Buddhist, Samadhi by the Hindu, Christ Consciousness by the Christian mystic and Cosmic Consciousness by the philosopher" (Masters 1:8).

As we have seen so far, we have begun our journey with the physical body, with the profession of chiropractic philosophy and treatment of the physical body. We have addressed the transformation of the ego to the soul through the modalities of Reiki, remote viewing, the etheric body, and how it functions within the psyche regarding mental faculties. We have examined CST and SER and the light body. We have explored the reconnection and reconnective healing in relation to their function and activation of the astral body, and we have learned of the importance of the University of Metaphysics and the University of Sedona in activation of the spiritual body and the role in becoming one with God.

Divine clarity-----spiritual-----spiritual body----divine memory > ego construct

Intellect----------mental---------etheric body---------mind------------humanness

Reason---------emotional-------light body----------soul----------unconsciousness

Logic-------------physical---------astral body-----------body (heart)—brokenness

The above chart shows the alignment of the corresponding bodies and how they relate to their positioning and function in the psyche, including the ego. The only difference is that after going through spiritual growth, the divine memory is replaced by the spirit and is translated into the flesh by the astral body when the Word becomes flesh.

Paul Ferrini, in his book *Reflections of the Christ Mind*, comments on the proper attitude and appropriate perspective to have when addressing the physical body, which may also be applied to the etheric, light, astral, and spiritual bodies: "The body is a vehicle. It is a means for learning. Please do not disrespect it or demean it. Please do not make it into a god that you worship. Don't make it more or less important than it is" (218).

Affirmations are important because they state the true conditions of our spirit and soul in beingness and in mystical union with God. This gives the mind a goal or objective to strive toward, compared to the current state of the individual in experiencing dysfunction or disease. Affirmations work on all levels of health and being, and once mystical union with God is achieved, they work on others as well as oneself. Connection through soul awakening helps them to become more effective in the restorative nature of the vibration they were created at. Louise Hay, in her book *You Can Heal Your Life*, gives a mystical affirmation that transcends all dysfunction and disease: "In the infinity of life where I am, all is perfect, whole, and complete. I recognize my body as a good friend. Each cell in my body has divine intelligence. I listen to what it tells me, and know that its advice is valid. I am always safe, and Divinely protected and guided. I choose to be healthy and free. All is well in my world" (143).

In *The Nag Hammadi Scriptures* edited by Marvin Meyer, *The Wisdom of Jesus Christ* mentions an invisible body and a body of light: "The savior appeared not in his previous form but invisible spirit. He looked like a great Angel of Light, but I must not describe his appearance. Mortal flesh could not bear it, but only pure perfect flesh, like what he taught us about, in Galilee, on the mountain called Olivet" (287).

One modality that deserves its rightful place in metaphysics is the modality of holistic iridology. Holistic iridology is a tool to evaluate levels of health in the body, mind, and soul and is epigenetic in that it can uncover illness decades before onset and possibly avoid disease altogether if intervention is given in time before onset.

Holistic iridology is needed as a gauge or barometer for assessing health on a spiritual, mental, emotional, and physical basis through reading the iris, sclera, and pupil of the eye. As one becomes awakened on the levels mentioned in this paper, challenges arise with each body to appropriately heal and integrate into the whole of one's being. This can be a challenging event at times, especially during the integration and incarnation process. It allows validation of signs and symptoms of a consciousness nature that medicine will miss and brush off but that the patient will feel. It will reveal positive findings as one completes a segment of growth and healing and will confirm also negative findings when there is a challenge to one's being on any or all levels of one's being. It allows one's journey to be tracked and accounted for and may reveal potential health challenges down the road in the future. The Bible verse "If thy eye be single thy should be full of light" applies not only to the third eye of consciousness but also to the eyes of the body, which reveal the state of one's soul in relation to the physical and everything between the two.

Hand reading, or palmistry, is an art and science of revealing self-knowledge and health, with purposes dating back more than four thousand years in India. The hand, like astrology, reveals strengths and weaknesses of the individual as well as changes that take place that the individual is trying to make. Ellen Goldberg, in her book *The Art and Science of Hand Reading*, says, "The changes that occur in the hand come from the subconscious mind" (2). She also mentions that "a neurologist would tell you that there are more nerves between the hand and the brain than between any other two points of the nervous system" (2–3). Palmistry can point out the broader goals and chart the connections of what an individual can grasp and understand.

Holistic iridology, which also works through the nervous system and subconscious, can point out what a person can see and learn to grow from, leading to greater health and well-being.

The Anatomy and Physiology of Spiritual Growth and Healing and Being

The divine memory accesses the etheric body (mental level) to bring up illusion, belief, layers, patterns, constructs, thinking, and memory associated with the lesson or pain God wishes to teach the individual soul about. At the same time, the light body brings the light of awareness from God's presence to the emotions and underlying issues and feelings, as represented in the astral body. The light of awareness in the light body (emotional level) brings awareness and discernment to the contents of the etheric body (mental level) and the astral body (physical level). The light shines on the darkness and differentiates what is true from what is false. Discernment distinguishes what is to be discarded and what is to be integrated for educational and growth purposes. The truth is revealed through this process and is explained in a context that is comprehensible and understandable to the individual soul. Validation of the process and of the experience of learning and spiritual growth is then compared to the spiritual body, which is divine awareness. Divine awareness validates for the individual soul what it has learned and God's account of the phenomenon or experience just processed and accounted for. At this point, clarity is gleaned and gained from the experience, and free will can now be used to make an informed choice as to how the individual soul would like to resolve the conflict in an appropriate manner, taking proper responsibility for his or her feelings, thoughts, and emotions to learn; grow; understand the self, others, and God; and move forward in purposeful alignment with God, true faith, and intelligence, not ignorance, to eventual mystical union with God and beyond.

Each body governs, translates, and downloads disease (ego) or health (soul), depending upon the state of being or lack thereof of the organism or life-form. The etheric body governs, translates, and downloads disease pathology associated with illusion, belief, layers, patterns, constructs, thinking, memory, and feelings of humanness, causing discomfort or pain on a mental level. The light body or soul governs, translates, and downloads on an emotional level, in a disease state of pathology by the ego, negative emotions associated with feelings of unconsciousness. It's also associated with the astral body, which contains the primordial feelings associated with the ego in an ego pathology disease state, feelings of brokenness on a physical level. The spiritual body is untouched by ego or pathology, and when the ego is the predominant consciousness, the divine memory is fully activated and transformed into a fully alive manifestation of a living, breathing, sustainable, fully conscious life-form of spirit, which then takes over the process of healing and homeostasis of the life-form, governing, translating, and downloading vibrant vitality. Every level or body of existence is transformed into beingness. The etheric body, or mental level, is associated with the feelings of humanness and is governed by the living Word of God, which transforms the feelings of humanness, giving life, health, and vitality to the mind in thought and inspiration. The light body is fully conscious with the presence of God and its awareness on an emotional level, identifying negative emotions and feelings of unconsciousness and converting them into positive, conscious ones that contribute to well-being and stability. It acts as a warning system of other life-forms in need of help. The astral body, or psychophysical level, is converted from brokenness to wholeness and governs, translates, and downloads divinity of the divine spiritual level into the physical body, restoring health and radiating vitality to the body.

Pain of any kind on any level is governed, translated, and downloaded in the system and processed as described in this paper. Pain starts on a psychophysical level, meaning the mind affects the body, and the body affects the mind. Pain leads to discomfort. Discomfort leads to tension, tension leads to agitation, agitation leads to disruption, disruption leads to dissonance, dissonance leads to incoherent vibration, incoherent vibration leads to decreased vitality, and decreased vitality leads to disease. Healing, as described in this paper, takes the incoherent vibration and dissonance from the ego, with its out-of-phase lower-energy frequency and vibration, and transforms it into coherence, which leads to well-being and the reestablishment of vitality, through the process just described, addressing the psychospiritual, psychophysical, parapsychological, and psychological anatomy and physiology of the psyche of an individual and the process of disease. There is healing in becoming a human being from being just human. Once this process is complete, then the spiritual body, integrated with the etheric, light, and astral bodies, enters into and completes oneness with God in mystical union with God, becoming one with God in God's mind, heart, soul, and presence in samadhi, saturated with the profound peace that passes mortal understanding.

Gary Zukav, author of *The Seat of the Soul*, states that pain with an understanding serves a worthy purpose: "Suffering is meaningful. Suffering can be endured because there is a reason for it that is worthy of the effort. What is more worthy of your pain than the evolution of your soul?" (195).

Pain is God's navigation device to guide the soul where it needs to go to become free of all attachment that limits its potential to become all it can be, who it really is, and who it was created to be. Pain, when it is first encountered, needs awareness, discernment, and understanding, along with love and compassion, to be recognized and handled appropriately. Pain is a signal to the life-form that something within itself needs attention to be cared for, loved, and released in forgiveness—a thought, emotion, or feeling that has fulfilled its purpose of what it has to teach the life-form for growth. Pain can be unbearable because the ego is judging it as something alien to it, rejecting the pain outright, further alienating it, adding to the intensity, making the pain even more unbearable. Love and compassion in the spirit of truth are needed to bring comfort to the pain and begin the process of disentangling the pain from the life-form. This resolves it into its constituent parts of feeling, thought, and emotion and allows the pain to tell its story by being acknowledged, heard, and forgiven in a way that the pain can understand, as well as the life-form. Understanding each other leads to forgiveness of each, releasing the entanglement between the two, and in its place, the grace of God soothes and sublimates both the pain and the life-form so that both become whole and complete, resolving the conflict appropriately.

The ego avoids pain at all costs, which contributes to making it unbearable. When any kind of pain is encountered, awareness and discernment are needed to discern if the pain comes from the life-form itself or from another source in a potential conflict. Awareness will shine its light on the pain in the darkness within, and as soon as the light shines within, discernment determines the nature and origin of the feeling, including what it is about and where it came from. Once identified, the pain will need to appropriately be handled and released in forgiveness to return to its source and then return to God. Whether the pain belongs to the life-form or is from another source, the remedy is the same: choose forgiveness. Even if it feels as if forgiveness cannot be given, choose it anyway. Next, choose to forgive God, yourself, your parents, and the world. Next, release the pain into God's presence, and exercise faith, believing God will do His part, as you have appropriately and responsibly done yours. Next comes the time when you enter eternity with God in the process of freeing your soul and heart from the entanglement that caused the pain to begin with. The releasing process can be long, and one can still experience the pain as the piece of the soul being recovered crosses the abyss within. It may seem one gets lost or loses faith. This is the memory associated with the loss of the soul part that is being released in the process, and when it reaches this point, it is important to keep the faith, as liberation is near. The Christ light shines within and releases the pain to its light, freeing the life-form of its pain, completing the cycle of creation from start to finish. This accomplishes four things: (1) recovering a lost or fragmented soul or heart piece; (2) healing, with the Christ light, that part or piece; (3) placing it back where it came from; and (4) making it better than it was before the breaking process began. Once every fragment is accounted for, true wholeness is experienced from the soul through the mind to the body, leading to mystical union with God, which involves a purified soul and heart becoming one with God's soul, mind, heart, and spirit.

David Hawkins, an enlightened psychiatrist, describes the mindset of someone going through and coming out of this experience, in his book *Healing and Recovery*: "We come out of the depression willing to look at the fear, at the way it was set up and how we got set up. We experience the anger about that and then use the energy of that anger to want something better for our self, now having the courage to face how it all came about" (390).

DISCUSSION

The light body is born in darkness. As it illuminates that darkness, it reveals the mysteries contained in that darkness. It is extremely aware and, thus, capable of understanding complex concepts and systems. The astral body is dark and is born in the daylight, and it learns about itself as a result of being in the light. All the mysteries of the shadow will come into the light to be known. The etheric body is born in consciousness and reveals the mysteries of consciousness itself, and it has access to the light and astral bodies. The spiritual body is born in the water-like dimension and chamber of the holy of holies and is in the medium and substance of akasha, or the primordial creative substance of all living beings and creation. Its purpose is to be perfection of beingness and express that perfection of God through God's mind as a vehicle of God's love.

Healing processes through the spiritual, etheric, light, astral, and physical bodies as the divine memory, following God's will, cues the soul, mind, body, and spirit as to what is to be used as far as growth, learning, and healing are concerned within the organism and life-form. God's will has the soul's purpose in mind and will tailor the process of becoming a human being from just being human in a way that is both insightful and helpful, reflecting the needs of whatever that purpose will be. God is comprehensive, thorough, and complete, with universal God mind, which means all lessons learned will benefit all people from all walks of life. Relatability, creativity, wisdom, insight, and knowledge regarding any kind of creation or construct of the ego will be applied to transforming that construct of ego into soul or spirit. Once the process of spiritual growth has been started, it continues, using free will to keep choosing growth in a forward direction. All past lives will be evaluated as to what needs to be healed according to God's will and the soul's purpose. Any issues and unresolved feelings will be brought up to be evaluated and processed through the anatomy and physiology of spiritual growth, as described in this paper. The unresolved issues and unresolved feelings are coordinated with the heart and soul or ego and soul, consisting of past lives, strongholds, karma, illusion, belief, constructs, layers, patterns, memory, and thinking. The experience of going through this will be a three-part process consisting of heart on the left side of the body, soul on the right side of the body, and ego connecting to both heart and soul. Pain from the soul, which is not able to express itself and who the person is, is accompanied by pain from the heart, which is not able to be who the person was created to be. This is further complicated by the pain of the ego in not getting its own way as this process cycles through the mind, body, and soul, processing all karma, strongholds, illusions, beliefs, constructs, layers, patterns, memory, and thinking of sublimating and dissolving the ego.

This process continues until all unresolved issues and unresolved feelings are appropriately processed and integrated according to what is useful to keep from the experience as far as serving the soul's purpose and what is to be discarded regarding outgrown experiences of the ego. The process will cycle left to right or right to left within the mind and is experienced in the body in the head region. Liberating the etheric, light, and astral bodies activates awareness, discernment, and healing qualities associated with each body and the overall process of embodiment, integration, and eventual incarnation.

A healing treatment consists of using all modalities as needed to bring about healing, harmony, and balance to the life-form seeking help. The ideal healer or practitioner, to be integrated as far as soul into heart is concerned, will use at his or her disposal all healing modalities the soul has learned and accessed over its career in becoming a healer. Each modality, under the guidance of God's presence, working with the divine memory or directly with the soul or both, assists the life-form seeking help with a condition as a catalyst, and sometimes source, of healing. An integrated soul guided by God's presence uses the different modalities like a skilled spiritual surgeon, knowing exactly how to pinpoint the cause of dysfunction, disease, or both and also how to heal and release the unresolved issues and unresolved feelings responsible for the dysfunction, disease, or pain. Also, the integrated soul knows how to harmonize and balance the area being treated and return vitality to the area in question, raising the life-form's vibration to a level of strong coherence and well-being. Each area found to be dysfunctional, diseased, or causing pain is addressed in this manner, until all areas are accounted for and reintegrated back into the presence of God in the life-form seeking treatment to be processed and healed as a unit. This process may need to be repeated on a reduction-frequency basis to resolve the problems experienced by life-forms, until they are better and their complaints are fully resolved. Since all levels have a healing modality associated with them, the process is thorough, comprehensive, whole, and complete. The process never overburdens the life-form or overwhelms him or her in a negative way but is effective also in what it is achieving in an appropriate, loving, and compassionate way to heal the life-form with dignity and respect for the life-form's divinity, whether the person is aware of it or not.

A healing treatment consists of light touch palpation of the entire body from head to toe in a twofold approach, or modified laying-on-of-hands modality. When an area is touched, it is evaluated for degree of dysfunction, tension present in the tissues, and how it relates to overall beingness with the mind and soul. As the areas of dysfunction are scanned, they are treated simultaneously as the presence of God and God's mind work through the modalities of the practitioner to directly transmit healing energies and frequencies to the patient or life-form. Once transmitted, the healing energies and frequencies clear the feeling, thought, and emotion responsible for the dysfunction and reestablish harmony and balance, as well as raising the life-form to a greater state of coherence and well-being. Feedback is given to the practitioner through intuition, palpation, or both. The tension that was present is now gone, eliminated, and cleared from the life-form on all levels. As a result, the life-form will feel lighter and better.

A healing treatment starts at the feet to check the person's understanding and, if needed, treat it so the life-form can accept the healing about to be given. Next, the lower legs and knees are checked for flexibility of mind needed to help life-forms learn if they are rigid within themselves and how this contributes to their dysfunction or disease. Next, the hips are evaluated to clear any blocks in their ability to move forward from where they are. Next, the abdominal organs are evaluated for congestion or a lack of vitality to determine the causal issues and feelings that apply to each one found. Each organ has a feeling, thought, and emotion associated with it that must be evaluated, cleared, and healed. Next, the thoracic cavity, containing the lungs and the heart, is evaluated for tension in its systems and cleared accordingly. Next, the neck and head are evaluated for any signs of imbalance on any level. The subconscious mind is checked for any ailments to well-being and vitality.

The life-form is turned over, and the spine is evaluated for tension, starting at the coccyx and toward the head, up to the shoulder area. Each level is palpated for tension, released, and healed until the entire spine is free from tension. The life-form's posture is reevaluated and compared to the posture he or she had when standing before the treatment, and observations are noted as far as corrections made, allowing the life-form to stand straight and erect. Range of motion may also be checked at this time to note improvements as well. A healing treatment can be used for isolated conditions or be used as a method of growth to assist as needed for one to be who he or she is and was created to be.

"Success in metaphysics must have as its first definition, the good, the uplifting, the bringing forth of God's potential, the healing that you give to others in your doctoral work" (Masters 49). This quote from Dr. Masters sums up what a healing treatment should encompass and deliver to the life-form. This is from his MBA degree program consultation (73).

In addition to the laying on of hands as a healing modality, the living Word of God from God's presence within a healer can also work wonders and miracles. The living Word of God speaks its works into creation, being the source of all creativity from the bright, radiant white light of God's presence within the healer. The living Word of God, as scripture says, never returns empty or void. It is always enlightening and enlivening all it comes in contact with. As far as healing goes, it works on a metaphysical level on all levels of being and nonbeing states. Because it created all the levels to begin with, there is nothing it cannot transform. Its purpose is closely aligned with Christ consciousness, and its primary objective is mystical union with God to make human beings or realized divinities. In the psyche, the living Word of God will clear the feeling, thought, and emotion causing the block leading to dysfunction, disease, or pain. Once the feeling, thought, and emotion are cleared, the living Word of God will pass by the soul level of mind in the patient, recover a lost fragment, heal it, integrate it, and make it more whole than before the encounter with the living Word of God. It establishes an authentic connection with the life-form and God and between the life-form and God. It also creates interest in the mystery of creation itself, leaving the life-form with a wondering curiosity, to instill motivation and a desire for more of the same as far as healing and growth are concerned. When the living Word of God has completed its mission, it returns to the presence of God in the life-form, and with it comes a realization of all that has taken place as far as growth, healing, learning, and education in God's mind.

Deep down, people crave this education, but they don't know how to get there. As metaphysicians, we are uniquely qualified by God to be able to help such people when the need arises. The living Word of God is not restricted to any limitation, as it is both infinite and never-endingly creative. Counseling of any kind that is spiritual in nature is a viable path for healing, as it can be used directly for healing in counseling or during and with a healing treatment. It has infinite applications because it is infinity itself. Once the gift of itself has been accepted, the process of growth and healing continues with the living Word of God to eventually meet its divine destiny in returning to its source, having made the creation it originally was created from in the life-form, becoming a realized divinity, or the Word made flesh one with God in mystical union with God. It can also be used for other applications as well, such as helping to guide and manage a business or enterprise. These successful practices lead to prosperity for the one who follows their guidance and advisement in such matters. The applications are endless and are not limited by anything or anyone. Once the living Word of God returns to its source, then the cycle of life is complete.

An important consideration regarding spiritual growth is the phenomenon of a traumatic past-life passing or death. This can be from an accident or sudden, unexpected death or can be more violent, such as a killing or murder. All these events have a high degree of energy that is negative and a high degree of karma that go along with them. The charge, emotionally and spiritually speaking, is of a high magnitude because of how the ego is formed in the next life after the traumatic death. The powers and principalities break open the heart and soul to help form the ego and then also help to repress the content of the karma back into itself, enclosing the whole unit into the subconscious mind, where it stays until the awakening process starts, and spiritual growth begins.

The events and the level of development of the soul will determine how difficult a predicament is to overcome and recover from. The energy can overwhelm the life-form, leading to psychiatric illness, until the life-form can successfully navigate and work through it, doing his or her part and letting God do God's part in it. The energy will need to be transduced down and decompressed from the repression, and this takes time, effort, and motivation. Therapy will help the life-form to release attachments associated with the ego, so it can continue to move forward to meet its divine destiny: being sublimated into God's presence in the collective unconscious. The experience of the life-form will be one of repression, suppression, and depression, as this reflects what the life-form had to go through to become human. The greater the resilience of the soul is, the greater the efforts needed to suppress it will be. This equates to the valuableness of the gifts the soul has to give and share with the world. The greater the obstacle to overcome is, the greater the gift the soul has to share with the world is. This should be a source of motivation for the life-form to keep it from giving up.

As long as the soul keeps choosing to grow and get better, progress will be made, and little by little, or sometimes with leaps and bounds, the life-form improves to get to a better place. Life-forms will have to be nurtured, and progress will need to be pointed out to them because of the deceptiveness of the feelings they are processing. The feelings are based upon illusion, so they will try to fool and confuse a life-form until their very end, up until they are processed and released. It is a matter of going two steps forward and one step back. That is how it cycles to give the life-form time to contemplate and realize what needs to be learned from the experience so the educational value of the experience is complete, and the soul learns the reasons for the experience.

Because of this latent tendency in life-forms, great care needs to be given when assisting them with their growth. If one's intuition is picking up that this may be the case, then caution should be exercised to allow the process to unravel and unfold as easily as possible in a way the psyche of the life-form can handle. Therefore, techniques or practices that are more aggressive toward mystical experience should be avoided, with gentler ones employed in their place. Kabbalah, from Judaism, is a gentle practice that utilizes all five bodies, as mentioned in this paper. Sometimes how it unfolds can't be helped, and the life-form will experience hardship, but also, the person will be given assistance from God to soften the blow, and it is temporary and will resolve with time and the right care. There is nowhere in society that educates or prepares one for experiences like this. That is another reason metaphysicians are needed in the world: because they understand it and have been through it.

The progression of healing modalities from the physical to the spiritual flows as such: (1) medical treatment and intervention; (2) supplements, such as vitamins and minerals; (3) herbs, homeopathic remedies, and flower remedies; (4) essential oils; and (5) consciousness work, such as meditation, laying on of hands, affirmations, yoga, and prayer. All of these have their place and purpose in the world and will be needed at some point in a life-form's lifetime to help maintain and heal from the growth and changes that come from and with life.

The cost of becoming a chiropractor or medical doctor is more than the cost of becoming a healer. A medical doctor's education is approximately $350,000 in today's world. The cost of becoming a chiropractor is $150,000 to $200,000, and the cost of becoming a massage therapist is approximately $9,000 in comparison. The cost of becoming any kind of doctor is prohibitive and is primarily funded through the use of student loans, which are the worst kind of loan to have should one become injured or disabled. The educational background is ideal to learn about what science has discovered physically about anatomy and physiology but not necessarily essential, as God's education is much more thorough, comprehensive, and complete. What is taught in medical schools, chiropractic colleges, and massage therapy schools constitutes the bare-bones basics of long-held traditions of established practices, with minor upgrades to those practices as science evolves. It is not necessarily what will be the best course of action, depending upon the presenting condition of a patient with a problem.

It has been my experience that what gets people well is found outside the mainstream flow of society in postgraduate seminars, conferences, and workshops. The benefit of such events is that you learn cutting-edge technology and techniques and also get to benefit from that same treatment performed on yourself by another. Partnering in workshops gives the perspective of being both a patient receiving a treatment and a healer giving a treatment. Most workshops are for three to four days on average. The cost of the workshops covers the cost of the treatments you receive and, as a bonus, the knowledge and experience you gain as a result. It is something a healer can use immediately to start helping people. For Reiki, to become a master is approximately $1,000, or less than that for level one and level two. Attunements are given to activate the modality.

Remote viewing is the only modality that is not hands-on as far as laying on of hands is concerned, but people have reported that their hands get hot or activated in the process. These seminars are more intensive and generally run $500 for a four- or five-day workshop. Remote viewing activates intuition and converts the mind from ego to soul consciousness through the etheric or mental body. Craniosacral therapy and SomatoEmotional Release activate the light body as an angel of light from God's presence. Seminars here run about $600 each, as there are levels one and two for both CST and SER, a total of four, plus advanced classes, which run higher: $1,500 for an advanced class, plus $400 for administrative purposes to obtain a diplomate status.

The light body brings awareness to the darkness to be able, with the etheric body, to lead to the spiritual growth process leading to wholeness. The reconnection is $333 and activates the astral body, which is important to use the ego as a vehicle of spiritual growth and, when finally sublimated, is used to translate the spiritual body into the physical body as the living Word of God becomes flesh. Reconnective healing costs about $400 to receive the transmission of frequencies and attend a three-day workshop.

The University of Metaphysics and the University of Sedona cost $1,290 for bachelor's, master's, and doctorate degrees with a scholarship. Cost without a scholarship is about $4,500. These universities transmit the consciousness of Dr. Masters to those who are ready and open to receive it. The God mind is the highest level of consciousness the heart can reach in its union with God. It is a purely purified state pristine from any mortal consciousness. It is a supreme and generous gift of Dr. Masters to have made this possible for all who come to his universities. The gift of enlightenment Dr. Masters bestows cannot be given a price, because it is priceless in its value as to what is gained in the process. Postgraduate work, such as a doctorate in theocentric psychology, is $990. This degree in metaphysics was $275 and helps to impart Dr. Masters's wisdom and insights in the field of metaphysics. Additional doctorates other than those mentioned are $490 and offer those who seek them a validated spiritual education that is not of this world but thoroughly from God.

So far, we have looked at the costs involved from the healer's perspective, along with the benefits involved as well. We will now look at the costs from a patient's perspective for each. The cost of an adjustment from a chiropractor varies from about $40 to $80, depending upon specialty, experience, and location. Those in major metropolitan areas charge as much as $300 for an adjustment. The cost of a massage generally runs from $50 to $100 an hour, with metropolitan areas and resorts charging more than that. Specialty work, such as CST or psychic-level work, can be as much as $200 an hour. The reconnection is $333 for a healer or a patient. For spiritual healing, Dr. Masters's MBAM program (consultation 12, page 59) cites $50 for weekly practitioner work. Other costs involved include whether to rent space and start an office or practice out of one's home. A holistic iridology evaluation can cost anywhere between $20 and $50 or more. Chiropractors, because more money is involved, may purchase an existing practice, be an independent contractor, or be an employee of an existing practice with a chiropractor in his office. Massage therapists generally rent space to practice out of because they don't make as much as chiropractors do. An average salary for a chiropractor is about $65,000 to $70,000 a year. Massage therapy can vary from $25,000 to $40,000 a year.

Costs of insurance are as follows: Professional liability (malpractice) for a chiropractor is $800 a year for a part-time policy (twenty to thirty hours a week). Business liability insurance is $525 a year. The cost of renting space varies from $500 a month to $1,500 a month, depending upon location. Operating out of one's home has tax advantages and write-off benefits. If practicing out of your home, you can use approximately 35 to 45 percent of your home's square footage and deduct that same amount from expenditures, such as utilities, homeowner's insurance, and direct operating costs for doing business, as expenses.

As one can see, there are numerous costs involved in becoming a healer. The most cost-effective way is through the route of becoming a massage therapist. The cost of massage therapy school, as mentioned, is $9,000, coupled with $6,000 for a diplomate in CST, including SER and levels one and two for each. Advanced classes are as follows: $1,000 to be a Reiki master; $1,500 for advanced-level remote viewing; $333 for the reconnection; $400 for reconnective healing; $1,290 for a doctorate from the University of Metaphysics with a scholarship; a diplomate in holistic iridology for $2,500; and a class on hand reading for $300. The total comes to $22,323 to become a complete healer or metaphysician. Healers will be able to do for themselves and others work where the limitations of the healing professions leave off because they focus strictly on the physical and further fragment from there into multiple subsidies and subspecialties, with the costs going higher and higher the further it is fragmented. The costs become less and less the more whole the mode or philosophy of health or well-being becomes.

The process of being who you really are (soul) and becoming who you were created to be (heart and mind integrated with the soul and free from the ego) naturally unfolds over time with the help of healing in the form of meditation, laying on of hands, or both. Divine awareness, through the spiritual body and spirit, guides and directs with the help of Christ consciousness. Through the divine memory, it deconstructs the ego into its component parts. The intellect of the etheric body or mental body handles the feeling of emotion associated with humanness. The faculty of reason is converted on an emotional level through the light body as an angel of light. This identifies thoughts and thought forms, cues them for growth and transformational purposes, and is associated with the feeling of unconsciousness. The faculty of logic is converted from ego expression in the physical to feelings of brokenness in the growth and transformation process. Together all four metaphysical bodies interact, are interdependent upon one another, and work together in the mystical process of spiritual growth, directed by Christ consciousness. This leads to the ideal state of being: a perfection that fulfills Christ's words "Be ye perfect even as your heavenly father is perfect."

After achieving this state, one is like God, just as Jesus Christ was and is today. The divine blueprint of the vibration spoken by the Word of God in creating a human being has been validated and realized not only by God but also by His creation in the realized divinity human. There is oneness through God's mind, and the divine will of God is now accepted. In the preferred will of His creation, there no longer is a struggle with the limitations of the ego. Being a realized divinity means there are no longer any remnants of the ego left to confuse, puzzle, or mystify the life-form to the contrary to God. The inner world matches the outer world, and there are no issues of compatibility within or with the soul, mind, body (heart), or spirit. There are no dysfunctional behaviors, pathologies, gender identity issues, negativity, discontent, uncertainty, or confusion. There are no more illusions, beliefs, constructs, layers, or patterns of thinking, and thinking itself is replaced by intuition directly from God's presence and God's mind.

These modalities, working mystically and metaphysically with the spiritual, etheric, light, and astral bodies, help people to achieve their best and, if they choose, become who they really are and who they were created to be.

The astral body is key as a dual-purpose metaphysical body, translating ego or spirit into the physical body and also making the decision when the moment of truth arrives. The astral body is in transition while it is in the collective unconscious within the collective ego when reconciling the ego to the soul and God's presence within the self. It is both giving up the ego and, at the same time, translating the spirit within to take its place. This goes on until the moment of truth arrives to determine and decide whether the ego will completely surrender to the soul or whether the ego will continue on as the predominant consciousness of the life-form. The choice presented is to become who you were created to be or not be who you were created to be. The choice is presented in the form of a temptation to sin and follow one's ego or make a higher choice to follow one's soul. The temptation is directly linked to one's unbelief and the inception point where the life-form's experience of ego began. The experience of temptation, through one's unbelief, is enticing and not easy to resist unless one is accustomed to using such experience for spiritual growth by not giving in to it in the flesh and acting out the impulse with another. This same temptation is used as leverage to take back strongholds related to it. The temptation will also be tied to sin, or more than one sin, for the soul to learn from and be victorious over. Once the temptation is presented, it is either acted on or not, and when it is not, it reverses the process of unbelief, cleaning the mind of all past, present, and future lives associated with it, including the present moment. Soon after that, one is a master of the collective unconscious and a master of the collective ego.

The temptation and trial reveal the flaw of the individual, and he or she is given the choice to live out how things were before the process of spiritual growth started or become something new as a realized divinity, or the Word made flesh. King David sinned at this point with Bathsheba, arranging for her husband to be killed in battle. His offspring, King Solomon, became lost once he entered the collective unconscious and collective ego, as evidenced in his writings in the latter part of Ecclesiastes, where it becomes evident that wisdom into such matters was missing in his life.

CONCLUSION

Becoming a complete healer or metaphysician is a pragmatic, practical way to become who you really are and who you were created to be. The journey is beyond compare as far as educational value of life and love. Learning about God and God's creative mind and presence is what life is really about. How everything works and works together is sublime perfection, and once one is perfect as God is perfect, it all makes perfect sense. The goal of all such endeavors is to be better or the best one can be and, once that goal is attained, live from that perspective with God as one's everything, as God intended for all. The cost involved is reasonable compared to that of other healing professions the world has to offer, and a healer will exceed and succeed where others have limitations and will see a greater cross-sectional variety of dysfunctions of the ego than those in other professions. The work will be invigorating and interesting and keep one on his or her toes with the variety of cases and presentations. Spiritual growth is both challenging and rewarding at the same time and is the only way to become who you were created to be. With body liberation come activation and connection to God and each corresponding level: spiritual, mental, emotional, and physical. Once one is connected, affirmations have greater effectiveness.

Spiritual growth ends with sublimation of the last remnant of the ego portion of the astral body in the collective unconscious within the collective ego, culminating in your becoming who you were created to be. Progress can be evaluated and marked through holistic iridology and palmistry, or hand reading. It is important to be guided by God mind to be aware of what the field of metaphysics and areas considered outside it offer and what is useful for God's plan for fulfilling one's soul's purpose. The final product of this process, a realized divinity, a human being, saves not only money but also other precious resources valuable to God, self, and others: time, energy, and consciousness. Being streamlines the process of living and is cost efficient and cost effective in all its methods and ways of meeting its immediate and long-term needs to be successful and prosperous in every aspect of life as an extension of the mystical fulfillment of being with the spiritual, reflecting the internal state of beingness with the outer aspect of being successful in all endeavors that extend from it. Being healed and whole means having a healed, whole, and free soul, mind, and body (heart). That's the way God intended it to be.

WORKS CITED

Ferrini, Paul. *Reflections of the Christ Mind*. New York, NY: Double Day, 2000.

Gerber, Richard. *Vibrational Medicine*. Santa Fe, NM: Bear and Company, 1996.

Goldberg, Ellen, and Dorian Bergin. *The Art and Science of Hand Reading*. Rochester, VT: Destiny Books, 2016.

Hawkins, David. *Healing and Recovery*. W. Sedona, AZ: Veritas Publishing, 2009.

Hay, Louise L. *You Can Heal Your Life*. Hay House, 1987.

Masters, Paul Leon. *Master's Degree Curriculum*. 2 vols. Burbank, CA: Printing, 2011.

Meyer, Marvin. *The Nag Hammadi Scriptures*. New York, NY: Harper Collins Publishers, 2007.

Pearl, Eric. *The Reconnection: Heal Others, Heal Yourself*. Hay House, 2001.

Upledger, John E., and Jon D. Vredevoogd. *Cranial Sacral Therapy*. Seattle, WA: Land Press, 1983.

————. *Somato Emotional Release and Beyond*. Palm Beach Gardens, FL: Upledger Institute Publishing, 1990.

Walther, David S. *Applied Kinesiology*. Pueblo, CO: Systems DC, 1988.

Zukav, Gary. *The Seat of the Soul*. New York, NY: Fireside, 1990.

6

The Transitions of Transition Transitioning

A Dissertation Submitted in Fulfillment of the Requirements
for the Degree of Doctor of Philosophy, Specializing in
Metaphysical Counseling, on Behalf of the Department
of Graduate Studies of the University of Sedona

RAMON LAZARUS
MAY 18, 2020

INTRODUCTION

The Transitions of Transition

Transitioning is the process of change that accompanies the death of a loved one, such as a parent, sibling, or spouse, and includes the changes and challenges involved if the family member fulfilled his or her familial spiritual responsibility to the best of his or her ability while alive in the body before transitioning. This dissertation claims that this is important, as grief is a part of life at some point, and that metaphysical counseling can help one to overcome not only active, acute grief but also anything that is giving the person grief, including whatever issues or feelings he or she is dealing with at the core level, based upon the illusions created. This dissertation will examine the spiritual growth process as it is relevant to health, grief, and grieving and show how it relates to healing and the recovery of beingness in returning to love. Obviously, this can vary from one who is awakened and has made considerable growth to one who is in need of healing on all levels: physically, mentally, emotionally, and, in the case of sin, spiritually.

Generally and specifically, the roles of the individual (survivor), the family of origin, and the individual passing and transitioning will be examined in relation to the heart, soul, and relationship, with the previously mentioned roles regarding this topic. The concept of virtue will be briefly referenced, with an overview of the twelve virtues of the soul. This is important to contrast with and provide for distinction with awareness and discernment. The level at which this paper will elaborate and expand on is from the concept of sin, the illusion of sin, other associated illusions that go along with sin, and the dynamics and static representations within and through the spiritual, causal or etheric, emotional or soul, and astral levels. It will compare what is at one end of the spectrum—transcendence—to its opposite, which is literal and fear-based and the apparent limitation of sin. It will quantify and qualify the journey of the individual, the family of origin, and the individual passing through the death and dying process to transition the soul and the spirit to the eternalness of the Most High God, culminating in a return to love and a coherence and integration with spirit.

The phenomenon of the physiology of a feeling will also be looked at from a higher-consciousness perspective regarding its processing or being interpreted correctly, using the faculties of God and beingness and, beyond beingness, through the heart and head in the context of the mind.

REVIEW OF LITERATURE

Webster's Dictionary defines the word *transition* as follows: "A passing from one state, stage, place or subject to another." This dissertation, "The Transitions of Transition Transitioning," will explore the process described in the introduction through the spiritual relationship of the inner child (true spirit heart) and the soul and how these changes interact not only with the metaphysical aspects of being as experienced through the spiritual, etheric, soul, and astral bodies but also with the physical expression of existence and manifestation in the material world from the spirit.

Important aspects of the spiritual path are the journey and the destination. This paper will guide the reader to such a state of being and consciousness and beyond. It is important first to understand the process and how it works and then to apply it to the subject matter and topic stated in the statement of purpose and introduction.

In the book *Proof of Heaven*, which explores awakening through a near-death experience, Eben Alexander, MD, shares his insight about how important it is to stay on the spiritual path not only for the discovery of one's self but also for other discoveries regarding how to make the world a better place and why and to do the growth work required.

He writes, "Another aspect of the good news is that you don't have to almost die to glimpse behind the veil- but you must do the work. Learning about that realm from books and presentations is a start- but at the end of the day, we each have to go deep into our own consciousness, through prayer or meditation, to access these truths" (157).

Part of the spiritual work required involves working with healing our inner child in relation to our soul. The soul can represent both the inner child and our inner adult. When awakening occurs, the soul becomes enlightened as an extension of the light of the presence of God. The heart also becomes enlightened, awakening the spiritual component of being until both are healed and whole from their brokenness, unconsciousness, and humanness and restored and transcended to a fully realized divinity one with infinity and creation. The time spent in the ego and dysfunction of a lifetime until this point gets worked on and converted to the newly awakened and enlightened consciousness to go beyond it into a state of mystical union with God with a fully integrated heart and mind and a healed and whole soul and spirit. The spiritual dynamics of how this works will be explored now in this section of this paper.

The inner child is more than a concept, intellectually speaking. It is a living, aware consciousness with a state of beingness. Physically and spiritually, anatomically, it resides in our gut, and a spiritual representation of it from head to toe extends from the stomach to the reproductive organs. Once made whole and integrated, it becomes a regular spirit within our beingness and being. Our souls reside throughout our physical bodies once enlightened and integrated. The soul receives wisdom and knowledge directly from the presence of God and other sources, including the inner child. Both work together to bring about and work through issues and feelings important to both, with the common goal of wholeness and expression of that wholeness through mutual cooperation with each other and God's presence through the Holy Spirit.

In the book *The Second Brain*, Michael D. Gershon, MD, shows and proves an intelligence within the physical body that resides in the abdomen, or gut, within the intestines. It has, like the brain, central nervous system, and heart, its own consciousness.

"The enteric nervous system is thus an independent site of neural-integration and processing. This is what makes it the second brain" (17). Gershon also states that if the cranial nerve that helps to service the organs of the gut, mostly the small intestines and large intestine, the enteric nervous system were cut, the ENS would still work and carry out its functions and tasks. Gershon goes on to state the key discovery and link to wholeness and beingness, as evidenced in this passage from his book: "...Confirming that is due to an action of serotonin on nerve cells and not a direct response of the smooth muscle of the stomach. These observations... between nerves and smooth muscle are... in the important crosstalk that goes on between nerve cells" (45). Gershon next discloses his discovery: "The nerve cells that specialize in this type of kibitzing are called 'Interneurons'" (45). The interneurons are intricate and complex and distinguish themselves from the peripheral ganglia outside them. Gershon concludes, "Because of its interneurons, the enteric nervous system can modulate and process information it receives" (45). This not only is significant for the health of the gut itself but also provides a linkage to the mind, and the presence of neurotransmitters in the gut provides evidence that it can not only modulate and process information but also think for itself. This science shows that gut health is responsible for mental and emotional health and well-being. More serotonin is made in the gut than in the brain. This provides a solid platform for the inner child to use and work from in the process of achieving wholeness and well-being while doing the work of spiritual growth.

The inner child helps the soul or adult on a spiritual and mental level, and the soul helps the inner child on a feeling and emotional level, or, simply, heart and soul. The reason for the inner child's need for healing is not only to heal the woundedness of becoming human but also to overcome any excessive negative programming of its upbringing. The brain-wave state for children from birth to six years of age is theta, wherein the child's mind is like a sponge and absorbs everything, positive or negative, from its environment. One reason the world is in the shape, state, and condition it is in today is because dysfunctional children are being raised or have been raised by dysfunctional parents, and the fallout from that has led to gaps in consciousness and understanding in a segment of the population. They don't know they are in this state, but even if they did, they might not know where to get the appropriate help to get out of it.

The mechanism of spiritual growth, in a nutshell, is the mental construct, complete with associated unmet need, illusion, narrative of the illusion, and belief. This is presented by the inner child to the soul (awareness and discernment) to reveal what is false and untrue about the issue and feeling so it can be compared to the truth presented by the spirit and then transformed into wisdom and knowledge for self and others. Whatever is outgrown or no longer needed is archived or released altogether and then downloaded and translated into the physical for vibrant, vital expression of who you really are and were created to be.

In his book *The Resilience of the Heart*, Greg Braden cites the recent discoveries in research based upon the heart and its wisdom and intelligence and how it works with the central nervous system. Feelings arise through the craniosacral system through the cerebrospinal fluid, or CSF, to the heart, to specialized nerves called sensory neurites, which compose a little brain in the heart. "...the heart brain is an intricate network of nerves, neurotransmitters, proteins and support cells similar to those found in the brain proper" (12). It regulates blood chemistry, including hormones, and also converts chemistry into the electrical language of the nervous system so that it agrees with the brain. Other functions of the heart include "wisdom or heart intelligence, deep intentional states of intuition, precognitive abilities, and communication with other organs in the body" (13).

This little brain in and of the heart has been found to function in two distinct yet related ways. "It can act independently of the cranial brain, to think, learn, remember and even sense our inner and outer worlds on its own. Also in harmony with cranial brain to give us the benefit of a single potent neural network shared by two separate organs" (13).

The Physiology of a Feeling

From here, a feeling, after being acknowledged, is sent to the brain, where it begins to be differentiated into an intelligible experience for cognitive abilities for learning and educational purposes. It first goes to the subconscious mind, to the medulla, or brainstem, where such functions as heart rate and respiration have their origin and function. These are involuntary to the conscious mind. Here the light body, or soul, is also part of the awareness, discernment, and emotional intelligence that reside within the brain. Next, after the decoding of the emotion, where it came from, and whom it belongs to, it travels to the right temporal lobe for spiritual discernment as to its etiology and origin. Then it goes to the left temporal lobe, where language discernment puts it into a context that makes sense to the mind and brain. Next, it travels to the right parietal lobe for spiritual recognition as to its significance to itself and others. The relay station for all of this is the thalamus. Then it travels to the left parietal lobe for the concept or idea it is trying to make. Next, it goes to the occipital lobe, where an image or picture is made, and a construct based upon visual sensory data constructs an understanding based upon all levels of being if enlightened. Here it is comprehended, and then it goes to the frontal lobe, where it is understood as to context, meaning, and purpose. After this, it travels to the cerebellum, where healing is initiated, prompting movement to a place of sanctuary to integrate, take shelter, or contemplate the whole experience. It then returns to the medulla, learning wisdom, which is then sent back to the heart to be realized. The wisdom learned is then applied to the situation and circumstances involving the feeling, returning to God's presence in the soul, deep within the heart, mind, and body, resulting in healing and well-being.

Dysfunctional pathology of a negative feeling is bypassed from the cerebellum to the sympathetic branch of the autonomic nervous system, engaging the flight, fight, or freeze emotions. The chakra system integrates the physical, emotions, mental, and spiritual aspects through the soul, heart, mind, and spirit and communicates with the central nervous system, or CNS, and with the venous and arterial circulatory systems to download health or disease. The sympathetic NS needs mitigation and balance from parasympathetic NS to restore or attain health and wholeness.

Doc Childre and Howard Martin go deeper into the heart in their collaborative work with the Heart Math Institute in their book *The Heart Math Solution*. They have solid scientific evidence for how the brain and heart communicate with each other and the rest of the body: "neurologically (through the transmission of nerve impulses), biochemically (through hormones and neurotransmitters), and biophysically (through pressure waves). In addition scientific evidence suggests and points out that the heart communicates with the brain and body energetically (through electromagnetic field interactions)" (28). Also in their book is a comprehensive definition of stress: "Stress is the body and mind's response to any pressure that disrupts their normal balance. It occurs when our perceptions of events don't meet our expectations and we don't manage our reaction to the disappointment. Stress- that unmanaged reaction- expresses itself as resistance, tension, strain, or frustration, throwing off our physiological and psychological equilibrium" (55).

Stress that is not chronic and is well managed is not a threat to well-beingness. However, stress that is chronic and not well managed is a threat to and negatively affects well-being. The two main systems physiologically responsible for downloading stress are the autonomic nervous system (sympathetic branch) and the hormonal system. The two main hormones activated by stress are cortisol and adrenaline. When these hormones are in balance, they play an essential role in functioning to maintain health within our bodies. When they're out of balance, when levels get too high, they can cause "impaired immune function, reduce glucose utilization, increase bone loss, promote osteoporosis, reduce muscle mass, inhibit skin growth and regeneration, increase fat accumulation (around the waist and hips), impair memory and learning and destroy brain cells" (55).

In their second book, *Heart Intelligence*, Doc Childre and Howard Martin also discovered that "...what we feel influences and is influenced by the activity of the physical heart and that our feelings are a key aspect to unlocking 'heart intelligence'" (25). Childre and Martin go on to elaborate and conclude their research up to that point in time, in 2016: "...cultures around the world spoke of the heart as an access point to the wisdom of the soul or a higher source. Although we cannot say that nonlocal intuition research described above proves that we have a soul or that there is a universal source of intelligence, it does indicate that the heart is indeed connected to a source of intelligence not bound by the limits of time and space" (57–58). Childre and Martin are on the cusp of proving not only that the soul exists but also that God exists. Perhaps it is just a matter of the intelligence of the heart making the connection with their souls to provide the insight to do just that. Perhaps this has already happened but not yet been realized. They theorize that there is a connection between the physical heart and the energetic or spiritual heart that has greater expansive and inclusive capabilities than "...implicit processes" (58).

Childre and Martin's work led to what they call *heart rate variability*, or HRV, which is the variability of the heart physiologically speaking in deciding when and how its next heartbeat will occur, which is ultimately linked to and decided upon according to our state of beingness. Spiritual, mental, emotional, astral, and physical components of being all figure into this process of HRV, which is becoming a marker or predictor of health or disease, scientifically speaking.

For metaphysicians, it is comforting to learn that solid science is catching up to what we've known for time eternal. The wisdom, insight, understanding, and knowledge we know and apply with love and truth in the capacity and beingness of Christ consciousness and Jesus Christ Himself will open a door both in heaven and on earth to bring more people to their true essence and beingness, upgrading the world to where it needs to be to support this endeavor.

Why did I include this information and these insights in this paper? Because they prove and validate that the Most High God's creation of a human being comes equipped with all it needs to be whole and complete and that its true, inherent nature is to constantly and continually adapt, adjust, and improvise to change with change as change or change as a constant with the process of living.

Caroline Myss, in her book *Why People Don't Heal and How They Can*, summarizes succinctly why change and one's ability to be flexible are so important: "Yet the truth is that healing and change are one and the same thing. They are composed of the same energy, and we cannot seek to heal an illness without first looking into what behavioral patterns and attitudes need to be altered in our life" (47). Once these aspects are discovered, action in faith must be taken, and that means change.

Healing wounds is the work of change through spiritual, mental, emotional, and physical growth and healing. The purpose of healing is to empower where powerlessness occurred in order for one to go from minimum expectation and irresponsibility to great responsibility to fulfillment and wholeness, transforming the negative perception of the wound and ego. One realizes nothing was ever taken or stolen from oneself and returns to love and trust in God once again. For the wound or wounds to be healed, the light of the soul enters the darkness. The darkness itself is just to give the experience of a contrast of light and dark. Wounds can affect the heart and, if deep enough, the soul and also the mind, which joins the two. The shadows of the ego veil the ego itself. Primarily, the ego is usually secluded in the darkness. If it isn't aware of itself as an expression of the light, it must become aware of itself, differentiate what needs healing from itself, and transform and integrate itself, transcending it as spirit. Once the ego (negative expression of the heart) is transformed, then divinity in the body is experienced, or the Word made flesh.

In his book *The Psychology of Consciousness*, Robert Ornstein includes this contrast, labeling it a duality in his comments on the two sides of the brain: "Yin-Yang symbol neatly encapsulates the duality and complements of these two poles of consciousness" (81). It's important not only to understand the workings of how beingness operates in a healthy capacity but also to understand dysfunction and how it relates to pathology, resulting in diminished capacity.

The feelings of humanness, unconsciousness, and brokenness, if not transformed and healed, can cause dysfunction, disease, and degeneration. These feelings are generated from the primal wound of becoming human, and all other wounds are derivative of this wound. If a life-form doesn't get the opportunity to successfully heal these wounds, then this presentation can manifest behaviorally and be acted out in dysfunction and may become sin.

In the book *The Aquarian Gospel of Jesus the Christ*, Levi comments on sin and its relation to sickness: "The laws of nature are the laws of health, and he who lives according to these laws is never sick. Transgression of these laws is sin, and he who sins is sick" (41).

Charlene Proctor, PhD, in her book *The Oneness Gospel*, addressed the concept of sin: "Sin is pursuing erroneous habits in thinking and the actions stemming from polluted thoughts" (150). It is missing the mark, being in error, or not getting it. All of these are the basis of confusion. God is not the author of confusion, and confusion is not of God.

Feelings create thoughts, which create emotions. Emotions form illusions, which have masked, unmet needs. These form beliefs, leading to layers of beliefs and then patterns of beliefs, which in turn lead to constructs. If the feelings are divine from the presence of God and one's soul and spirit, they translate health, well-being, wholeness, and completeness. If the feelings are from the ego, then dysfunction, disease, and degeneration can occur.

For the purposes of this paper specializing in metaphysical counseling, I will examine and explore the limiting beliefs that lead to potential sin and some of the illusions that lead to those beliefs. This will be contrasted with the virtues of the soul to establish the goal to work toward once the dysfunction has been identified through awareness and discernment from meditation, prayer, and dreamwork interpretation to strengthen the apparent weakness, empowering the individual to succeed from the dysfunction to regain health, vitality, and wholeness, recovering well-being. If people find themselves with dysfunction or potential sin, then it is a clue that a loved one who passed had much spiritual growth work to do while passing or after he or she passed. If there is mild to moderate dysfunction, then that is a clue that the loved one who passed did some, if not all, of his or her spiritual growth work.

Norman Paulsen's book *Christ Consciousness* lists the twelve virtues of the soul, along with the aspects of right living to maintain and carry out one's existence. The virtues are charity, faith, loyalty, patience, honesty, perseverance, temperance, humility, courage, equanimity, continence, and compassion. Charity is love for one's fellow human beings. Faith is belief and trust in and loyalty to God. Loyalty is the quality of being loyal. Patience is the capacity of being patient. Honesty is fairness, as well as straightforwardness of conduct. Perseverance means to keep at something despite difficulties. Temperance is moderation in feeling, thought, or action. Humility is humbleness. Courage is mental or moral strength to withstand danger or difficulty. Equanimity is evenness of emotion or temper. Continence is self-restraint, especially in the face of bodily temptation. Compassion is mercy for others, aroused by the suffering or misfortune of others.

Virtues are needed to establish goals for the life-form struggling with a limiting or false belief to work toward to heal, achieve comprehensive completeness, and be free. This requires time, motivation, and determination by the client or patient—a commitment that must be made and adhered to for success in the desired outcome. Life-forms can have a good soul, heart, and mind and find, with the loss of a loved one, that sin or potential sin is a hindrance for them if they don't know what to do and where to turn.

It is important to note that traditional counseling from a psychologist, psychiatrist, or therapist works from the outside in, working with life-forms' consciousness but limited to the feelings and issues of the ego or literal heart. Metaphysical counseling works from the inside out and is less about the trauma of the negative emotions, as psychotherapy is. However, both can work together in determining what is best for and more comforting to the life-form. Traditional psychotherapy is mainly concerned with managing the ego to regain function to a level to maintain a basic level of life or lifestyle. Metaphysical counseling looks for comprehensive resolution of the issues and feelings of the ego to transition to soul and beingness with true heart consciousness, which is at a level beyond and above ego, leading to a true new beginning. In both traditional counseling and metaphysical counseling, the ego must comprehend, learn, and understand to decide on forgiveness or revenge to either transform and move forward or stay in the past with no relief or resolution.

Dr. John Upledger, DO, in his book *Cell Talk*, summarizes the dynamics between consciousness and energy-to-matter states within and beyond time and space, which has also inspired the title of this paper, "The Transitions of Transition Transitioning," as it is applied to the topic and statement of purpose outlined in the introduction.

> As with the concept of the states of consciousness all being on a continuum, I suggest that energy to matter states are connected on a density continuum, with an infinite number of states between the two extremes (if there are extreme end points). Further, it would seem that the states of energy to solid matter and back again are in a constant state of flux. That is, the particles that make up energy are the same particles that make up matter, and they're constantly flowing back and forth. (16)

This passage beautifully describes that change is the very nature of consciousness and being and that energy and matter, guided by consciousness, are always evolving from matter to energy and consciousness to evolve and from consciousness to energy to matter to establish evolved states of beingness. The preceding passages provide the background and scientific evidence that humans becoming human beings are equipped with the hardware and software to make the transition to being human beings. Part of the growth and transformation process is in transforming and converting the mind and ego from being human to being a human being.

This process involves converting thoughts or thought-form constructs in the mind based upon unbelief, illusion, and limiting or false beliefs into awareness, discernment, beingness, and feeling by the human being. The first commandment given by God to Moses dealt with having no other God other than the Most High God and not worshipping false idols. The ego uses the worship of false idols as a mechanism to avoid feeling, along with thinking. The idol is constantly thought about, creating an entire belief system with its own narrative and perspective regarding its origin and why it was created. Its main purpose is to operate as a distraction from the soul and to compete with it as well. Because of the illusion of it in time and space, the ego, through the five senses, makes it appear real. So an idol, with thinking, provides an illusion as a distraction within an illusion or time and space within an illusion. It is witnessed by the five senses and validated and verified by the ego. So the ego has a significant, reinforcing feedback mechanism and loop that can be added to through repression or suppression through depression or subtracted from. These multiply and, exponentially at times, can progress through growth.

A Course in Miracles, a combined volume published by the Foundation for Inner Peace, comments on the significance of idols: "Idols are limits. They are the belief that there are forms that will bring happiness, and that, by limiting, is all attained... Behind the search for every idol lies the yearning for completion. Wholeness has no form because it is unlimited... It never is the idol you want. But what you think it offers you" (630–31). An idol prevents not only feeling but also whatever else is involved to become truly whole.

Gary Zukav, in his book *The Heart of the Soul:Emotional Awareness*, adds these insights regarding idols: "An Idol worshipper ignores her inner signals and acts as she thinks she should act. Those inner signals are her emotions. ... If an emotion does not fit the role you think you must play- the idol you worship- you attempt to substitute an emotion you think you should feel" (202). Zukav characterizes the average population regarding these statements as follows: "The idol most people worship every day and every night is an image inside themselves of what they think they are, or what think they should be" (200).

Whether persons seek enlightenment, religion, or some other philosophy and whether it is from the inside out or outside in, they will eventually all get to and be complete with wholeness from God as long as they persevere in being who they really are and were created to be. Eckhart Tolle comments on this in his book *The Power of Now*: "...as far as the unconscious majority of humans is concerned, the way of the cross is still the only way. They will only awaken through further suffering, and enlightenment as a collective phenomenon will be predictably preceded by vast upheavals. This process reflects the workings of certain universal laws that govern the growth of consciousness and thus was foreseen by some seers" (187).

In *The Gospel of Philip*, Jean-Yves Leloup describes a more mystical process of growth regarding an idol and transformation: "Truth did not come into the world naked, but veiled with images and archetypes; otherwise it cannot be received; there is a rebirth through the image of rebirth. One must truly be reborn from this image; this is resurrection" (97). This next passage gives insight into what early Christianity was about from a mystical perspective: "The name Christian is welcomed with anointing, in the fullness and energy of the cross, which the Apostles call the union of opposites; then one is not just Christian, one is the Christ" (97).

These passages describe the process currently and of more than two thousand years ago and show how the past and future are important to the present moment.

Past lives relate to whether future lives are necessary as far as what has been learned and can be applied to the current lifetime or present moment. Brian Weiss, MD, comments on this in his book *Same Soul, Many Bodies*: "Our individual immediate futures in this life and those shortly to come depend to a large extent, as we have seen, on our choices and actions in the present" (214). Weiss also adds that long-term future is more of a collective phenomenon: "The closer we get to a particular future, the more accurate we can be in predicting it. ... We will not stop our progress toward the one" (214).

This passage points out the underlying goal of all growth through counseling or personally directed by God: to change the world to be a better place, first by changing ourselves and then by helping others who yearn and desire to do the same.

Eckhart Tolle describes the mindset of the overall goal of all counseling regarding the process in his book *A New Earth*: "Who you are requires no belief. In fact, every belief is an obstacle. It does not even require realization, since you already are who you are. But without realization, who you are does not shine forth into this world" (189).

Deepak Chopra, in his book *The Path to Love*, shares three distinct realizations in achieving liberation from the ego and establishing beingness in the soul: "I Am That, Thou Art That, All This Is That" (274). The realization "I Am That abolishes all separation between The Soul and God. This is the moment when the drop dissolves into the ocean, when a person looks at all good and bad things in his existence, the struggle between light and dark, the contrast of virtue and sin, and sees them all as equal" (275).

The realization "Thou Art That denotes the sacred nature of the beloved, for 'Thou' is both God and Lover... One can gaze like a loving parent on every person" (275). This can involve two souls or just one soul in individual counseling.

The realization "All This Is That is an expansion of the first two realizations to encompass every particle in the universe. ... the Individual ego finds that it is actually cosmic ego. 'I' is no longer an isolated speck, a viewpoint bounded by time and space. ... I sense myself as infinite consciousness expanding with infinite speed through infinite dimensions" (275).

Don Miguel Ruiz, in his book *The Four Agreements*, comments on a life-form that has reached this level of consciousness and beyond: "This way of life is possible and it is in your hands. Moses called it The Promised Land, Buddha called it Nirvana, Jesus called it Heaven and The Toltecs call it the New Dream"(128).

A life-form must be freed at the level of the soul, mind, body, and spirit. Illusions, limiting or false beliefs, and limiting emotions must be and receive light awareness, discernment, comprehension, and understanding so they can be transformed and integrated into wisdom and applied to lives individually as well as take their place in the circle of life collectively.

Charlene Proctor, PhD, in her book *The Oneness Gospel*, addresses maintaining one's self and a potential pitfall once one is liberated and infinite: "The Bible teaches spiritual attainment, not religion. Jesus taught that we should worship nothing outside ourselves, for if we do, it will negate our own ability to experience union of body, mind and spirit" (334).

Dr. Masters, in his book *Mystical Insights*, comments on the process of the universe manifesting and unmanifesting in harmony and oneness, which is the goal of God, soul, and spirit and the purpose of this paper and metaphysical counseling:

> The symbol of yin and yang corresponds to this great mystical truth. ... In an absolute sense the yin and yang symbol is saying, "I Am in God and God is in Me." There is no truth that is any higher in understanding one's relationship between body, mind, soul Universal Consciousness, Spirit or God, for upon this one great mystical truth rests the entirety of physical and human existence. (51)

Dr. Masters also comments on the fluctuations between consciousness energy and matter: "Balance is constantly being gained or lost as the Soul self passes through various stages of Spiritual awakening to its ultimate oneness with God" (34).

Dr. Masters expresses his hope for a better and more well-balanced world from the mental health community:

> Only when the mental health sciences of today have developed to where they are aware of such simultaneous states of conscious activity can clinical evaluations of such occur as psychosis, split personality and a whole host of other dysfunctions or mental ills be approached and treated from wisdom and true knowledge, rather than only from a limiting behavioral science secular scientific perspective. (39)

Norman Paulsen comments on the pure self, the Christ, in regard to the consciousness assuming the throne of beingness and what takes place in his book *Christ Consciousness*: "It now takes place possession of the throne, at the pituitary center, where the Heavenly heart pulsates. ... Here from the throne room, the now awakened soul, The Pure Self with Christ, rules the physical, astral and causal forms of your body. What a miraculous event it is!" (488). It is important to note that in the baptism of fire, a spiritual vortex that descends upon the person obtaining Christ consciousness, the female and male energies travel through the body, with the feminine descending to the base of the spine and the masculine descending into the heart. They meet in the heart before ascending to the head and merging together. Christ child and Christed soul work together for the highest good of the person. They are holy.

From the New King James version of *The Holy Bible* comes this scripture validating and sanctifying the life-form who has gone through this process, quoting the apostle Paul: "Now may the God of peace Himself sanctify you completely; and may your whole spirit, soul and body be kept preserved and blameless at the coming of our Lord Jesus Christ" (1 Thessalonians 5:23).

The Way Bible gives another interpretation of 1 Thessalonians 5:23: "May the God of peace himself make you entirely pure and devoted to God: and may your spirit and soul and body be kept strong and blameless until that day when our Lord Jesus Christ Comes back again."

Metaphysical counseling is essential to help people transform not only their limiting or false beliefs regarding grief but also illusions and emotions or feelings supporting those limiting beliefs or illusions. Wholeness is the goal, complete with total resolution of issues and feelings associated with limiting beliefs. It directs people deeper into themselves to resurface once again as whole and complete on all levels in mind, body, soul, and spirit if it is their desire to become who they really are and were created to be.

DISCUSSION

Having established the psychospiritual, mental, emotional, and physical model for the scientific evidence of growth from the review of literature, we will now look at the roles in which growth takes place: from the child (heart) and soul (adult), in an individual child (survivor), as a child of an adult and parent (individual passing), and the overall dynamics within the family of origin.

We start our journey with the functional workings of the psychospiritual dynamics of a projection. A projection is an unowned part of oneself that is perceived to be negative both in its composition (thought form) and in the feelings and associated constructs and is projected onto another that the life-form thinks is responsible for it. In an individual, there is a projection on each level: psychic or astral level; emotional or soul level; etheric, causal, or mental level; and, in the case of sin, spiritual level. Each level needs healing in regard to the age when the life-form's projections took place. The inner child and the soul adult need to work together to methodically and systematically sort out the feelings, thoughts, and emotions involved in each level and age to put together, transform, heal, realize, and grow.

The first projection is becoming human and takes place at around six months to a year old on the physical or astral level (survival). The next two, the emotional level and the etheric or mental level, take place from one's family of origin, primarily from the parents. The emotional or soul level usually, if the individual is male, will come from his father. The mental or etheric level will come from his mother. Through the mother and father projections on the mental and emotional levels, other projections from siblings or other family members will work. The spiritual level will involve a spousal relationship and come through the spouse, and it can and will use the other levels to project unfinished business back to the individual it concerns to use as an opportunity for growth. However, oftentimes, it is used negatively to control (which is an illusion) and to reject the individual's feelings and project other feelings onto the individual, rendering him or her unable to function, because the projector fears this will be done to him or her.

A projection is in the current lifetime for the life-form. A projector is emotionally spiritual, is from current and past life-forms, and may involve other lifetimes and unfinished business that kept people from becoming who God created them to be in those lifetimes. These are used as lessons for growth in the present lifetime. So a projection can carry multiple levels of projections, going back generations and lifetimes simultaneously.

A projection can be used to dump or project all levels onto another life-form or source or be used for spiritual growth. Each projection will have a spiritual, mental, emotional, and physical component to it. With awareness and discernment, like a detective, one must determine the spirit; where it came from; the thought or circumstance involved; the emotional charge associated with it; and physically where it is felt in the body, soul, and spirit in the form of sensations, feelings, or both. For example, the individual child will have an original wound from becoming human (psychic level, survival) and, on top of that, a wound at the emotional level from the father of rage, which can be from the father himself, from his parents, or, as in this case, his mother. Next, a wound on the mental, etheric, or causal level from the mother who was projected on by her sister growing up. This originated with the mother and mother's sister and father or generational, which involves a mental condition or an affective disorder of mentally having difficulty in disseminating emotions, in this case jealousy, projected to the mother by the mother's sister or the individual's aunt. This is also projected onto a sibling, a sister of the individual, and then projected to the individual. All three—the mother, the mother's sister, and the individual's sister—can be conduits for the spirit, thought form, and feeling to work through. The projections, as conduits, can also be used positively once the individual has done the hard work of spiritual growth to transform and heal from them to eventually become who he or she really is and was created to be.

One must overcome survival emotions to get access to feelings and thought forms associated with the projection. Excessive worry sustained over a period of time leads to paranoia, which is an emotion associated with the thyroid gland and adrenal glands (anger and fear over not being able to figure it out). Worry is associated with the stomach and spleen (apathy or inability to digest the situation and circumstances).

Excessive worry turns into paranoia with continued exposure to a negative stimulus or behavior, emotionally speaking, and is perceived to be a threat of the cessation of life-force energy. The inner child, through its perception, interprets the event as a threat of life ending, which causes panic attacks, which are based upon an illusion. The negative cascade of events through projection on all levels mentioned thus far establishes a belief in fate versus destiny.

One overcomes the belief in fate by challenging the illusion of fate, and both are eliminated successfully from all levels when complete. Jesus Christ arrives at the exact moment when fate appears imminent and almost certain and snatches victory out of the predicament, securing His and God's victory for a redeemed life (reconciled to God).

Destiny refers to a positive outcome with positive results and good fortune. Fate is an illusion made by the ego during wounding. It is negative-karma-based, which leads to cause-and-effect experience and outcome and negative fortune. Verbal drama, negative touch, or projection through touch will give the illusion of one's not being in control of one's being or destiny, which triggers anxiety based in fear, worry, and paranoia that one's life will not be fulfilled and one's destiny will not be obtained. If it's perceived by the inner child as negative, then conscious repression is engaged for survival. If not enlightened, it can be from self, others, or both.

Conscious repression involves pushing emotions and feelings back down into subconscious mind. They will come up again to be acknowledged and processed. They can be from the self or others above the inception point of the origin of the ego in the subconscious mind. Unconscious repression is repression of feelings of humanness, unconsciousness, and brokenness by powers and principalities. These are core feelings of the ego only accessible by the soul, which is anchored in the bright, radiant white light of God's presence. The soul navigates and processes, using free will, love, and forgiveness, below inception point (unbelief) in subconscious mind.

In addition to projection is the unfinished business of the life-form's parents going back many generations. Overcoming this requires working through the survival emotions, or the emotions of the lower three chakras or ego, and the negative expressions of them. This is important because this comes up with grief and grieving. It comes up in an unorganized way logically, but from an enlightened perspective, it will make perfect sense. The time necessary to get through it is determined by how many go through the process. First ones take longer than others that follow. Once the trail is blazed, the work being done shortens, and time is conserved. The first fruits of Jesus Christ's labor (symbolically speaking) of love more than two thousand years ago are starting to gain number, significance, and volume.

Jesus taught two Christianities: an outer one through parables when dealing with the public and crowds, so they would not become frightened by direct teaching, and an inner one, which He taught to His disciples. The outer Christianity is one of preparation, and the inner one is of differentiation; integration; and the art, science, and philosophy of the applied practice of becoming who you really are and were created to be: a Christed being.

Healing of the whole person and being includes soul, body, heart, spirit, and mind if needed, and all levels and components thereof are affected. As stated earlier in this paper, feelings generate thoughts, and thoughts generate emotions. If the feelings are of low vibration, energy, and frequency, then illusions are the result, which alter interpretation and create a false reality. From illusion, there is a need not being filled or perceived as not being filled. This leads to limiting beliefs, which form layers of a belief system, which forms patterns that lead to constructs, which form memories, which then become the basis of thinking.

Material needs have to be met to connect and ascend higher than the basic drives of humanity, which means connecting to all of a life-form's feelings so union with God can be achieved, establishing peace, love, joy, spiritual rapture, and ecstasy. For the preceding to occur, a spiritual practice of purification and connection needs to be established and maintained. For complete wholeness to be attained, reconciliation of one's own heart is a choice on the spiritual path. For those seeking wisdom, this is positively advisable.

Reconciliation with God is established with the realization of wisdom and love. Having learned from the past, present, and future, one is in harmony with God. This process continues until soul, spirit, body, and heart are free of all conflicts. All feelings, thoughts, and emotions are accounted for, and one is aware and has worked through and healed them all. This leads to understanding, prompting forgiveness and resolving conflict where hurt was involved, considering the level of development on all levels and extenuating circumstances. This is an ongoing process and will go on for however long is necessary. Achievements are made and reflected in the blessings people receive in life for having the courage to transform themselves with God's presence and Jesus Christ's help to be the best they can be.

The divine memory, once opened, establishing a connection to God either directly through itself or through the soul, is a place where prayers are answered and where prayers are offered up to God. It is the place where feelings are offered up to God to transform and heal. When the inner child asks, it receives from God, fulfilling scripture from the Holy Bible: "Ask and thou shall receive."

Tools of the Metaphysical Counselor

In addition to prayer, meditation, dreamwork interpretation, and other modalities of interpretation and healing, three thorough and comprehensive tools of therapeutic interpretation with diagnostic, discerning capabilities are holistic iridology, HeartMath HRV components and software, and the counselor's clinical assessment and intuitive faculties. All can help patients to identify (recognize), recover, and understand their reason for the office visit so they may heal and move forward with their lives. Iridology identifies patterns in the eyes, particularly the iris, looking not only for what is positive but also for potential health risks manifesting as dysfunction or disease on any level of being, along any component in the sequence of perceptual reality among which limiting beliefs are found. HeartMath HRV software is an evidence-based tool that measures HRV, or heart rate variability, which is a measurement of how well a patient is managing his or her stress level, which is monitored between the parasympathetic and sympathetic branches of the emotionally regulated autonomic nervous system. Limiting beliefs create emotional blocks and vice versa, depending upon the spiritual orientation of the patient's literal heart-based spirit. The counselor's clinical assessment and intuitive faculties use all the modalities he or she is versed in, and the God mind of the counselor discerns, through all the relevant information gleaned from the patient visit, when, how, and why the limiting belief was created, interacting with the patient, sharing the wisdom and knowledge gained, and presenting it in a compassionate manner that makes sense to the patient as to its validity according to the patient's process of beingness and where he or she is at with it at the time of the presentation to the counselor. Holistic iridology provides a comprehensive epigenetic picture of the issues (emotions) or feelings that are active currently, those that are past, and those that are yet to be. HeartMath HRV software measures, with the emWave Pro monitors, integration of feelings from emotional transformation as well as coherence of positive creativity, which includes soul, mind, body (heart), and spirit for the inner child independently and as part of a whole being, part of the adult (soul) located as a spirit in the abdomen, or gut, with heart and literal and transcendent spirit as well as the head from the bottom or feet up to the head.

Feelings in need of healing may be from any type of negativity, dysfunction, or disease and are likely to be from abuse experienced directly, indirectly, or both. If abuse is sexual in nature, then healing on all levels with all components in the sequence of perceptual reality must be addressed, including limiting beliefs, in a thorough, comprehensive, and complete way so the patient may successfully heal. The sequence is from the inside out: feeling, thought, emotion, illusion, belief, layers of beliefs, patterns of beliefs, constructs, memory, and thinking.

- Literal heart is on the immediate plane of terrestrial existence. Flesh connects literal with spirit but is limited in both its expression and its experience of lower-heart, lower-mind manifestation. It's literal spirit.
- Transcendent heart is Christ consciousness with soul and mind. Its expression and experience have no limitations. It exists at all planes of existence, higher mind, and higher heart. HRV is less than or equal to ten beats per minute when processing a feeling.

When a life-form is stuck, that is low coherence. When limiting beliefs and emotions are cleared, that is high coherence, or greater than or equal to ten beats per minute HRV. HRV is based upon the patient's state of beingness and is not a fixed-rate variable but a variable variable that is constantly adapting and adjusting for its highest and best expression of itself and the life-form it is in.

- Meditation brings awareness to the darkness to discern what of the literal heart needs to learn, grow, heal, comprehend, and understand to gain wisdom from the trauma and experience, therefore increasing coherence between the transcendental heart—consisting of the head and heart as well as the gut (where the inner child, anatomically and spiritually speaking, resides within the life-form)—and the literal spirit. Coherence of abdomen, heart, and head is the pathway for the holy breath as well as feelings brought up to feel if necessary to experience and process.

Mysticism Is the Realization of Knowingness

In meditation, once one reaches the threshold where the conscious mind meets the autonomic nervous system, below it, mental or verbal commands can be given to influence physiological responses to stimuli real, imagined, mental, emotional, or spiritual or feelings thereof. Returning reaction or response back to balance, equilibrium, and homeostasis; conserving HRV, or heart rate variability; reducing stress; and raising the threshold for an overwhelming stimulus response, wherein the sympathetic nervous system is agitated or hyper to neutral or zero, allows parasympathetic tone to activate, repair, regenerate, and manifest healing measures to the organism. Lower heart, head, or literal spirit needs to become aware, discern, recognize, comprehend, and understand, which leads to healing, recovery, wisdom, reconciliation with God, and true wholeness. With this arrives restoration of gifts, talents, and dreams meant to be used to bring ultimate fulfillment, joy, and happiness if God's attributes are used with love, compassion, and forgiveness not only given but also chosen, until one becomes love again.

This is important to determine not only for the client but also for the counselor. Ideally, it would be wise and spiritually astute for the counselor to have journeyed and experienced the complete life cycle of birth transition and resurrection at least on a spiritual level to be able to help anyone from any walk of life, no matter his or her race, gender, orientation (spiritual and emotional), or circumstances. This is important because the metaphysical counselor needs to be able to ascertain where the client is spiritually, mentally, emotionally, and physically, as well as where he or she has been on all levels and would like to go. And how would he or she like to get there? To help discern this, I will discuss the light, the dark, and the shades of gray, which are used to get a feel for the client's spiritual orientation.

The Light (White), the Dark (Black), and the Shades of Gray

People who are incomplete often seek refuge in the gray of an issue or matter, which will temporarily allow them to be right and wrong at the same time. It's an in-between place where they don't have to use their free will, and they think they have the best of both worlds, which is an illusion and not true. Jesus Christ addressed this dilemma when he said, "You are either hot or cold but if you are lukewarm I will spit you out of my mouth." This means the gray in between black and white is the ego's attempt to seek salvation by not dealing with itself in between right and wrong. The "hot or cold" refers to actually using free will to choose right or wrong. The ego is afraid of choice, because deep down, it knows it really doesn't have one, and it is afraid of the soul, which actually has the faculties of God and choice. Therefore, the ego doesn't want to choose, because it is afraid of beginning the process of its own demise, so it remains stuck indecisively in the gray area. The good news is that God will forgive and allow another choice if an unwise choice is made or continues to be made. He understands this predicament that people find themselves in at some point in their lives.

By doing this, God is trying to nudge the person to make a choice, right or wrong, to begin the process of growth and evolution. He will support one in doing so, even if a wrong or unwise choice is made, as judged by the ego. To continue to hide in the illusory comfort of the gray is not acceptable to God and will not be supported, because it is a position of fear, not faith, and to remain in it without trying is not trusting God and believing that God can overcome any seemingly insurmountable obstacle and restore wholeness and well-being to any situation or circumstance.

People who find themselves in this dilemma or predicament will not take sides in an issue or feeling—not because they are wise but because they don't want to deal with it to begin with or be singled out for taking a stand, because of what has happened to those in the past who have. Understanding right and wrong, or good and evil (soul and ego), is important for every soul and life-form. It is equally important to understand the many varieties of gray in between the two areas that appear up close as black and white. With a more complete perspective of the big picture, the black and the white appear gray from a distance. It is important to understand how the black and white become black and white and how, from another perspective further away, they appear gray. It is equally important to realize the gray not to make an excuse or justification for it (ego) but to learn from it and take appropriate measures to bring awareness to it to determine the choice to be made, understanding the gray as both temporal and transitory. It is a phase of perspective to allow one's consciousness and that of others to experience illusion, realize, and understand it for what it is so free will can be used to discern the components of the gray. People must learn how they got there to determine where they are and where they wish to go. Once that's done, the gray disappears, leaving only light, or white, illuminating the mind. The light appears the same from both close up and far away.

An idol is an ego-created idea or concept of worship first in the mind and then in the heart. People see it as an ideal concept or idea to worship, thinking that worshipping it will bring all they desire into life. However, it produces the opposite effect, creating a dysfunctional cycle of avoidance and abuse, avoiding the discovery of the truth of one's beingness through consciousness, and preventing one from feeling and becoming whole and complete.

The first commandment says not to have idols, worship false gods, or have any other God than the Most High God, Source of utmost truth. Idols compete with God and lead away from God. Idols are extensions of the ego and are based on it in both etiology and morphology, in its configuration individually and collectively. Making and having an idol can lead to control and manipulation without feeling and can become a problem for the person making the idol or the person projected upon. All ego-based conflicts can be reduced to idols.

Idols are eliminated through release of feelings, emotions, illusions, and beliefs at their core or the basis of their dysfunctional creation. Also released are disappointment, the reaction to that disappointment, and what it represents to one's working concept of oneself. The idol, without a feeling connection, can compete with one's putting God first, to potentially avoid growth or difficult feelings. Idols block the stressful feelings of the literal heart and spirit. Processing of feelings leads to healing. Idols are sinful because they deny the life-form's beingness an opportunity to heal, grow, learn, and evolve to reach a higher state of being and God. Confusion results, if not discerned with awareness, from survival emotions. Feelings of joy, transcendent heart accepts existence. Feelings are neither right nor wrong, but one needs to discern them with awareness to know what the soul is feeling, as experienced through the heart. Feelings in relationships can be judged in error, rejected, and projected back, creating an illusion in the projectees of fear. They therefore have an experience of being rejected. The ego creates idols to overcompensate for its imperfections and to excuse and justify them at the same time, so it doesn't have to live up to them.

The love of idols doesn't make them inappropriate in the eyes of God, but the worship of them is being in error, missing the mark, not getting it, and eventually, if sustained long enough, sinning. Through the literal heart and spirit, the scripture "All have sinned and fall short of the glory of God" was declared. This spirit and part of the heart need healing because they're where the limiting beliefs and emotions are found, along with incongruent thinking and painful memories. The false personality ego needs to be healed so the true personality of the heart can be integrated in the Word made flesh.

The false-spirit literal heart is what psychotherapy is based upon. It is temporary and a projection, entity, or both.

The true-spirit transcendental heart is spirit, eternal, and mystical union with God.

Not being in touch with true spirit or soul will leave individuals with two deficits. They're (1) unaware of the awareness or the soul and (2) unaware of the awareness of the true spirit. That's why Jesus Christ said, "Let the dead bury the dead." So there are two spiritual bypasses that can happen in spiritual growth. Limiting or false belief works on the integration of the personality with the soul, mind, and spirit and uses the representative illusion presented to the inner child through the use of the intellect to provide a narrative, creating with it the limiting or false belief, which follows the format and programming of the ego to resolve any discrepancies between the ego and the limiting belief so that it makes sense according to the ego and how it was originally formed.

> Illusion > voice of illusion > unmet need > intellect > limiting belief > belief system > layers > patterns > constructs > memories > thinking > individual consensus reality

Holistically, fully, and functionally healed, whole, and complete, the limiting belief is identified as incongruent with beingness of the soul, mind, body (heart), and spirit. At this stage of the spiritual journey, the soul, astral body, etheric body, and spirit or spiritual body are all awakened (enlightened) and integrated (mystical union with God), merging the true personality of the true heart (transcendental) with the rest of the formerly mentioned bodies and components of being and beingness to achieve total and true wholeness and also working with the astral body to complete the incarnation process of the Word becoming flesh, or a realized divinity, or a human being.

The mindset of the process working to move forward must revisit and integrate the past. Reexperiencing ego—going back to move forward—gives an experience of illusion. One seemingly is reentering illusion but, in reality, is reexperiencing part of one's self to integrate into wholeness and the true transcendental heart of one's essence, complete with personality. During this process, if there is any residual negative karma from the present lifetime, it will be up to the life-form to address it in the current lifetime, or not, in the hope of reaching peace and a return to love in forgiveness and reconciliation if the offended is other than one's self.

Also, a working knowledge of one's astrological natal chart; numerology; and a familiar understanding of the chakras and their levels of development, meaning, and symbolism, both positive and negative, are helpful but not necessary. As Dr. Masters points out in his weekly broadcast titled *Astrology, Karma, and You,* focusing on the positive and the negative will take care of itself. This is true most of the time, and the other part of the time, the issues and feelings will need to be addressed, differentiated, transformed, integrated, realized, and released.

Remember, astrology, numerology, and the chakra system are tools to guide you in being who you really are and were created to be. They are not to be made into idols or illusions, because the infinite and creation are limitless, and our true state of being is exactly that: limitless and expanded.

Childhood projections are received from birth to seven years of age for the child. Then the inner child develops as a result of a negative projection at the age of parental projection. Unconsciously conscious projection results in repression and then, as a result, becomes a component in the grief process to be accessed and worked through at a later date.

Grief is a generic term to attempt to describe when life-forms enter their shadow side of their hearts and personalities as related to their beingness and self. Grief is the price one pays for becoming human.

The affirmative prayer for taking back these strongholds or ground given is the following:

> In the name of Jesus Christ from creation and the infinite Most High God mind, I ask the merits of Jesus Christ's holy, precious blood to cover, neutralize, and dissolve sin and its constituent feelings. I ask the bright, radiant white light of Jesus Christ's resurrection and God's presence to transform and metamorphose everything into purity of radiant spirit. Amen.

Realization—recognition of sin specifically—will be named and revealed (e.g., greed and lust) in the relationship with a sibling, parent, spouse, or other. Once you realize it, confess it to God in the heart, and God Most High will give immediate feedback regarding if it is yours to repent or is from another life-form or source. If it is from familial origin immediate or generational, God will inform you of where it resides, with which family member (parent, sibling, or spouse), and its link to the person. This will stop neurotic and psychotic behavior of the spirit and allow recognition and realization that the compelling compulsion behind it is not worth striving for if it is hurting loved ones. Then a realization will take place that reveals others within the family unit of origin don't know many of the things that a person discovers on the way to attempt to become whole. An accompanying realization will occur: that others can't take anything away from another, which is an illusion and a component of sin. Ask for forgiveness, choose love and forgiveness, let go and let God, go with the flow of the Most High God, and be grateful for the goodness in life.

When the ego is formed, it is comprised of others' literal feelings at the first-chakra level. When processed, the feelings are transformed, and when they are transformed, they are sent to God. God sends them back to their source in others, and when they arrive, they will signal the life-forms in current possession of them. They'll signal life-forms through their spirit, soul, mind, and, finally, body, through the nervous system, circulatory system, and lymphatic system. The literal feelings are shared to create bonds of love and mitigate negative feelings of jealousy or envy to deter sibling rivalry among life-forms.

The nervous system receives input from sensory afferents of the heart and central nervous system from feelings and discerns and disseminates the expression of the feelings, leading to experiences, positive or negative, for the organism.

The circulatory system provides nourishment and biofeedback and recycles what can be used and downloaded to the body.

The lymphatic system provides an exit for waste products that can't be recycled as far as metabolites of metabolism.

Feeling of the feeling will start in the mind of the inner child, in the spirit located in the stomach portion of the gut. Then the feeling returns to the inner child's body releasing it or letting go with the bowel or soul. Things speed up, going from ego to heart and soul and from time and space to eternalness and feelings.

This will manifest symptoms signaling the life-form that it is time to release the feelings he or she acquired long ago and that it is time for growth and discovery for both life-forms involved in the acquisition of each other's feelings for educational, learning, and growth purposes. This is involved in the grieving process and is why there is familial drama at the death or loss and transition of a parent, sibling, or spouse—because it is a wake-up call to all life-forms involved in the exchange to decide what they need and want out of life so they are fulfilled with wholeness, peace, love, and joy in all aspects of their lives and can share what God and they have accomplished so others can be helped to do the same.

All in the family lose and gain. In losing a loved one, they regain themselves, but they do not realize that until afterward. When it is happening, family members think the person is theirs, so they try to hang on through drama and projection, not yet realizing the truth. They do not yet realize it was in illusion, which is integrated after their realizing it. They didn't know what happened or what it was because it was sin.

Sin has to be broken down into its constituent parts after it is confessed to God and forgiven. Then God informs you about it: if it is yours or not, where it came from, and what to do about it to heal and return to peace. A piece of one's heart and soul returns to him or her from a time when the child needed physical, emotional, mental, and spiritual support, shelter, and refuge. If there was a need for emotional healing, then during the grieving process for the loved one who is transitioning, this is passed on to the survivors to be worked on in the process of their grieving to be returned to wholeness. When something is in sin, it is like a game of keep-away tag in which a participant thinks that something that belongs to it is separate from itself and that others have it, which is an illusion.

In addition, one may enter into the grief of one's being to become human, which is why it is a difficult time for those who are in it and go through it. If one is enlightened, he or she has a distinct advantage over one who isn't enlightened. As Jesus Christ said, for man, it is impossible, but for God, all things are possible. Confusion arises if sin is present and when family members try to hang on to what isn't theirs anymore, which the part in question is returning to its source.

Sin	Belief	Positive Affirmation
Sloth	Powerlessness: Why bother?	I Am Powerful
Pride	Invincibility	I Am strong but also vulnerable to grow and understand others.

Gluttony	It's OK to abuse myself and others.	I Am disciplined.
Wrath:	My anger is justified to hurt. whoever hurt me.	I Am is a perceptual state of Equanimity and temperance.
Envy	Taking from others is OK.	I Am content with what I have and count my blessings and know Godwill fill my needs.
Lust	It is OK to gratify my desires no Matter who it hurts.	I AM secure in my sexuality and Value it as an extension of who I really am created to be.
Greed	Wanting more than I need is justified. Because I have to survive and survival Is hard. The world is against me.	I Am prospered sufficiently to fulfill God's will, learning my Soul's and heart's life purpose.

Ego Dysfunction	Illusion	Positive Affirmation
Unconsciousness	Illusion of imperfection	I Am conscious and aware with discernment.

(Covers chakras one through four upon awakening and embodiment and chakra two upon integration.)

Brokenness	Illusion of perfection	I Am whole and recognize and recover my wholeness.

(Covers chakras four through seven upon awakening and embodiment and chakra one upon integration.)

Humanness	Illusion of separation from God.	I Am protected by God.

(Emotions that protect brokenness overcompensate for powerlessness. Covers chakra one through seven upon awakening and embodiment and chakra three upon integration.)

Aspects of Sin

Sin	Chakra	Spiritual	Mental (Thought)	Emotional	Physical Behavior
Sloth	7	Idle,	can't do anything right,	depleted	busy, doing nothing menial tasks

Pride	6	ego, self, Importance	I know I can do it, and don't have to prove it	egotistic	looking for validation
Gluttony	5	Excessive Activity	indulging to not feel	overly sympathetic.	Always hungry.
Wrath	4	Rage at injustice,	justified anger; wrong to hurt others.	Anger and Fear	depression; sub-merged anger.
Envy	3	Coveting others, Desires or possessions	it is OK to take from, Others if it makes You happy.	Lives through others.	always wanting Unfulfilled.
Lust	2	Desire for sex; lack of: Love or material things:	fills desires for the satisfaction of the Physical	Unconsciousness vs. feelings/ emotions	sexual addiction or frustration
Greed	1	obsession with power Overcompensating for Survival.	lack; too busy too survive.	survival Brokenness	lack; being poor.

Unmet needs lack of:

Love: material needs of the body.

Joy: lack of connection to feelings.

Peace of the mind that proceeding needs are met.

Ecstasy: Connection with God.

Chakra: Needs: Ego Traits: (worlds projections) Emotional Release 7 connection to God laziness Enlightenment 6 wisdom hubris; arrogance insight 5 expressing understanding overindulgence understanding (letting go) 4 love war comprehension 3 shelter conceited discernment 2 clothing/ protection Vanity awareness 1 food power/negative use of money grief (released) Joy returns. Limiting beliefs > Layers > Patterns > Constructs > Memories > Thinking can be, to an extent, self-sabotaging and can lead to negative predominant thinking and unhealed emotions, which will lead to toxicity of the mind, body, and soul if not addressed and healed and can contaminate one's beingness. People may act upon it in the physical in an attempt to seek relief from it internally, and when this happens, it becomes sin if it produces harm to another, oneself, or both.

It's OK to be sexy and express sexuality positively as long as it is an expression of who you really are and were created to be in the image and likeness of the Most High God as spoken into being by the living Word of God. Free will means having a choice at all times in all circumstances and situations, regardless of how it appears to be through perception in time and space.

Stress is a dysfunctional response or reaction to a negative stimulus that is perceived to be real and is not recognized or understood as dysfunction or an illusion.

Sin is not a lifelong process in which one has to keep being dependent upon a savior. The reliance on such is designed to be on an as-needed basis as it applies to one's life, situation, or circumstances. God gives free will, and if one is in the vicious cycle of sin and death or, at a deeper level, karma, then free will is not being used as God intended. If this is the case, then one's ego is in control of the person, not Christ or the soul. The ego is the culprit who devises elaborate illusions to justify its continued existence in the face of truth. Accepting Jesus Christ as one's Lord and Savior without becoming conscious and aware is disempowering to oneself, playing into the ego's hands and keeping one separate from God and out of the kingdom of heaven. To intellectually utter allegiance and loyalty to the ego's illusions is to create a false god or idol. Worship of that idol is called *religion* or *theology of ego*. Masquerading as spirituality, it has no depth or connection to God. Proclaiming that one is saved without going through any in-depth process is hubris of the ego at its extreme and doesn't amount to anything, unless it's accepted by the collective ego, whose consensus nonreality is shared by others in that mindset, in which spiritual bypass and nonaccomplishment of spiritual growth are valued.

Most create the illusion that Jesus has already done everything for them, because the alternative is perceived to be unbearable. The flogging and subsequent crucifixion of Jesus Christ were as bad as it gets as far as suffering is concerned. What many imagine and perceive can be far worse than what Christ went through. They wish to share in divinity but not take responsibility for their egos' pain and, therefore, end up sharing grief and misery with one another, rather than true joy. It is an unconscious process. The joy they do share usually involves the changing of life circumstances and the ego's self-contrived salvation. They do not know God or have a connection to God. Many make Jesus Christ into an illusion by their egos because they really don't know Him or what He taught or was about, only what they have been told by others or in church, both of which teach about love and truth not from the soul's or Christ' perspective but from that of the ego, complete with laws, rules and regulations, cause-and-effect thinking, and theological doctrine and dogma.

This serves to manipulate and control people and maintain order for a given society to be ruled over or governed as subjects or citizens by egos who are pompous, obnoxious, bombastic, and neurotic to serve as examples of what is acceptable behavior for subjects or citizens of such a society. Therefore, so-called free societies are not free; they are only as free as they are freed from their egos. This is, sadly, a by-product of the human condition.

The ego thinks in terms of right and wrong and cause and effect, which it learned from its own convoluted thinking and the world. The soul is concerned with being and expressing love and compassion. The ego seeks refuge from its offenses in its own contrived theology. The soul (Christ) does not know sin and unconsciousness but is aware of it if growth is required. The ego is separate from God because of unconsciousness and if its behavior manifests in the physical there is sin. The only way to correct sin and unconsciousness is to become conscious by being aware in the awareness of the soul, or Christ. As Saint Paul said, when in Christ, it is impossible to sin. Attempting to address sin at the level where it is created, which is unconsciousness, only leads to more unconsciousness upon unconsciousness or illusion upon illusion. It doesn't solve the problem and only adds to it by contriving more elaborate illusions to cover gaps of unconsciousness and thinking to fool and outmaneuver reason. Convoluted thinking uses the intellect as a template to contrive new illusions based upon the original illusion contrived to manufacture the ego based upon a systemic error of being. The ego does not deviate from its internal dictum of avoiding love and truth at all costs to maintain its illusions, which bring it comfort because of the pain of its contents. The ego is perfect in its own mind but imperfect because it is based in error and illusion.

The ego searches outwardly to seek comfort in whatever seems to agree with its perception, particularly when it comes to defending itself and justifying the perceived existence. It seeks to commiserate with others, seeking their comfort and hoping others will join its ranks, using scripture, such as "All have sinned and have fallen short of the Grace of God." The ego distorts scripture with its illusions of itself to seek strength in numbers against a perceived threat or enemy (stress). It exerts control and rejection of others' feelings when confronted with love and truth. Jesus Christ said, "Be perfect as your heavenly Father is perfect," which means to become aware and conscious and carry one's own cross, doing the necessary spiritual growth work required to go through the process of becoming perfected in God's image and likeness as spoken by the living Word of God from infinity to creation or from darkness into light.

Unconsciousness is what separates people from God and keeps them imperfect. Becoming conscious and aware in Christ (the soul) is the remedy designed for sin and unconsciousness by God through Christ. It is not an intellectual exercise but something much deeper and thoroughly more complete, which eventually leads to integration and incarnation of the soul and God and to becoming one in heart, mind, soul, and spirit. The ego's contrived answer to this is, of course, illusion, and its convoluted thinking is based in error, resulting in cause-and-effect circumstances. Because of its illusory nature, the ego thinks that if it contrives an illusion, it will produce an outcome or effect that is desirable to itself, regardless of whether it is true or not. Its primary objective is to alleviate pain at all costs and try to make itself feel better. An example of this is "If I create this, I will get that. If I accept Jesus Christ as Lord and Savior, I will have eternal life," however that is defined by the ego and its illusions.

The ego has limiting beliefs that are in the way of the true heart's and soul's surfacing, which prevents the true reality of the scripture often quoted during the beginning step in faith and results in cause-and-effect, lower-consciousness theological doctrine that follows the law of Moses, which leads to the law of the ego and an attempt to be perfect. Jesus Christ said you cannot enter the kingdom of heaven by following the law. In other words, eternal life cannot be entered into by cause and effect or the law of being good and avoiding evil. The ego is quick and convenient in its attempts to have life and, especially, God on its terms in dealing with a future based upon the past and the psychological instability it overcompensates for.

Jesus Christ's mission, which is still being carried out in time and space and eternity in spirit, is to help others to obtain eternal life in the presence of God, regardless of which phase of life they find themselves in. Jesus Christ assists all to help them first successfully obtain this for themselves and then reach out to help others. Jesus Christ does not do everything necessary for this, except when His assistance is needed, nor can He, because that would violate one's free will given by God. The ego assumes that God is at its level and that it can interact with God at its level, and therefore, it creates contrived illusions about God and its future, based upon its separateness from God. As long as one is separate from God, there is no connection to God, and all the illusions the ego makes cannot establish connection to God. Only through the soul's integrating and incarnating until there is oneness or union with God is connection possible and established. One does this by becoming conscious and aware; taking responsibility for one's soul, heart, and mind; carrying one's cross to be perfected by God; and enduring the process from beginning to end, letting go of everything that is not true, which is primarily the ego, with all its contrived illusions, which no longer serve the highest good of the life-form once all that has been stated here is understood. When feelings of acute, deep grief come up and out of a person, they are projected outwardly if there is an element of control involved regarding the person who is passing to transition. It can be perceived as sin because of the control and associated illusion. However, once the control is realized, the illusion begins to break down, with joy, love, and peace taking its place. In addressing the layers of feelings that created the pattern upon which it was built, one will need the attributes of God—perseverance, love, compassion, and forgiveness—to work it down to the limiting belief and behavior that caused the feelings to be projected in the first place. Once this is done, the feelings are transformed and integrated with the realization that one has completed the cycle of successfully processing one's acute, deep grief, and he or she can now confidently move forward with dignity and grace. A realization takes place that there is no death or sin. As soon as these realizations occur, a coronal discharge of resurrection transforms the literal heart's spirit, establishing deep transcendence and liberating the soul to be free. The stone is rolled away from the tomb. The resurrection of Christ levitates to prove to itself it is so, and so it is.

The three days to resurrect represent the three lower chakras.

The twelve tribes of Israel represent the twelve signs of the Zodiac.

There are twelve main acupuncture meridians and fourteen overall.

The two-hour interval in each sign or meridian accounts for two extra meridians (heart and soul).

There are four levels: spiritual, mental, emotional, and physical.

$3 \times 4 = 12$ (hours in half a day)

$2 \times 12 = 24$ (hours in a full day)

This creates the time-space continuum, sanctifies it to God (Most High), and covers eternity so life-forms can do what this paper reports on their journey to wholeness through the life cycle. The mesenchymal matrix is the extracellular fluid medium of exchange in the body and mind between cells to interpret the environment outside and inside cells. It acts as a sensory afferent apparatus for the organism, as well as an efferent milieu to differentiate and download internal signals, light, and information as well as external signals from its environment, constantly monitoring what is useful or advantageous for improving or maintaining the organism and what may or may not cause potential harm to it.

> Energy, frequency, vibration > mesenchymal matrix > cell membrane > DNA > nucleus > cytoplasm > blood > CNS > autonomic NS > tissues, organs, glands > stimulus to move or adapt in or from environment

A realization, after manifestation of the presence of the Christ child, determines if Christ's coming will be vengeful or peaceful. The Christ child, soul, spirit, heart, and body, freeing the mind, are in control. Those who oppose it will have an opportunity to face themselves and grow authentically or face the consequences of their actions. So it's their choice if they want a vengeful Christ or a peaceful one.

The I Am has taken the blame for millennia, but God's plan for redemption includes healing and eliminating blame, so there is no one to blame wrongfully, as the ego does. One takes responsibility for one's actions, thoughts, feelings, and emotions, which is the reality of the Most High God.

In eliminating blame, you choose love and forgiveness when in grief and, particularly, in sin. Working to become free of it will mitigate God's wrath from being carried out before it hurts another. One does this as soon as possible after realizing it has taken place. The last illusion is one that is created by illusion itself: the illusion that pain and suffering will never end. Suffering does end with God's presence and Jesus Christ's love and light, which equal inexhaustible mercy, compassion, and forgiveness and lead to reconciliation with God once established in a life-form.

An illusion of illusion within an illusion, once transformed, reveals the truths that wholeness is and was always present and that the inner child was always in God's presence and Christ's love the whole time in the experience. It also reveals that apparently limiting beliefs are not limitations but lessons to learn and expand from to experience the love of the Most High God.

The apparent limiting and false belief in illusion itself by the inner child ends the family-of-origin drama and nightmare, freeing one's self from the tyranny and oppression of all members of the family as well as the life-form's transitioning. This heals the startle reflex, the inception point of the ego, all projections that are negative in origin, and any remaining unbelief.

If life-forms going through this process are aware of how they can impact others negatively and cause suffering, this leaves them feeling as if God is against them for something, which is false. This is an illusion because God is for everyone ever created and deeply yearns for His creations to thrive and flourish under His care and love, therefore reminding them that they have a choice. The belief that they don't is another illusion and a reminder of a remnant of the ego that may or may not be in sin.

Limiting Beliefs

Ego Formation (Chakra)   Ego Elimination (Chakra)

1 others are after me 7
2 not meant to grow or have a 6
Family if wanted one.
3 Not sure one could make it on 5
One's or my own
4 afraid to love or be me
5 Chaos/confusion 3
6 Control: afraid to use my mind because 2
It could hurt someone.
7 Ego 1

Working toward Reconciliation

When in sin, the heart, soul, and mind, through Jesus Christ, have a choice guaranteed by the crucifixion, resurrection, and ascension of Christ to work through the issues and associated feelings to discern with awareness; learn how to free the inner child (the heart) and the adult (the soul); and rejoin God, reconciled, whole, and complete with the mind and spirit, or true heart (transcendence) of being.

Layers build up in the collective unconscious, obscuring inner light at times. When this happens, it creates an illusion of literal interpretations that can become sin if acted upon in physical reality in and through the body. Releasing this grants freedom to ascend and achieve enlightenment. The realizations will follow after mystical experiences of proof of having worked the conflict all the way through to the conscious mind from the subconscious mind, with both connecting to the superconscious mind, or onement with God.

Working through apparent sin teaches life-forms which virtue they need to practice and behold to heal their heart. So sin it is, until it isn't, and once it is not, it isn't anymore. This doesn't mean to go out and deliberately sin. But if life-forms, through circumstances beyond their control, find themselves in sin, there is a responsible and appropriate way to handle it and save the self from destruction or destructive behavior. One example of this is found in the psalms of King David in the Bible. His sin was in arranging for Bathsheba's husband, Uriah, to be killed after coveting her and committing adultery with her. David's sin was premeditated and happened in time and space before Jesus Christ's incarnation, so the remedy for such a situation was deeply expressed through his writing and music. This is different from what has been described here in this paper, but the remedy is the same. David needed a confrontational event from the prophet Nathan to get him to confess his sin to God and then go on to write, inspired by his love for God through his grief, many of the psalms and inspiring books in the Bible. God forgave David, and He will forgive all if they seek Him with a contrite soul and spirit.

Outside In and Inside Out

The mystic experiences the veracity of reconciling feelings to God through Christ and the presence of God. Mystics know from experience and, from this knowing, use belief to deepen their faith and go further on their path and journey. Those who try to believe to develop faith suffer pitfalls associated with unbelief, false or limiting beliefs, and the associated illusions that go with them. This is problematic to growth but not impossible. It is a slower, more inefficient way compared to the mystic but serves a purpose as a prerequisite to becoming a mystic. Dogma is not truthful, and doctrine becomes outdated and legalistic and only serves an independent intellect that doesn't know itself, based upon the assumptions and guess of the ego.

Configuration of Spirit	Aspect of Being	In Sin	In Health
Spirit	"	Figuratively	Transcendent
Mental	"	Metaphorically	Figuratively
Emotional	"	Symbolically	Metaphorically
Astral	"	Literally	Symbolically
Physical	"	Real	Real

In sin, the astral is an illusion thought to be literal because of inception or the startle reflex that is part of the inception point and origin of the ego. Patterns overlap, and then come diffusion and reabsorption back to the source.

What determines if a sin is a sin? The motivation or attitude with which the decision is made. In other words, why was it committed? Was it selfish, and if so, for what reason? Was it something that could have been helped or avoided? Was it conscious or unconscious or both? Sin stems from not knowing one's true nature, source, or identity in Christ through the Most High God. God deeply desires for His beloved to know God as God knows God.

Acts people commit while not knowing God are forgivable by God because they are under the illusion that they are separate from God, which is not entirely their fault, because of how the process of becoming human is carried out. However, it is the person's responsibility to decide what to do about it once it's done, seeking forgiveness and reconciliation with God. Is sin a sin? Yes and no. Yes if it is an act that violates boundaries and harms another or self in a negative way or offends love. No because it is not entirely a person's fault, because of how a human, being human, is made.

The motivation for sin is dysfunctional. The penalty is God's love to correct it, not to punish but instead to instruct and teach life-forms and educate them on what is responsible and appropriate behavior concerning such an offense and the circumstances involved. So it is sin, until it isn't, and the interval of eternity and the time are determined by how quickly a life-form can use its free will with God's help to work through it. The penalty of it is that the life-form will become aware of the separation from God, which is a blessing, in addition to the other illusions that contributed to the alleged sin or offense.

Darkness is condensed, contracted light that folds or bends in on itself, forming a limit congealed or shadowed. Shadow after shadow, superimposing itself on itself, gives the illusion of darkness but is really light. Light, expanded when confronted or presented with darkness, shines even brighter in the case of Christ consciousness and resurrection, until it forms and reaches eternalness, which creates life-forms of the light, such as angels or beings of the light. Darkness forms life-forms of the darkness.

Within light and darkness, there are darkness and light both internally and externally, as symbolized in yin and yang.

As in the case of Jesus Christ's resurrection, suppression, oppression, and repression of yang, or light, create a tremendous magnitude of pure, radiant white-light energy that consumes all darkness and its initial limits imposed on it. It shines eternally and infinitely, without beginning or end, and remains constant with beingness and beyond and within it.

If yin energy is contained by the light, then there is condensing of light. It is contracted and congealed with limitation, and organic life or life-forms will be without feeling or comprehension of themselves because the component and fuel for growth will be without conscious comprehension of self and be isolated from the condensed light of yin by the light of yang, with only the yang and what the yang knows about itself without yin, which will be limited because of its suppression of yin.

The light, or yang, is transcendent spirit; the darkness, or yin, is literal spirit. The contractions or limitations are limiting beliefs created by the illusions of the ego until they are transformed in a purified heart consisting of soul, spirit, body, and mind. Then darkness and light are the same, but instead of illusion, there is a feeling of awareness, discernment, love, and truth.

In the grieving process, if family are fortunate to witness the loved one's transition, then both the loved one's spirit and the soul can be observed and witnessed by the survivors in the loved one's family. The spirit of the loved one passing will appear to the growth or awareness level of the surviving family members, usually intradimensionally at the level and age it was stuck at due to some limitation, whether sin, illusion, limiting belief, or energetic or emotional block. It will appear vibrant, radiant, and whole. The soul is more of a presence similar to God's presence, only individualized into human form. Communication can and does take place at this time and beyond it, bringing comfort to the ones left behind, who often learn more about the intimate details of the loved one's life through the transition than in life. Were they abused in any way, and by whom? Were those wounds and tendencies healed, or did they get passed down to the survivors? The heart is the last component to heal completely on a holistic level, as it is the first to get hurt when potential wounding takes place on whatever level the offense occurs. Each family survivor member goes through the process described and discussed in this paper to some level and degree. With perseverance, commitment, dedication, hope, faith, and love, all can successfully get through the process of transitions of transition transitioning and be better and wiser for it. It will be a time of preparation for each family member who succeeds in getting through it.

Any discrepancy will be uncovered on any level, sometimes more than one, such as mental or emotional disorders, spiritual crises, and physical symptoms of these and others. It is a time of growth. Love and forgiveness are the only way to any fruitful outcome and positive resolution for all involved.

Individually, as the literal spirit heals, such as at a childhood level of a one-year-old, the next literal spirit that needs healing takes its place, giving the illusion that the joy experienced in healing is being stolen by someone or something else. In reality, it is contributing to a critical mass within, leading to resurrection and the permanent restoration of joy.

The grieving process usually initiates before the loved one passes, and it continues through the passing and past it. The more growth and awareness the life-form has, the better the chance of not only getting the most out of it but also, equally important, getting through the acute stage of the event or difficult time. Being rooted in God's presence and Christ and having reached and obtained mystical union with God provide tremendous advantage in how long it takes to heal and integrate that spirit on the levels it needs to learn and grow. It's a struggle or very limiting or incapacitating if a person has not done so yet. This will vary, as family members are unique, but also, they can complement one another and can help one another greatly to comprehend and understand what is needed to be able to effectively grieve and bless and release not only the loved one but also other surviving members.

This is a time of revealing sins of omission, secret loves and lovers, and abuse, perhaps for the first time. As members go through the process, the loved one's journey can be quantified and qualified by how they are progressing through their own journeys as well as the journey of the loved one transitioning, who has been through it already. Thoughts, feelings, sensations, images, and communication take place between the loved one and the surviving family members, in whichever stage of grief they are in or if they have returned to love, experiencing joy. Going through the process multiple times is not uncommon, as childhood often has much to heal from at different ages on different levels, and sin includes all levels and ages that were affected by it. In sin, there is stasis of being. With beingness, everything is in motion, able to respond and adapt to change. With mystical union with God, spirit is free, complete, and whole.

Acceptance	Transcendent Spirit> Heaven
Depression	Etheric Spirit > Mental
Bargaining	Light Spirit > Emotional
Denial	Astral Spirit > Physical
Anger	Literal Spirit > Ego

Any of these can occur in any order at any time anywhere, but once the cycle is complete, one moves on to what's next to be felt, grieved, and processed.

The goal of metaphysical counseling is to meet life-forms where they are and try to get them into a spiritual practice that will work for them to increase their awareness so they can discern and comprehend their feelings and awaken their heart. This will give them the courage to face themselves and their apparent limitations, whatever they may be and whichever levels they are on. Meditation accomplishes both, but affirmative prayer will work as well. Once a realization is experienced by the client, it will lead to a positive belief, increasing or birthing faith to move forward with confidence with continued experience, as Dr. Masters eloquently states in these passages from his doctor of theocentric psychology degree program:

> The mind responds to the power of your belief, because belief becomes faith when the basis of belief, is enforced by a spiritual premise to give its possibility credence. ... The closer that one is to God, the greater the possibility that the person's Soul will touch the Universal Spirit whose nature, being part of constant renewal, will infuse the Soul with energy of its newness. It will thus, translate that newness of divine energy into thought that is discernable to one's conscious mind as an inspiration, to enliven one's sense of life and living to start anew. (2/40)

The HeartMath freeze-frame technique stops the movie of life within at a single picture or moment and then connects to a positive feeling. It then uses heart intelligence to learn what it is all about and, if negative, a better way through it, balancing head, heart, soul, and mind. This manages the startle reflex of the inner child's inception point of the ego. HRV, or heart rate variability, is a phenomenon of the heart through the soul and spirit. It determines every heartbeat from the heart as related to the soul or beingness, which is what the transitions of transition transitioning are also about in a positive sense.

Forgiving oneself for all transgressions against oneself brings one completely out of the illusion of sin and further solidifies one's understanding of the security of one's being in Christ, Christ consciousness, and God's presence, which moves one's being permanently into the resurrection and ascension of Christ and into heaven, fulfilling the Old Testament and the New Testament.

Modern-day Christianity focuses on the literal heart and, therefore, bypasses the mental and emotional levels of growth and development. Without the reclaiming of these strongholds, they can be used for creating idols mentally and imbuing them with emotional energy, creating a false or limiting belief or belief system and something to compete with the Most High God. This is the reason modern-day Christians struggle so much with sin. This is because of dysfunction itself and the origin of the dysfunction generator in their psyche. That is why regular attendance and participation are required for their services and activities—because the questions "Why?" and "How?" have not been answered to satisfy the inner child and free it from the dysfunction of its family of origin and the inception point of its ego when it was created.

God allows things to happen and play out as a trial to determine what a life-form will do, given the situation it finds itself in for the greater good of all.

God's will is what God does—and wishes to do, accomplish, or resolve—and results in freedom in and of beingness on all levels of mind. Each level of beingness and component works individually and as a unit as an infinite creation of God for the greater good of all.

CONCLUSION

A Return to Love

Love loving love being in love with love.

The transitions of transition transitioning, simply put, means accepting change throughout the life cycle. That is what this paper is about: becoming a realized divinity. With this comes the realization that love is what guides a life-form through the process of becoming a realized divinity. It describes the phenomena and experience of the state of beingness of the soul, mind, body, and spirit as an integrated, whole, complete creation of the Most High God, reconciled to God through the grieving process.

Love is discovered again overall but for the first time for the inner child who became overwhelmed with the idea or concept of change from a different perspective than what it was used to in its short existence of life. Wisdom is love finding its way out of the darkness and knows one's way of discovering and reconnecting with the light of creation, or God presence, the bright, radiant white light. People carry the world on their shoulders and back when they are young, and the world and God carry them when they have matured and are complete enough to become who they really are and were created to be. The inner child needs to return to its faith of its youth and upbringing, to the religion it was raised in, to have a positive experience of it as an adult at all levels of development, so it can realize, learn, and discern that all religions have a purpose and are stepping-stones on the way back to God. In addition, all people are going through change and are in the process at one stage or another. Every person, through the divine memory or soul, heart, mind, and spirit, has a pathway and a portal to the Most High God.

One is in love with love as love, being love. Love is experienced with a oneness with life as an experience, a realization accompanied by another realization that the whole process is a blessing. Tears of joy precede these realizations, and the heart fully opens again in resurrection, reconciled, whole, and complete. One experiences heart wisdom, which includes restoration or discovery of dreams, gifts (soul), and talents (heart), which joyfully express themselves with the soul, mind, and spirit, both within the body and transcendent to it simultaneously.

I'll conclude with a quote from Sister Joan Chittister's book *Becoming Fully Human: The Greatest Glory of God*. She quotes from Confucianism: "Experience, Confucianism teaches, guides us through life at its dregs and provides the final test of enlightenment; who we are on the other side of pain and loss is who we are at our best" (99).

WORKS CITED

Alexander, Eben. *Proof of Heaven.* New York, NY: Simon and Shuster, 2012.

Braden, Greg. *Resilience from the Heart: The Power to Thrive in Life's Extremes.* USA: Hay House, 2014–2015.

Childre, Doc, Howard Martin, Deborah Rozman, and Rollin McCraty. *Heart Intelligence.* Water Front Press, 2016.

———. *The HeartMath Solution.* New York, NY: Harper Collins, 1999.

Chittister, Joan. *Becoming Fully Human: The Greatest Glory of God.* UK: Rowan and Littlefield, 2005.

Chopra, Deepak. *The Path to Love.* New York, NY: Three Rivers Press, 1997.

Foundation for Inner Peace. *A Course in Miracles.* 3rd ed. Mill Valley, CA: 2007.

Gershon, Michael D. *The Second Brain.* New York, NY: Harpers Collins, 1998.

The Holy Bible. New King James Version. Thomas Nelson, 1984.

The Living Bible: The Way. Wheaton, IL: Tyndale Publishing, 1971.

Leloup, Jean-Yves. *The Gospel of Philip.* Rochester, VT: Inner Traditions, 2003.

Levi. *The Aquarian Gospel of Jesus the Christ.* Marina del Rey, CA: Devorss and Company, 2001.

Masters, Paul Leon. *Master's Degree Curriculum.* 2 vols. Burbank, CA: Printing, 2011.

———. *Mystical Insights.* Arizona: University of Sedona Publishing, 2016.

Myss, Caroline. *Why People Don't Heal and How They Can.* New York, NY: Three Rivers Press, 1997.

Ornstein, Robert E. *The Psychology of Consciousness.* New York, NY: Penguin Books, 1972.

Paulsen, Norman. *Christ Consciousness: The Emergence of the Pure Self Within.* Buellton, CA: Solar Logos Foundation, 2002.

Proctor, Charlene M. *The Oneness Gospel.* Minneapolis, MN: Two Harbors Press, 2001.

Ruiz, Don Miguel. *The Four Agreements.* San Rafael, CA: 1997.

Tolle, Eckhart. *A New Earth.* New York, NY: Penguin Group, 2005.

———. *The Power of Now.* Novato, CA: Namaste Publishing, 1997.

Upledger, John. *Cell Talk.* Berkeley, CA: North Atlantic Books, 2003.

Webster's College Dictionary. Barnes and Noble Inc., 2003.

Weiss, Brian. *Same Soul, Many Bodies.* New York, NY: Free Press, 2003.

Zukav, Gary. *The Heart of the Soul (Emotional Intelligence).* New York, NY: 2001

The Wisdom of Wisdom Being Wise Is Love

A Dissertation Submitted in Fulfillment of the Requirements
for the Degree of Doctor of Divinity, Specializing in
Bible Interpretation, on Behalf of the Department
of Graduate Studies of the University of Sedona

RAMON LAZARUS
APRIL 25, 2022

INTRODUCTION

This dissertation will develop a functional frame of reference and perspective in which to learn to grow from dysfunction to wholeness of function by changing the frame of reference and perception from negative to positive by defining and redefining word definition, usage, context, historical background, logic, precedent, and inference relating to interpretations inspired by the Bible. This new frame of reference will guide and reawaken the literal and the transcendent spirit to discover the truth of one's being, which is love. This is important and essential because one's choices and decisions are based upon either one's perception or one's perspective, leading to unhappiness or happiness, respectively. The proper perspective is paramount for vitality and well-being.

When the heart and head are not in coherence (connected to each other) and congruent (working together), the default function is perception from the ego (just the head working in dysfunction), resulting in a political process and a political outcome or decision.

To change perception, a frame of reference is needed for a basis of basic understanding to work with. This frame of reference is either dysfunctional or functional to a point, as it is able to accept the internal explanations that are adequate to each, until it is challenged by life or until one's circumstances cause it to be questioned in the quest of wisdom, knowledge, truth, and love within the individual. Key to understanding this process is one's interpretation of one's perspective, and higher consciousness and higher awareness, if not present, need to be awakened to understand the negative emotions and feelings based upon illusion and dysfunction and the apparent absence of positive ones from the constructs of mind involved. If based in dysfunction or based in the light that then becomes dysfunctional, both situations need to be illuminated to redefine the terms and concepts used to challenge associations and, subsequently, interpretations made regarding comprehension, leading to frame of reference and, therefore, perspective.

Perception distorted in each frame of reference mentioned from the basis of dysfunction and where the light gets distorted by the apparent limitations of the darkness is mainly ignorance from unconsciousness. This perception is unable to interpret it as such based upon illusion (which they interpret well but don't realize it doesn't apply to God's reality) that was created by apparent dysfunction of the dysfunctional ego. This is evident when reconciling the past in one's life. People may find they have become stuck or confused about their critical, basic understanding of life itself; the healthy, functional processing of feelings; and psyche functioning overall. The ego is based upon literal spirit, and it justifies itself through projection, deflection, and blame when challenged directly by truth. It thinks this will temporarily relieve itself of its pain it carries and protects within itself. This can be seen in politics and domestic disputes, which are the most common areas in which people are incapable of listening to one another and instead talk or shout over one another, with the ego preempting every attempt internally of God's Word in communicating to persons' hearts. People are intimidated by the emotion, fear, and narrative the ego has created in its confusion to stabilize itself in a dysfunctional way by making a narrative according to the ability of the intellect to interpret its experience. It reaches error when the experience goes beyond its limit to comprehend and understand. Therefore, the ego doesn't know how to communicate this, except when contrasted with positive experiences of God's presence, either through its own soul or through the divine memory. A person could get stuck or confused several times in the course of a lifetime.

In either perception mentioned, both are reluctant to trust each other enough to grow. This reluctance doesn't allow their perceptions to be altered or changed in any way, let alone positively. This is important for communication with self, others, and God to have a healthy frame of reference and perspective, because both perceptions are resourceful in resourcing references to support their political positions.

This paper will use the Bible and other references, along with God's presence and the Word in Christ and the Holy Spirit, to reveal the middle ground needed to grow and get past political positions so that each perception is deconstructed. These perceptions are not new in current society but have been around since the beginning of humanity, returning to heaven from earth, moving from head to heart and both head and heart from the Old Testament to the New Testament and beyond.

It is important to have a positive interpretation of the Bible to address each perspective, as each person is important to God, and more people will eventually turn to God through the Bible for guidance and advice on how to apply it to their lives.

The Bible is the relationship of God to man and man to himself in relation to God and others, until eventual mystical oneness with God and integration of the ego into the light of God's presence. By learning wisdom from the process of the experience, life-forms can realize and come to the conclusion that they, like God, are love in essence and beingness.

This process redefines who they are from ego, gives them a purpose to use for positive purposes in God's plan, recontextualizes their mindset and historical meaning regarding their past as it relates to the present moment, and makes sense following logic and agreement with their spirit, giving them a testimony that is relevant and relatable to others because it is based in love and truth and because the process is based upon mystical experience and the realizations and revelations that take place within life-forms as it happens, making all these things possible. The only conclusion that can be reached is that one becomes God's masterpiece of infinite love, brought about and created from the infinite and God's presence of creation. This is the ultimate drive of human beings' life-force energy, along with their spirit: to attain and maintain this objective for their lifetime and beyond.

The concept of divine design is a whole and a working process of the whole. The parts consist of both whole and process, containing details needed by the life-form to implement the process initiating it with its consciousness and awareness, which become awakened and enlightened. Prior to this point, the components of being—heart, soul, spirit, and mind—are compartmentalized into pieces, all separate from one another, woven by the intellect to conceal and protect its wounding and how it became that way. All are subordinate to the ego, with the erroneous conclusion that it is separate from itself, its environment, and God. Once aware and conscious, using discernment through meditation and healing, one can use the process to deconstruct the ego; release the components of being from their separate captivity within the mind; and work on unresolved feelings and issues, replacing emotional blocks and limiting beliefs with positive, affirming realizations. This leads to Gestalt revelations, or seeing things from a higher view, where growth and success gain the faith needed for the person to become who he or she, in the image of God, was created to be. This process recovers all components of being and pieces of one's soul, heart, and mind to be discerned, embodied, integrated, and realized, inspiring and empowering the life-form to accomplish all tasks required to achieve the objective of being and becoming God's masterpiece.

DEFINITION OF TERMS

For the purposes of this paper, the following terms will be defined as follows (definitions of *heart* and *wisdom* come from *Dictionary of the Bible* by John L. McKenzie, SJ):

- Ego: False heart that is in between soul, spirit, and mind within, along with true heart. It is literal in its viewpoint, resulting in perception that is separate from God, others, and its environment. It thinks it is alone in this predicament.
- Heart: "Associated with psychic activity... chief bodily focus of emotional activity. ... Discernment of the spirit of wisdom and revelation and the knowledge of Jesus Christ enlighten the eyes of the heart" (McKenzie 343–44).
- Soul: Supernatural life and salvation, illumination. Brings light to the psyche and illuminates it so the heart may learn of its contents and not be afraid of them. Helps with emotional healing of itself, the heart, and the mind.
- Spirit: Literal spirit associated with ego and earthly life. Transcendent spirit associated with heavenly, cosmic life and associated with the soul and infinity.
- Mind: Consciousness that is a repository for the above-mentioned items in the psyche when ego is dominant. Becomes purified with mystical union with God and transcendent spirit.
- Wisdom: "The Wisdom of Yahweh is Knowledge of how to do things and the Knowledge which lies behind the greatest of all works, creation, is the highest of all Wisdom" (McKenzie 930).

- Transcendent spirit: The fear of God is the beginning of wisdom because it contrasts and exposes the literal spirit, which is the lowest and furthest away from God. It is this spirit that undergoes growth through faith and ascends eventually to transcendent spirit, highest of all wisdom.

- Perspective: "The power to see or think of things in their true relationship to each other" (*Webster's College Dictionary* 662).

- Perception: The by-product of the ego's narrative based upon itself and its limited mindset incomplete of God's reality, reduced down to sensory data or input.

- Refraction: Negative, dysfunctional projection seeks to find God by means of negativity to prove to itself God is to be held accountable. It thinks by blame and is direct. It goes through the surface of heart but does not know the light. Therefore, it cannot discern or use awareness to learn to educate itself to alleviate its burden of error without knowing and realizing the true nature of itself.

- Reflection: Positive-idea Gestalt and feedback when love is shared with another life-form. It is not projected but emanates and flows from the God Source within and with grace that reveals to all hearts present to it the truth of the matter, situation, or circumstance presenting itself as discerned, fake, negative, and untrue, which is threatening to others who don't know or want to know the truth of their own situation. Individuals have a choice to go along to get along or face humiliation, which aggravates the pain of being human. Both choices are not really choices, because both are void of love. It validates love and the positive as well.

- Refraction and reflection of light: Needed to grow to learn and learn to grow. Independently, on their own, they will eventually lead to discontent and a longing for something more out of life. This leaves life-forms with a negative emotional condition of inwardly living a life of quiet desperation while outwardly facing peer pressure to fit in with whatever consensus reality they encounter that vies for their support to feel justified. They may side with their political disposition regardless of whether they really agree deep down with it or not.

- Metaphysician: A soul who has awakened in consciousness (heart) and awareness (soul) and spirit; who has integrated these components into beingness to a certain extent; and whose purpose is to help others to heal and grow to achieve the same for themselves. A metaphysician reflects light (transcendent spirit naturally reflects light) and does not project in a dysfunctional manner. Its challenge is to heal its heart enough or completely to accomplish and carry out life's purpose. In order to do this, it may have unfinished business in healing its heart regarding its past and, if so, may project directly (refracting light) in the hope to heal, learn, grow, and understand the lesson and purpose for it as it is experienced and processed accordingly. Spiritual being having a human experience.

- Fundamentalist: A being who has taken the initial step to awaken the heart but, because of the dynamics of the ego (forgetfulness), thinks that there is no more to do or become and that others must change so it can feel comfortable about its positions. This is a more difficult way to achieve beingness and oneness with God. It needs further awakening in consciousness to become aware of its soul awareness, heal them both if needed, and discern the ego from the other parts of its being to integrate it in healing, leading to realization of wisdom and, from this, who it really is, which is love. The fundamentalist projects in a dysfunctional way (refracted light and literal spirit) and needs to learn to reflect light accordingly.

The introduction, the terms defined, and their subsequent conceptual meanings elucidated provide a changeable frame of reference with which to work in transforming perception into perspective.

REVIEW OF LITERATURE

In everyday life, from the beginning of humanity to today, there have been distractions in the world and society vying for our attention to try to tell us what we need or want for ourselves, based upon the world's standards and priorities. This component of the world creates chaos, confusion, indifference, and a whole host of emotions and responses, whether it is dealt with at its level or not. The major by-product it creates is stress, both outside ourselves and in our subconscious ego (which is the same thing), with the world trying to manipulate for its goal of making money from it and by it and to control it for power. The overall stress can create even more stress if it becomes chronic and constant, causing disease or illness. Then people will stop to reevaluate their lives and start asking questions: "Why is this happening to me? And what can I do about it?" If pondered long enough, these will lead to deeper realizations. Are they inspired or empowered? And if not, how can they achieve that? Many turn to others first, but if that doesn't solve the problem, then they turn to their higher power or God.

The word *perspective* isn't mentioned much in the Bible, if at all, but one word that is mentioned many times is *consider*. According to *Strong's Concordance of the Bible*, in Deuteronomy 4:39, *consider* means to allow, make room for, or weigh another way of looking at a point. *The Good News Bible* states, "So remember today and never forget: the lord is God in heaven and on earth. There is no other god. Obey all his laws that I have given you today, and all will go well with you and your descendants" (193–94). In this passage from this Bible, the word *consider*, in *Strong's Concordance*, is phrased as *remember*: to remember, recall, and use the mind to adhere to instruction and correction if needed. To consider or remember is to challenge current thinking with a new or different teaching or to recall teaching that was given in the past that is truthful and will stand the test of time and beyond.

Dr. John Upledger, DO, in his book *Cell Talk*, comments on chronic or prolonged stress and what it may do to individuals the longer they are exposed to it: "Human beings, when put under severe and prolonged stress of any sort, may regress in their behavior and become more childish as the stress goes on. During this regression the human often becomes obsessed, compulsive, and more unreasonable. When the human cell becomes stressed for any reason, it may also begin to regress"(305). This kind of stress can produce major disease in the mind and body on any or all levels and will require each level affected by it to be healed to produce a positive outcome in which health, well-being, and vitality are restored.

The Bible uses the terms *consider* and *remember* in conveying teachable moments that provide students with a safe place outside themselves as well as a safe space within themselves, where they will not be judged for where they have ended up in their circumstances, condition, or perception. They'll see things as they really are in relationship to each other, which is the definition of *perspective*. This allows them to grow to learn and learn to understand. Whether it is base mortal consciousness or divine, perception or perspective, there are not really two different entities at play but only one, in that they are both energy.

Lynne McTaggart, in her book *The Field*, declares this realization from experiments done with the zero-point field: "The Einstein Equation $e=mc^2$ was simply a recipe for the amount of energy necessary to create the appearance of mass. It means that there are not two fundamental physical entities—something material and another immaterial- but only one: energy. ...As they would write later, that mass was not equivalent to energy; mass was energy" (33). Energy is neither created nor destroyed but conserved and changes phase and state of phenomenal existence based upon the observations of the one observing it or interacting with it or both. Perception is low energy; perspective is high energy. Perception is subconscious, nonconscious, or unconscious. Perspective is conscious and aware to realize these things and itself and its environment in relationship to God, itself, and others. Perception is the heart, with the ego as its reference point. Perspective is the soul, with its awareness to provide contrast to the heart to illuminate it to help it to discern, grow, heal, and integrate the lessons in life it is meant to go through to become pure and merge in mystical union with God. The goal of this process is to transform the inner isolation of the separateness of the ego in the inner-world experience after awakening and embodying the soul to bring the purified inner heart to become one with the outer experience. This leads to coherency and congruency between head (Old Testament) and heart (soul, spirit, New Testament) to work with each other connected to infinity and God. This relationship of the being seeking help has a new relationship with God, itself, others, and its environment because it has perspective instead of a perception that is bound in the reality of itself in relation to its experience.

Two key figures from the Bible who are significant in illustrating this process and the wisdom their lives gave to humanity with their respective contributions are King David from the Old Testament and Jesus Christ from the New Testament. King David's life represents the limits of the Old Testament and living in and with the configuration and mindset of the heart, primarily consisting of the ego. King David slew Goliath in his youth, representing his outer world, but transforming the ego heart is something that had to wait for the incarnation of Jesus Christ to add to the legacy of God and man, transforming the inner world and bringing it outward to the outer experience of people. King David's limitations were evident in his affair with Bathsheba and the plot to kill her husband. For these sins, David suffered greatly, as expressed in his psalms to God, which express the full range of emotions and feelings a human could go through at that time. Jesus Christ healed His outer life by healing others, and His mission was and is to heal His inner life and help those who need His help to heal their inner lives as well. To satisfy the requirements of this paper, I will examine two scriptures, as outlined in the statement of purpose in the introduction. For King David, Psalm 23 will be evaluated and interpreted. For Jesus Christ, Matthew 6:9–13 will be evaluated and interpreted. This is otherwise known as the Lord's Prayer. Both scriptures will be from the New King James Version.

Before I interpret these two scriptures of the Bible, it is important to engage in a short preparatory meditation and breath work to open the heart and calm the mind. Because different people are at different levels of spiritual growth and awareness, different interpretations will be gleaned when interpreting the Bible. The Bible references meditation in Psalms, when its author is seeking God. In the book *Meditation in Christianity*, Swami Rama mentions numerous references to meditation. Psalm 1 describes "the righteous person as one who meditates on God's law by day and night, asserting that his roots are securely planted beside the stream of life" (Rama 23). In addition to meditation, which greatly enhances the opportunity for advancement of insight and oneness with God, is breath work. In the book *The Miracle of the Breath*, Andy Caponigro's reference to *pneuma* for the inner breath, or prana or chi, refers… "to mystical union of spirit soul and breath … God within the breath" (7). This is important to get the most out of the awakening when consulting the Bible by focusing, preparing to study it by first meditating, and focusing with breathwork to invite God's presence to be present within and be part of the dissemination and interpretation of the scriptures referenced for illumination and awakening.

And now let's look at Psalm 23:

> The Lord is my Shepherd; I shall not want.
>
> He maketh me to lie down in green pastures; He leads me beside the still waters.
>
> He restores my Soul; He leads me in the paths of righteousness for his name's sake.
>
> Yea, though I walk through the valley of the shadow of death I will fear no evil;
> For you are with me: Your rod and staff comfort me.
>
> You prepare a table before me in the presence of my enemies;
> You anoint my head with oil; My cup runs over.
>
> Surely goodness and mercy shall follow me all the days of my life:
> And I will dwell in the house of The Lord. Forever. (Psalm 23:1–6 NKJV)

The key word from verse 1 is *Shepherd*. In *The New Jerome Biblical Commentary*, Raymond Brown comments on the usage, context, and meaning of this world according to the time it was used and before this scripture was written: "Shepherd—A universal image of the king in the ancient world, emphasizing leadership and providence for his subjects" (530).

According to Greg Braden's book *Wisdom Codes*, the definition of a shepherd from this scripture is... "To watch over, to care for, and to provide for the creatures that depend upon him for their lives and well-being" (126). This psalm, according to Braden, was written early in King David's life, when he was a shepherd tending to his flock.

A shepherd of the Lord, as stated here, offers contentedness associated with being a shepherd. With the Lord, all needs are provided for to the shepherd and his flock. The language of this scripture is metaphorical, poetical, and symbolic. A case for a literal interpretation will be made in the discussion section of this paper.

The key words or phrases from the second verse are *green pastures* and *still waters*. For a shepherd, green pastures and still waters are important to sustain the life of the herd on a physical level. Symbolically, they reference communing with God and the accommodations God will provide for the shepherd. Taken further, it references meditation, stillness, and being led by God. It infers the logical process of wisdom through meditation, resting the whole time, perhaps contemplating his relationship to and with God.

The key words in the third verse are *soul* and *path of righteousness*. The soul is immortal and exists in eternity and experiences time and space through the vehicle of the physical body. It is a creation of God's presence individualized in human form. Restoring the soul infers something can cause it to erode or be adversely affected. This is a prophetic foreshadowing of his life yet to be, and being led in the path of righteousness agrees with wisdom. Used together, it suggests coming trials for the young shepherd in his later life.

The entire fourth verse is key. Walking through the valley of the shadow of death represents getting close to facing death or an ending of sorts. It suggests perhaps a surrounding with limited means to enter or exit. For David, facing Goliath and having an affair with Bathsheba certainly fit with the concept of death being near. Fearing no evil means encountering foes, things, or circumstances that are not for you. "For you are with me in spirit and symbolized by the rod and staff that bring comfort." This references the wisdom of Moses, who also had a rod and staff, which he carried as a source of God's transformative power and which gave Moses comfort as well. This verse infers a confrontation with things that are unpleasant and not for him, which, again, agrees with a running theme throughout the verse and chapter of wisdom and overcoming obstacles.

The entire fifth verse is key. "You prepare a table before me in the presence of my enemies." This gives further insight into what the confrontation mentioned in verse 4 is about: confronting his enemies in a banquet style, which was the custom of his time. It could also symbolically suggest confronting his inner demons and a transformative experience of having overcome his enemies victoriously, as symbolized by the banquet metaphor. Anointing means being sealed for holy purposes, such as a king to lead his people or, at the end of his life, to get ready to depart the world. "My cup runs over" bestows many blessings to come as a result of being wise and accepting God's invitation to learn wisdom.

The key words of verse 6 are the phrase and the verse. "Goodness and mercy shall follow me all the days of my life." This represents a reconciled past with God. Being followed by goodness and mercy is pleasant and comforting, an affirmation from God that everything will be all right for him. Dwelling in the house of the Lord forever depicts a successful life with residence in heaven and his name in the book of life. The theme of the psalm is that of a successful life and journey to the kingdom of heaven, following wisdom to get there. Most of the Old Testament deals with life and its associated issues and the resolution of them through drama, trial, and tribulation. David's life would be literally interpreted at times, as well as symbolically.

According to *Harper's Bible Commentary* editor James L. Mays, "The early church sang Psalm 23 as the baptized person emerged from the font and proceeded into the newly illumined Church for Eucharist. Contemporary churches turn to this psalm for holy-communion and funerals depending whether one stresses the early walk through darkness or the later banquet" (444).

We now look at what is known in the West as the Lord's Prayer, from the Gospel of Matthew 6:9–13 in the New King James Version:

> Our father which art in Heaven, Hallowed be thy name.
>
> Thy Kingdom come. Thy will be done on earth as it is in Heaven.
>
> Give us this day our daily bread.
>
> And forgive us our debts, as we forgive our debtors.
>
> And lead us not into temptation, but deliver us from evil:
>
> For thine is the Kingdom, and the power and the glory forever. Amen.

According to Neil Douglas-Klotz, creator of the audiotape series and study guide *Original Prayer*, the original language spoken by Jesus Christ is Aramaic. Klotz's translation of the Aramaic will be used and be interpreted from his work regarding this scripture passage and prayer.

The background for this interpretation, which is in the form of a prayer, was created from the Word of God made flesh in Jesus Christ. Klotz cites some historical evidence dating back to Emperor Constantine's request for the gathering known as the Council Of Nicaea (today's Turkey): "At this council of Nicaea from the hundreds of Gospels of Jesus' words and actions they were winnowed down to Matthew, Mark, Luke, and John. ... Simultaneously Christianity developed in the Persian Empire" (7). Jewish Christians who dwelled there declared they acquired Aramaic versions of gospels from initial accounts of Jesus. These Christians split from the Roman Empire's version of doctrine of Christianity,... "forced out of their traditional homelands in Eastern Turkey, Northern Syria and Northern Iraq as a result of world wars in this century" (8). "The Syriac Aramaic version of the Gospels that these Christians use, called The Peshitta, is the basis for the interpretations on *Original Prayer* or The Lord's Prayer" (8). "The Aramaic Peshitta Gospels also give us a window to his mindset that can't be found in any Greek version. In Aramaic, for instance, there is no ultimate separation of body from spirit. There is no separation of the realities 'within and among'—Aramaic contains only one preposition for both (b')" (8).

Klotz continues, commenting on the key experiential insight from his work: "Jesus' native middle eastern tradition, the sound of a word is considered to have innate power beyond the word's literal meaning. Because we live in a world of vibration, sound directly affects both our physical cells and our inner being. ... Sound changes the way we breathe thereby changing the way we feel our connection through breath to spirit and to all that is" (2–3). Klotz continues, further concluding that chanting and speaking Jesus's words in their native tongue of origin connects not only "to the feelings behind the words but to his consciousness itself which is beyond any translation or explanation of the words themselves" (3). It is Klotz's contention that "awareness of our breathing maintains a crucial thread of connection, deepening the wisdom contained in and beyond the words" (3). Klotz maintains that praying in the way Jesus did helps us to discover His capacity of His awareness of cosmic unity. Klotz says that one can discover the sacred I Am and that this is essential to comprehending, understanding, and finding meaning in the experience to awaken not only to what has been stated here but also to other mysteries of the universe and God.

In Aramaic, Jesus's prayer reads as follows:

> *Abwoon d'bwashmaya*
> *Nethqadash shmakh*
> *Tey tey malkuthakh*
> *Nehwey sebyanach ay kanna d' bwashmaya aph b'arah*
> *Hawvlan lachma d'sunqanan yaomana*
> *Wasboqlan khaubayn(wakhtahayn) aykana daph khnan*
> *Shbwoqan l'khayyabayn*
> *Wela tahlan l 'nesyuna*
> *Ela patzan minbisha*
> *Metol dilakhie malktha wahayla wateshbukhta l'ahlan almin*
> *Ameyn.* (2)

Now we will look at the key words or phrases from each line of the prayer.

- *"Abwoon d' bwash maya"* (2).
  "Our Father who art in Heaven (NKJV)." The key word from this prayer and scripture is *Father*, or *Abwoon* in Aramaic. The concept "our Father" symbolizes transcendence and invokes a parent whom a child asks for help when he or she needs help to understand something he or she doesn't understand. "The word Abwoon means seeking from the source of all creation present at the beginning and recovering spiritual nourishment through a birthing process to arrive at the present moment" (6).

- *"Nethqadash shmakh"* (2).
  "Hallowed be thy name" (NKJV). The key phrase in this line of the scripture is the entire line. "Hallowed be thy name" is a reference to make holy. *Nethqadash* means… "clearing space … and … making something central in our lives" (15). "Shmakh means light, vibration or sound and to focus through our connection our lives" (15). Klotz sums up the line as such: "Focus your light within us; make it useful, as the rays of a beacon show the way" (15).

- *"Tey tey malkuthakh"* (2).
  "Thy Kingdom come" (NKJV). The key phrase here is the entire verse or phrase. *Malkuthakh* means "kingdom" and, according to Klotz, points to an "empowering vision that solidifies one's life. It is a combination of vision and empowerment that allows one to say I can! to life" (17). According to Klotz, "In reality, the Aramaic malkuta and the word used in the Greek version of The Bible Gospels (basileia) are gendered feminine. Both would be more accurately translated as queendom" (18). Klotz answers this theological question: "Was this new reign or vision meant to be inside or outside? Was Jesus referring to the outer political change or inner spiritual change? The Aramaic word malkuta, when spoken by a prophet or mystic always means both" (18). To sum up, this phrase of the prayer, according to Klotz, is a… "deep inner sense of" I can" express itself both inwardly and outwardly" (18).

- *"Nehwey sebyanachaykanna d' bwashmaya aph b' arha"* (2).

  "Thy will be done on earth as it is in Heaven" (NKJV). The entire phrase is key. According to Klotz, "Jesus points to a unity, brought about by the delight of the universe, of both our individual existence (earth) and our communal, connected Life (Heaven). ...When we discover the pleasure power of the cosmos, these two worlds unite in Love" (21).

  The Dalai Lama comments on when the inner and outer come together in unity with the divine through the mind in his book *Dzoghen*: "But at a certain point, when outer and inner circumstances come together, the very nature of this unwavering state of mind is such that it is the basis on which a bare awareness can be experienced... but all penetrating and unimpeded within and without" (195). In his words, it is "primordially present mindfulness" (195). It is clear, light-purified mind and is signified by the above as the below, the inner and the outer, and they all become one.

  The Aquarian Gospel of Jesus the Christ by Levi chronicles Jesus's time in the Far East before His earthly ministry started. The scripture describes Jesus thusly: "This Hebrew prophet is the rising star of wisdom, deified. He brings us a knowledge of the Secret things of God; and all the world will hear his words, will heed his words and glorify his name" (54).

- *"Hawvlan lachma d'suhqanan yaomana"* (2).

  "Give us this day our daily bread" (NKJV). Here the entire phrase is key. This scripture, according to Klotz, addresses practical advice for living. It represents food not only for the body but also for mind and spirit. It emphasizes only asking for what is needed. It considers wisdom, or *hochma*, from *lachma*, which is "the daily bread of understanding contemplations to receive nourishment for the body, heart, Soul and spirit" (22).

- *"Washboqlan khaubayn(wakhtahayan) aykana daph khnan shbwoqan l' khayya bayn"* (2).

  "And forgive us our debts as we forgive our debtors" (NKJV). The key phrase is the entire scripture. According to Klotz, the Greek translation of this line is "Love your neighbor as yourself." In Aramaic, Klotz suggests, "Love your neighbor as your subconscious and your subconscious as your neighbor" (27). Boundaries both inner and outer can be crossed, which, when reduced down, are trespasses, which can form "spirit knots" (28). These knots need to be loosened, untied, and healed for one to realize salvation lives in knowing the fullest extent of our selves (the whole subconscious) so that this can be included consciously in *Alaha*, sacred unity. In short, this salvation lies in realizing "the purpose of our lives" (27).

- "*Wela tahlan l'nesyuna ela patzan min bisha*" (2).
  "And deliver us not into temptation but deliver us from evil" (NKJV). Key word *nesyuna*, or *temptation*, means "forgetfulness," according to Klotz. "It is opposite of the remembrance of Divine Unity, around which the spirituality of this entire tradition is centered" (29). The emphasis is on remembrance, and things that are superficial cause one to forget. The other key word here is *evil*, or *bisha*, which means "unripe," according to Klotz, or "out of tune with sacred unity." He says,... "It simultaneously affirms that Divine Unity (as well as our inner self) embraces all, including those qualities that are still coming into wholeness" (30). Remembering sacred unity to be in tune with it so one is ripe includes all and excludes none.

- "*Metol dilkhie malkutha wahayla wateshbuktha l' ahlam alman. Amen*" (2).
  "For the kingdom, the power and the glory forever. Amen" (NKJV). Key word *metol*, according to Klotz, means "to you belongs." *Malkutha* is the cosmic I Can from line three. *Hayla* is the embodied energy of the cosmos. The word *teshbuktha* indicates the song of harmony of the universe. "Lahlam alman means from gathering to gathering," a measurement of time... "by the seasons, the stars or festivals" (32). *Ameyn*, according to Klotz, is a word of power, affirming that "This is the ground of connection with unity from which my actions will come" (32).

To sum up, the Original Prayer, or the Lord's Prayer, with the Aramaic translation to English, according to Klotz, is as follows in its entirety:

> O Breathing life, your name shines everywhere!
> Release a space to plant your presence here.
> Envision your I Can now.
> Embody your desire in every light and form.
> Untie the knots of failure binding us, as we release the strands we hold of others' faults.
> Help us not forget our source, yet free us from not being in the present.
> From you arises every vision, power and song, from gathering to gathering.
> Amen: May our future actions grow from here. (2)

Pandit Usharbudh Arya comments, in his book *God*, on the spiritual nature of deity and relationships, how they lead back to God, and how they have purpose to reveal both maya (illusion and forgetfulness) and Brahman (infinite consciousness).

When Brahman, in its infinite consciousness, knows all of its potential, all of its shakti at once, without past, present, or future, it is Brahman. But when that Brahman knows that in all power, there are many powers, the moment the word *many* occurs, it becomes maya. When all is reduced to many, and when, from that many you take one, then you have relationships between that one and another one—you have relationships between different parts of the manifold. Then, when those parts and the manifold all fold back like a dream, folding back into the creator and dissolving, then it is Brahman again (65).

We have studied so far two central characters of the Bible: King David from the zenith of the Old Testament and Jesus Christ from the culmination of the New Testament. Both characters refer to each other. Darrell L. Bock's book *The NIV Application Commentary: Luke* mentions King David's referring to Jesus. King David refers to "Jesus as his Lord in The Psalms" (522). In *The Living Bible*, Jesus refers to David as being "David's root and his descendent." This is not a traditional person-to-person relationship, socially speaking. It is a spiritual relationship between two figures to reveal what level they are operating on in their lives, which is why they are in the Bible respectively. Both King David and Jesus Christ were in touch with their infinite consciousness (Brahman) and maya throughout their lives in various relationships, but the spiritual relationship to each other was key to both in discovering what was literal spirit as well as transcendent spirit for each and paved the way for God's people and humanity to be able to evolve from God with God to God from heaven to earth and back to heaven again. Psalm 23 of David and the Lord's Prayer from Jesus are sound-bites condensed into a simple bottom line for readers regarding what their lives were about and the events and processes they went through to get there. These two characters from the Bible represent a paradigm shift socially, psychologically, and spiritually. Dr. Daniel Amen, MD, in his book *The End of Mental Illness*, addresses the topic of a paradigm shift, the old ways of doing things, and what needs to happen to bring in the new and have it accepted. Dr. Amen quotes the work of historian and philosopher Thomas Kuhn on scientific revolutions and how they typically occur in five stages. This, in this instance, is applied to the field of mental health, as Dr. Amen is a psychiatrist who uses functional medicine and a unique scanning method to determine dysfunction from health and treats patients as a result.

> Stage 1: "The discrepancies show ... the standard paradigm begins to fail" (Amen 40). Traditional diagnosis of mental disorders leads to suicidal or aggressive behavior, causing more trauma and problems than it solves.

> Stage 2: "The disagreements start. Once the paradigm begins to fail, experts begin to look for small fixes" (40). "This leads to ... many competing schools of thought. More than 250 types of psychotherapies and myriad medications exist to treat metal illnesses. Kuhn wrote that no matter how wrong their models have become, the leaders maintain their beliefs and continue trying to tweak their ideas to preserve their power and influence" (40).

Stage 3: "The Revolution. Over time a new paradigm emerges that resolves many of the problems in the field. A new paradigm—such as 'Get your brain right and your mind will follow'—reinterprets existing knowledge, retaining the best of the old thinking and integrating the latest knowledge into a fresh model, a paradigm shift" (40).

Stage 4: "The Rejection. The new paradigm is then rejected and ridiculed by the leaders in the field. This is one of the most reliable stages of a scientific revolution. The old guard becomes frustrated that the new idea did not come from them and because they hold tightly to their own theories this period may last for decades until they retire or die" (41).

Stage 5: "Acceptance. The new theory is adopted gradually as younger, more open minded scientists accept it early in their careers and later become the leaders in the field. Kuhn also noted that professionals who are outsiders not wed to the status quo are often the ones who champion new paradigms" (41). "It takes courage to be the on the outside, but in the long run it pays off because everyone gets better care" (41).

What Amen mentions here, quoting Kuhn, is the type of situation going on across the board of all professions nationally and globally as well with the pandemic. There were times of turbulence both in King David's life and in the life of Jesus Christ as well, but they were successful in that their lives on earth have brought many to the truth of God, or infinite consciousness.

Throughout the Bible, angels are the Most High God's messengers, assisting persons with a need for their help. They provide God's perspective to whatever condition or circumstance is present in their lives. They provide God's perspective up and until the persons in need can provide that for themselves, apply it to their lives, and heal accordingly. There are many conditions physically, emotionally, mentally, and spiritually a person may need help in healing from. All the levels involved need to be addressed so one can heal appropriately.

Per the book *Ask Your Angels* by Alma Daniel, Timothy Wyllie, and Andrea Ramer, one such condition that qualifies for healing on all levels is addiction. "Addictions stem from feelings of unworthiness, just as all abuses come from a lack of caring or respect. These are a sign that love is missing. Abuse of alcohol, drugs, sex, relationships, shopping, gambling and food is an attempt to fill the empty place inside" (277). "Addictions are coping techniques for dealing with deficiencies in love. When an infant does not receive the handling, nurturing, bonding it requires, it grows up with a love deficit. This damages self-esteem and retards the development of healthy self-love. The less self-love you have, the more prone you become to feeding yourself with a substitute for feeling good"(277).

King David sinned sexually with Bathsheba, which suggests a need perhaps from early development in his life. Something was missing. Jesus Christ, being David's root and heir, had this predicament and condition to deal with, which He did to successful culmination on the cross.

Greg Braden states in the introduction of his book *Wisdom Codes* that "words can change your brain" (xiii). He adds that the language used to describe oneself and ..."share our thoughts, feelings and emotions and beliefs actually forms the framework for the unity or lack thereof that is experienced when we think and solve the problems of everyday life" (xiii). Changing from separation (perceptions) to unity (perspective) brings awakenings. However, persons may interpret the Bible from a literal perception and may have an awakening to the fact that they identify with separation rather than unity. If this is the case, then the aspirants need to go deeper within themselves until they experience an awakening of unity, and when they do, they will find themselves on the path of wisdom.

Wayne W. Dyer, in his book *There's a Spiritual Solution to Every Problem*, quotes Joel Goldsmith's book *The Art of Spiritual Healing* regarding disease, death, or sin involved in a person's circumstances: "When disease is called unreal, it is not a denial of the so called existence of these things. It is a denial of their existence as a part of God or reality. ... In the realm of the real, The Kingdom Of God, the discords of sense have no existence. That however does not change the fact that we suffer from them. ... The beginning of wisdom is the realization that these conditions need not exist" (184–85).

Words lead to perspective, and perspective leads to healing and resolution of perceived problems and circumstances. Such awakenings come about from interpreting the Bible or any other source the God presence within persons directs them to.

Joel Goldsmith, in his book *The Art of Spiritual Healing*, comments on supply as opposed to lack: "The secret is that the source of your supply is your own consciousness of God as supply- your developed state of consciousness" (153). He also states that people seek out healing or help, such as the Bible, because their own consciousness may not be developed enough to overcome their current health challenge or circumstance. "Infinity is the measure of God. ... The Presence of God does not manufacture some form of harmony: The Presence of God is itself the form of all good" (Goldsmith 157). This is the realization of the highest wisdom available to people, which will change their perspective and heal whatever needs healing in their lives in whatever circumstances they have. Contact must be made by connection in any way that is positive with God at the level, age consciousness, or awareness that is not coherent with God, so it can heal, learn, comprehend, and understand and have a realization, changing perspective. People are already whole in both their lives and life in the real reality of life.

Don Miguel-Ruiz, in his book *The Mastery of Love*, comments on the culmination of wisdom, which is love: "You can be so strong and so powerful that with your self-love you transform your personal dream from fear to love, from suffering to happiness. Then just like the sun, you are giving light and giving love all the time, with no conditions. When you love with no conditions, you the human, and you the God, align with the spirit of life moving through you. Your life becomes the expression of the spirit" (197). Ruiz finishes his book with this final line, which is appropriate to this section of this paper: "Life is nothing but a dream, and if you create your life with love your dream becomes a masterpiece of art" (197).

Dr. Masters, in his book *Mystical Insights*, shares his findings in exploring consciousness "as the final frontier in the exploration of life and the mysteries of existence" (13). Dr. Masters states two important things from his findings: "that intellectual analysis cannot answer questions because it is based on the speculations of the five senses and also ... to find truths of life, a person must go beyond the limitations of the five senses" (13).

Dr. Masters comments on resolving the unresolvable, when persons might consider making a change in their lives, and what happens when they do: "Whenever a person resolves to make changes in life, a dualistic conflict takes place, creating a stalemate where all remains unresolved" (31). This is key because it allows a person to seek guidance or wisdom, using free will to make a choice for the best interest of all, including the person seeking guidance.

Dr. Masters comments on the beginning of wisdom: "But Wisdom is a timeless Presence. When mystics seek guidance from God, it is wisdom that is active in their consciousness" (79). Wisdom is love, and love is wisdom. To seek it is wise itself, no matter the level of consciousness of the person seeking it. It is available to all if only they ask for it and seek it with all honesty and sincerity of their being.

DISCUSSION

Stress is a by-product of energy out of phase in relationship to perception, as opposed to the reality, or perspective. This simply means that perceptions that are not coherent or congruent with perspective (reality) produce stress, and the energy of it, as a result, produces the stress experience. Until enlightenment or enlightening experience occurs within a life-form, the default setting of its consciousness fluctuates between remembrance and forgetfulness but favors forgetfulness. Remembrance is light, awareness, God's presence, and Christ consciousness. Forgetfulness is darkness, ego, perception, uncertainty, half truth, and fear. This is why the Bible uses the terms *consider* and *remember* as a state of mind to monitor thoughts and feelings regarding living and the choices and decisions people make and how they will affect themselves, their families, and their descendants, especially if they have been brought out of or are being brought out of sin.

To remember or consider, in this context, as written in the review of literature, means to challenge, in addition to monitoring the mind for negative thoughts and feelings. Challenge them with the truth of the light of God's presence within. In addition to monitoring for negative thoughts and feelings, challenge them with God's presence to obey God within when God provides positive guidance on how to live, love, act, and behave. Awakening, or reawakening, is important to establish a firm foundation for comprehension, learning, and understanding; and perspective is needed to accomplish this with the Word of and presence of God to help transform and change perceptions into the reality of God's universe and creation. Without the aid of reason, love, and truth, this process is not possible, as love and truth verify and validate, within and without, if something is real or not, rational or irrational, true or false, significant or not.

The Physical and Metaphysical

The physical and metaphysical are one in love, truth, energy, frequency, and vibration. The physical is defined by an environment governed by the five senses and a limited perception concocted by the ego or lower-energy vibration. The metaphysical is defined by God's presence and the soul; has perspective, love, truth, and reason; and governs itself based upon these attributes of God, including intelligence and common sense, which leads to wisdom. The physical is governed by wisdom, and as such, when interacting with it, certain principles or laws can be formulated for the purposes of managing it to improve quality of life for life-forms and their habitats. The metaphysical is governed by wisdom and love and uses mystical insight to see and mystical hearing to hear as well as feel, acquiring data and information from the environment of infinity and creation to design and create solutions in those capacities as it applies to them and the physical. One such application to demonstrate this is water, or H_2O. Water qualifies for the physical because it has three phases of matter that it can exist in naturally in the physical and metaphysical environment. Water, or H_2O, is a solid, a liquid, and a gas, depending upon temperature of the environment, or all three, as in the case of a mountain peak and a body of water below it. The sun shining upon the mountain melts the snowcaps caused by cold temperatures at high altitude or elevation. Water consists of two hydrogen atoms and one oxygen atom per molecule. The atoms can be reduced further to their subatomic states at a quantum level, where they are energy. The phases of matter are the perceptions or limitations of it, but in reality, they are energy. In the natural world, wisdom governs water through order with other elements of existence in the environment. Metaphysically, water and its atoms and energy vibrate at a certain frequency, feeding back into infinity and creation to maintain harmony with self, God, and the environment to maintain safety (love) and order for all. When this harmony is out of harmony, chaos and destruction can occur, and this process changes boundaries or perceptions. Once order is restored, then the new perspective can be experienced as wisdom working through the laws of nature and God to reestablish new boundaries and phenomena to be experienced.

As in this example using water, it is the same for consciousness. Perceptions are the apparent limitations of phenomena identified by the five senses based upon the intellect's interpretation of them and its limited data bank, or ego. There can be mental blocks, emotional blocks, physical blocks, and spiritual blocks. These blocks have to do with limiting beliefs and their associated emotions or emotional blocks, which lead to physical and spiritual dysfunction, such as painful feelings associated with painful memories that need to be healed, forgiven, integrated, and released.

Perspective is the truth of existence, the reality of what and who we are and where we come from. Perspective is based upon infinity and creation; dissolves perceptions; and heals through transformation, realization, and revelation, restoring, renewing, and regenerating life-forms to their original condition, as they were created in the mind of God. The perspective provides directions, guidance, and wisdom of both light and dark and how to work through one to get to the other and coexist with and in both. This is the saga of life, or at least it is supposed to be.

Perceptions are contractions of phenomena, and perspective is expansion to and of reality. When this process is restricted or blocked, it doesn't flow or have harmony, coherency, or congruency and is a problem for the life-form in whom it is taking place in. The purpose is to learn that the inner life of a life-form needs to change and grow if that life-form's inner or outer life circumstances are negative, unsustainable, or life-threatening or have the potential to be.

The Old Testament's teachings represent transforming and healing the mind, eventually leading to and approaching healing the heart from outside in perception with a working perspective that is always changing according to the needs of the life-form going through the process. However, its drawback was in not being able to address the soul and spirit effectively to fully recover from negativity and sin through embodiment, which is an inside-out process and leads to coherency, congruency, harmony, and being in the flow of life and God. Ideally, a life-form can grow with God and the Bible, working and reading from the New and Old Testaments. Once embodiment takes place, the process becomes somewhat easier and more efficient in addressing the root origins of problems and how to successfully heal and transform them into positive aspects and outcomes in life.

Fear of death is the main pillar of leverage the ego uses to manipulate self and others who have yet to become who they really are and were created to be. It does this for the purpose of maintaining its control, hoping to dominate such people so it doesn't have to face its contents of emotions and feelings and face its fears and grow.

Three aspect indicators that are primary in astrology are the sun sign, or representation of the soul; the moon sign, which represents the reigning need of the personality or heart with or without the ego; and the ascendant, which represents the outer life in the world and is an indicator of overall beingness. The moon sign is the emotional disposition of the life-form and is where fears are faced, resolving unhealed emotions of the unhealed heart until the light of the Most High God is experienced and healed, transforming the heart. The sun sign, or soul, may have healing and fears to face and heal as well and is the illusion of a difficult, low vibration as far as emotions and feelings are concerned.

Emotions that appear to control serve a purpose under God: to help life-forms while working through and with their fears on the level of the personality as it relates to true heart versus the ego in respect to the mind, soul, and spirit. One learns to become love in the process. Understanding helps tremendously with realizing the truth, and with such understanding comes forgiveness as well as asking to be forgiven. Jesus Christ said to forgive and be forgiven. This leads to freedom from the emotions, allowing the creative life force to express itself through one's being as it is intended by God through creation to be able to express itself.

With this healing and restoration of feelings, the next important step is learning to trust again those things that appeared, through illusion, not to be what they were perceived to be at the time they were experienced. During and when concluding with this process, the true heart will learn and discern what is of the ego and is dysfunctional, releasing it as it reawakens and identifies the soul and spirit in wholeness, realizing the difference between them and where they are created.

The Paradox of Apparent Opposites (That Isn't)

Fundamentalist ------→	←------ Enlightened
By-product of the ego	view of Soul. Inclusive
Either/or mentality	Mentality both and.
"Black or white.	Black and white, plus gray.
"Right or wrong	What serves highest purpose
serves itself	serves self and others
Narcissistic	Capable functioning person

> Expansion <

Increase dimensionality

Life-forms must realize the role they play in the conflict and realize that ignorance, miscommunication, and misunderstanding were preventing comprehension of congruency, coherency, and cooperation to resolve it and realize wisdom and, from wisdom, love for self and others perceived as different.

Illusion of perception is seeing things not as they are but as one would like them to be, based upon the perception of the ego, which is *either-or* thinking: right or wrong, black or white. It has to be one or the other but not both. Failed illusions of love and happiness lead to resentment. That is resolved when a gaslighter (narcissist) is confronted. This leads to the discovery of the empath after one forgives oneself for being tricked by it to begin with as part of how one's past played into it. This realization no longer attracts negativity into one's life, and what is left of fear is transformed into positivity, bringing joy and well-being.

As mentioned earlier in the review of literature, two figures from the Bible who represent the paradox that exists until deeper evaluations are validated as being similar are King David from the Old Testament and Jesus Christ from the New Testament. King David was a fundamental narcissist whose sins led to forgetfulness, and Jesus Christ, as the enlightened being, after His inner transformations, had to find the courage to reenter the ego to redeem the inner world and experience back to God for Himself and all of humanity past, present, and future while overcoming His limitations through faith and others on His path.

Psalm 23 is similar to the Lord's Prayer in that both are condensed summations of their lives' stories and what they faced in their lives. Both scriptures were written early in their lives and summarize their lives succinctly. Psalm 23 suggests a successful reign, justice, and a wise reign for the future king by the "universal image from the ancient world symbolizing leadership and providence for his people" (Brown 530).

Verses 1 and 2 symbolically portray David as obedient to God and God's ways of communicating with him through meditation and prayer and time to contemplate them. It is evident David would be a wise king by inference of the first two verses of the scripture, as they logically make sense with the chapter intuitively as a theme throughout it.

Verses 3 and 4 are linked by the phrases "restores my Soul" and "the shadow of death." These provide insight into his life. Sin or limitation will happen but be overcome, and by going through the shadow of death, the illusion, he will be successful and get through the process with God's grace, protection, and mercy. This reveals an intimacy with God throughout the entire process: "For you are with me; your rod and staff comfort me."

Verses 5 and 6 symbolize success in the trials David went through. He succeeded as king in the presence of his enemies. "You anoint my head with oil; my cup runs over." He defeated his enemies in the physical world but spiritually had a problem and sinned as a result. The sins were adultery, greed, lust, envy, and wrath, which David confronted to the best of his abilities. He was successful in redeeming himself with God's help to remembrance and his repentance. As a result of this, David's hope of goodness and mercy followed him, until it came to his own family, and the unresolved drama from the unhealed emotional wounds of being human were passed on to his descendants, which Jesus Christ would heal for all mankind. Dwelling in the house of the Lord implies he obeyed God every step of his life and was rewarded for letting God and God's will be done in his life. Psalm 23 is a poetic piece of scripture, like the Song of Solomon or Lamentations. It is symbolic and metaphorical, and as such, the interpretation is conveyed by the presence of God in the reader to interpret according to his or her level of consciousness and its development.

Psalm 23, interpreted literally, would imply that the events of his life happened as described, word for word. After all, he was a shepherd when God called him, and he was anointed by prophet Samuel and faced Goliath not long after the first two events took place. He faced evil in Goliath and survived victoriously, and he was successful in many battles for God's people. Literal interpretation would attempt to justify David's sins and not repent, which David did. Had David not repented, then he would have added narcissistic pride to his list of sins. God took mercy on David, as mentioned in the chapter, and sent the prophet Nathan to him to break his forgetfulness and subsequent denial, until David confessed his sins before God and begged for His forgiveness.

Those who wish for a literal interpretation are hoping to be justified in identifying their ego's political position so it doesn't have to repent and change. Most of the time, scripture is symbolic. Occasionally, it may appear literal, and sometimes it is both literal and symbolic, as we will see with the Lord's Prayer.

The Lord's Prayer appears early in Matthew, and it also is at the beginning of the ministry of Jesus. The prayer is formulated from the Word of God speaking from Himself as if providing a template or flowchart for how to interact and be with others: by consulting God for instructions on how to do so first. Neil Douglas-Klotz's *Original Prayer*, the Aramaic translation of the Our Father, is an exemplary work. He posits that the listener can, through chanting and the use of body prayer, become one with Jesus Christ's consciousness, interpreting His thoughts and feelings regarding this segment of His life and experience.

Klotz's translation of the Aramaic in verse 9, "Our Father who art in Heaven" as *"Abwoon d' bwashmaya,"* goes "beyond transcendence to the source of all creation present at the beginning of creation through gestating to the present moment" (6). There is no higher wisdom than this, except to realize it and mystically experience it, which Jesus did. This was early in His ministry, before the transfiguration, when he became one with God's infinite spirit and then realized this line of the prayer. It also distinguishes His literal spirit from transcendent spirit and with others. It was His literal spirit that was asking for God's help.

In verse 9, "Hallowed be thy name" as *"Nethqadash shmakh,"* per Klotz's translation, "light, vibration or sound focuses through our connection of our lives" (15). This line is identifying the connection to the soul or divine memory. This is so the presence of God within will not only awaken but also embody and be brought forward to consciousness to guide and direct the one seeking its counsel.

In verse 10, "Thy Kingdom come. Thy will be done on Earth as it is in Heaven" is "*Tey teymalkuthakh nehwey sebyanachay kama d' bwash maya aph b'arha*" (2). This means embodiment or empowerment, which stems from embodiment so the inner self can express outwardly the presence of God or cosmic unity in the fashion of our earthly self and our heavenly self (soul) coming together in delight. This is a reference to the transfiguration, which would come later in Matthew's gospel. The Dalai Lama comments on the process in Buddhism. Dzogchen is a mind so clear it is transparent, with no darkness to it whatsoever. It signifies the inner and outer worlds' becoming one in unity, like in God's kingdom of heaven. This gives evidence that Jesus Christ spent time in the East as well, per *The Aquarian Gospel of Jesus the Christ*, at some point in His life.

In verse 11, "Give us this day our daily bread and forgive our debts as we forgive our debtors" is "*Havlan lachma d sunquanan yaomana; Washboqlan khaubayn(wakhtahayn) ay kana daph khnan shbwqan l 'khayya bayn*" (2). Klotz's translation of food is for the spirit and body, understanding contemplation to "receive nourishment for the body, heart and Soul and spirit" (36). Understanding leads to wisdom, and wisdom is connection to God. The process of forgiveness spiritually is complex, as it relates to inner and outer boundaries being trespassed. The goal for this is to liberate the subconscious of all that is dark or in forgetfulness and heal it so it may integrate with sacred unity within or God, which Klotz says leads to "salvation that lies in realizing the purpose of our lives" (27).

In verse 12, "Lead us not into temptation but deliver us from evil" is "*Wela tahlan l'nesyuna ela patzan min bisha*" (2). Klotz's translation of *nesyuna*, or *forgetfulness*, is opposed to remembrance, which is sacred unity, on which "the spirituality of this entire tradition is centered" (29). *Bisha*, or *unripe*, means being out of harmony with sacred unity and remembrance. It embraces all as an outward manifestation of our inner world that is coming into wholeness. This also is a connection to King David's unresolved, unhealed emotional drama as well as Jesus Christ's destiny and shows, at a high level of wisdom through God's spirit, how Jesus is David's root and descendent. That was answered in the book of

Revelation, and the answer is this: Jesus Christ is the first created soul from John's gospel, the first created light that experienced itself as light and realized itself as light being light. So this is how Jesus is David's root. Jesus is David's descendent through the sacred heart, which must go through all who came before Him and reconcile, heal, integrate, and embody it so one is whole and complete in beingness of heart, soul, mind, and spirit.

In verse 13, "For thine is The Kingdom, the power and the glory forever. Amen" is *"Metol dilakhie malkutha wchayla wateshbuktha l'ahlam alman. Ameyn"* (2). Klotz's translation "too you belongs ... the cosmic I can...Hayla is the embodied energy of the cosmos... in harmony with the cosmos or the universe" (32). It is a summary of the verses that come before it and affirms them to be true in agreement with one another. This is the nature of connecting with unity, in which right actions will come.

Both King David and Jesus Christ endured grief, and for a few moments of their lives, in moments of truth, they became their opposites within themselves. Each had to go deeper through grief and sin not only to heal it but also to succeed where others before them had left off, so the story could be continued with others.

Proverbs 3:5–6 states, "Trust in the Lord with all your heart and lean not on your own understanding; in all your ways acknowledge him, and he will make your paths straight" (NKJV). The key phrase here is "with all your heart," which implies components to the heart, such as true heart, transcendent spirit, and false heart, or literal spirit. Both spirits are tested through this scripture through faith. The transcendent must learn to trust God even deeper than it already has to get to the point of transcendence and any thought of reentering the ego it shudders at, but that is exactly what this scripture conveys. The literal spirit must trust beyond the fear of how it became literal spirit to begin with and transform into a hybrid spirit of both transcendent and literal spirit before becoming transcendent spirit. It is one of God's mysterious ways that gets demystified by going through the process it describes and ascribes the reader or seeker to consider to remember from forgetfulness to gain the perspective it is looking for.

This process shows the dichotomy all persons have inside from the by-product of their lives, whether they have gotten that far in their growth or not. All will go through it at some point in their evolution back to God in their lifetimes, at the time designed for it to happen. The ego is associated with literal spirit. The purpose of literal spirit is to experience an experience that appears real and that is compatible with earthly life, but in order to do that, it must also be a spirit, which it is, but with limited means and expression until it transforms into transcendent spirit. Then it can know and realize the truth about itself and realize and learn wisdom during and after the process has completed a cycle or phase. When reconciling the past of life, the process described here is the means by which God accomplishes His will with the life-forms going through it. Thus, they become whole and complete and are wise, understanding, and one with God, so they can live their purpose and enjoy the journey as well as the destinations. The purpose of the ego, once its time of learning concludes, is to transform. If it refuses, its own torment of itself will continue till it realizes that the most merciful outcome for itself is to do its spiritual growth work and face itself, versus the magnitude of its karmic debt trying to settle on its own terms what it owes. Then it realizes that God's just and that by doing its growth work, it will be given hope to someday complete it in as many lifetimes as it needs to pay the debt and make restitution to the offended parties. In that, it will find peace to heal and release the negative energy that started the debt to begin with.

Metaphysician	meets	Fundamentalist

Two sides of the same coin.

Inside out	Outside in
Spiritual being	Human having spiritual a
Having a human experience	experience
Understands shame and guilt	
	Understands Transcendence
And when first	but literal spirit limited
occurred as well	

As uncovered coming
to Christ at a
Later date than
becoming human.
Transcendent spirit liberated.

Realized Divinity

No longer overwhelmed or stuck.
No limiting beliefs, emotional illusions, astral (physical) blockages
Of any kind on any level or age of being.

- Divine human: Spiritual being who has a spiritual beingness experience of oneness or mystical union with God.
- Innocent ignorance: Unlearned, not knowing. Soul-based. Used for forgiveness and learning purposes.
- Complicit or prejudicial ignorance: Not knowing the truth about a matter but knowingly doing wrong in spite of knowing. Ego based upon societal values of right and wrong. No root to soul or spirit.
- Grieving the moment of passing or transition of the father in the family: Realization that one has a choice other than manipulation or being manipulated by the pain of being human (wisdom) or the pleasure of being divine (of wisdom). Then one can proceed forward in love. Love brings him or her through and to this choice. Love realizes the choice, and love makes the choice, for love is the highest good of the life-form, others, and God. The I Am, embodied in God as God with God within God, is love and realizes it is love, validating itself by the revelation and realization "I am love."
- Negative manipulation (narcissist): Ego using another for its own purposes, from which it thinks it might gain, devising and employing a strategy to fool and create chaos and confusion, using the shame or guilt of being human or the divinity of being divine to get people to second-guess their first impression of a person, place, or circumstance. This creates uncertainty and doubt as to the veracity of that first impression, which is the navigational system or perspective for interacting with and interpreting the environment and others. The degree of complexity of the intellect is directly proportional to the degree and complexity of woundedness for the life-form to cover up and enclose in the ego.

As we have evaluated, the lives and growth process of King David and Jesus Christ were based upon relationships with God, themselves, and others. Pandit Usharbudh Arya references this in his book *God*. It chronicles the flow of maya (illusion or forgetfulness) and Brahman (infinite consciousness or remembrance) and the nature of this relationship to know the self better. It is a process, as Klotz outlined in his translation of the Lord's Prayer, about loving others and loving the subconscious as the projections play out in the reality of God and illusion. Arya masterfully describes the process of this interplay or dance between maya and Brahman. It is a symbolic metaphor for how maya becomes maya and how Brahman reduces itself to form one-on-one relationships with itself, dissolving maya and becoming wiser and more whole and complete. Maya is perception of wholeness, and Brahman, when dissolving, folding back on itself, becomes whole and complete with the perspective of wholeness from the wisdom of going through the process, realizing all of its shakti, which is love. Both King David and Jesus Christ went through this process described in the review of literature and by Arya and discussed here in this paper.

The growth from God or heaven to earth has an effect on the levels below it from the spiritual to the physical, and society, or the world, undergoes what is known as a paradigm shift as a result of it happening. In the review of literature, Dr. Amen, in his book *The End of Mental Illness*, quotes historian and philosopher Thomas Kuhn and applies his methods to the field of mental health. Here, the discussion will be applied to the life of Jesus Christ to see how it applies, using Kuhn's model, and what changes came about as a result of His life being fulfilled by the Most High God through Him, in Him, and with Him.

- Stage 1: The discrepancies begin to show. Jesus's purpose was to redeem humanity's inner world or experience back to God through His life, death, resurrection, and ascension. During His life, He witnessed and encountered all the forms of wisdom and knowledge available to Him at that time, along with His connection and embodiment of His soul and spirit to God. He witnessed how the church failed the world and the people of not only His time but also the time span of the scriptures written by the prophets. The church knew what to do to help people but wouldn't do it for the people or themselves, because if they did, they feared, they would lose their power and control over them and, therefore, lose any bargaining power with Rome to maintain their traditions and customs, no matter how outdated they were. Jesus came to update and upgrade the church and the process of self-actualization and freedom that goes along with it back to the people. The discrepancies were the failed doctrine and dogma over time, which weren't really helping people to achieve this for themselves. Jesus's ministry, in part, meant to heal and address these issues.

- Stage 2: The disagreements start. Jesus, by challenging the Pharisees (conservatives) and Sadducees (liberals) of His day, initiated discussions and arguments with them, challenging the status quo, advocating for individual freedom on all levels. Jesus came to fulfill the law, which means to make it understood from God's perspective versus the limitations of man's perceptions over time as both man and God evolve over time. Jesus was to evolve both.

- Stage 3: The revolution. Jesus's ministry of miracles, wonders, and teachings resolves many of the problems within and beyond the fields of religion, spirituality, psychology, and philosophy. Jesus reinterprets the Old Testament and updates it to the New Testament.

- Stage 4: The rejection. Jesus was rejected and crucified, rose from the dead, and ascended into heaven. The church, led by High Priest Caiaphas, manipulated the people into calling for Jesus's death, versus the zealot Barrabas, because the church did not want to grow or update their vocations or lives.

- Stage 5: Acceptance. After Jesus's death on the cross and after everything He said came true, the church leaders relented, repented, and were willing to grow and change. They realized the fear, error, and dysfunction of their ways. As a result, Jesus Christ's life lives on today and is revered by many people to the present day. We, as a global society, have reached this point with the world today. With all that is occurring in it, it is evolving, although not in the way many would have hoped.

Angels are God's messengers who show up in persons' lives when they need help the most in a situation or circumstance that may be difficult to overcome. According to *Ask Your Angels* by Alma Daniel, Timothy

Wyllie, and Andrea Ramer, one condition that qualifies for angelic help is addiction. According to the authors, addictions are overcompensations the ego develops to stabilize itself during the formation of its sequence. They are based upon feelings of unworthiness and are deficient in love. If a baby doesn't receive the love it needs, it will suffer a deficit of love that will affect its self-image and image of God. It will search for a substitute for love to attempt to self-regulate.

A relationship in which addictions appear and are magnified is marriage. When two people get married, they do not become one with God per se; they instead, if it is traditional marriage, become one person split into two people. The female would reflect the soul of the male back to him so he could deal with his lower ego-based feelings of his heart to help himself grow with the aid of his wife in showing him the value of his soul. But sadly, most marriages don't go beyond that point, and worse, if the male and female involved do not want to grow, they regress into manipulation and control, trying to control the other in dysfunctional ways. This can be through deficits of character known as addictions, which can cause either to sin. When two people get married, everything becomes one with each other. In dysfunction, in sorting through the conglomerate of constructs, patterns, and feelings and working through it all, there is confusion as to whose feelings are whose, and there is blame for unclaimed baggage and feelings. There is blame for one's own feelings as well as those of the other, who doesn't take responsibility for them. This inevitably leads to spiritual divorce, beginning the individuation process in each if it hasn't already started in one or the other. Spiritual divorce serves a purpose for each to shed the ego and either rejoin through renewal of vows or physically separate and divorce. For becoming whole, the vehicle of marriage was created by God to fulfill each spouse. Becoming whole, and not being part of each other in a dysfunctional way, is the goal of it. Becoming whole, and living from that wholeness, is what it is supposed to be about. According to Retrouvaille, which is a branch of marriage management and renewal for troubled marriages, there are four stages of marriage: romance, disillusionment, misery, and awakening. It is feeling-based and includes the use of the five senses and memories to describe and communicate feelings in an attempt to sort out whose baggage is whose and bring peace of mind to the mind and love to the heart. To better show how couples are supposed to grow in such circumstances and know they're on the right track, I'll evaluate and discuss *The Alchemy of Marriage*.

The Alchemy of Marriage: Positive Male/Female Expression and Negative Male/Female Expression

Negative expression of masculinity (male) will manipulate (ego) and control the feminine or female into holding on to his heart and soul so he can indulge his ego in sin and not grow, not allowing the female in the relationship a chance to grow, as she is burdened with his responsibility and feels controlled. He must overcome his weakness, which is guarded by an addiction securing the stronghold for negativity and protecting the experience of pain.

Negative expression of femininity (female) will manipulate and control the masculine or male for possession of his heart and soul to keep from dealing with her own negativity, which may be undesirable compared to the male's heart and soul. This will render the male incapacitated and incapable of functioning, as he's burdened with the responsibility of her unprocessed, unforgiven feelings of humanness, unconsciousness, and brokenness. This leaves him feeling controlled. She must overcome her weakness, which is guarded by an addiction securing the stronghold for negativity and protecting the experience of pain.

Positive expression of masculinity (male) will take responsibility for his heart and soul, appropriately process and integrate his unresolved feelings, and transform them into beingness. Once he accomplishes this, he in turn helps the feminine or female to do the same.

Positive expression of feminine (female) will appropriately process and integrate her unresolved feelings and transform them into beingness and not manipulate or control the masculine or male.

Marriage based upon Adam and Eve is not whole but dysfunctional. Male and female are not one with God but one with each other. The female will take on heart and soul of the male to reflect back to him the virtues of his true heart and beingness of his soul. The male has the opportunity at this time to either indulge his ego in dysfunction and sin or work on transforming and integrating his ego in spiritual growth to become who he really is and was created to be.

Once this is obtained and accomplished, the male will be an example of wholeness for the female also to transform and integrate her ego in spiritual growth. Once that's done, the couple will exit the collective unconscious and the collective ego and live in the Garden of Eden or heaven, spiritually speaking, whole and complete with God as individuated souls, integrated with their hearts and minds one with God, sharing their wholeness with each other, instead of dysfunction and sin.

When a male and female get married, they become one with each other and not one with God. If both male and female don't want to grow, they will stay in dysfunctional oneness with each other, not whole, individually individuated, or complete. The male's being is divided and split into the male and female, and all the spiritual and emotional baggage of each is combined into one mess between the two. This dysfunctional oneness will cause discord between the male and female, and each will blame the other for how each feels about the negativity they experience. This will go on indefinitely, unless one or both make a sincere effort to grow and change to begin the process of journeying to wholeness, becoming one with God, and transforming and integrating the ego in spiritual growth. Once that's done, the honeymoon period is over in the marriage. Then comes entry into the collective unconscious and the collective ego, where one decides what one has to do to become whole and free, one with God. Spiritual divorce happens at this point to begin the individuation process between the male and the female. It is meant to happen so that codependency can be transformed into beingness and freedom.

The dysfunctional mess between the two who've become one will begin to organize from the chaos and, with awareness and discernment, get deconstructed into its individual parts of feeling, thought, and emotion to be processed and released in forgiveness back to God in exchange for beingness and freedom. Once this is done, the one who goes through it first will become the person he or she was created to be and give the same opportunity for the spouse to do the same.

The dysfunctional mess of oneness is a complexity of entangled feelings of constructs from the male's and female's lives. This will feel controlling to each and must be resolved completely for one or both spouses to be free of it and move on. While the dysfunction is entangled, if a spouse can't take the feelings, goes outside the relationship, and has an affair with another, that spouse is committing adultery as long as he or she is entangled to the spouse. The karma of such a dynamic will follow the spouse to each relationship outside marriage, until it faces its responsibility of appropriately dealing with its share of the dysfunctional mess. Each spouse has to take responsibility for his or her fair share of it and resolve, transform, and integrate it into their beingness, because if it doesn't go through the process of growth, it will remain for the remainder of one's life until he or she finally decides to do something about it in a positive way.

Up until this point, both live in the shadow of the crucifixion. The process of marriage was designed by God to get both the man and the woman to grow and enter into the resurrection, where they both become independent like the angels, integrated, incarnated, free from brokenness, whole, and complete.

The illusion of happiness is the illusion that is disillusioned for the truth of what was or is hidden underneath it, within perhaps many facades of the ego. It is awakened to the true meaning of love. This is a deeper acceptance of oneself, including loving oneself and not accepting abuse of any kind, to in turn be an example and testimony of the way one conducts him- or herself to be of service to others as a reflection of learning how to be a better example of faith or love in action instead of being overwhelmed with negativity in fear.

Pure joy is restored and gained, along with greater appreciation and gratitude for everything in one's life past and present to determine a future with hope and anticipation of the best it has to offer after confronting the worst of it and learning wisdom in the process and how to proceed forward accordingly with enthusiasm for life with abundance and joy to whatever destinations await on the journey to God and the origin of love itself. Learn that the things you think you want will not fulfill what you really need: love. Have appreciation and gratitude for where you have been, how far you have come, and what you have yet to discover.

The grief of the past is done when the final components and parts of the individual realize there is no more left to grieve at a childhood, teenage, or adult level. This is preceded by the revealing of the last strongholds the ego has at the childhood and adult levels. One needs to be conscious and aware of the age and development at the level perceptually speaking—in Christian terms, where ground was given, or, in enlightened terms, the inception point or beginning of the ego. This entails both the childhood and the teenage level and the encounters or experiences that opened them up to their inner world since the experience of the forming of the ego and the end of the negative projection process as a child. Was it light or darkness forming the ego? As Jesus Christ says in the Bible, how great that darkness is if one hasn't had any positive experiences of the light of Christ or God's presence. Being in the ego and experiencing darkness without any light or support can be a frustrating illusion for the life-form going through it. However, it still serves a purpose; through an enlightened perspective, it is the first opportunity in that life-form's life to grow and work through the fears, issues, and feelings associated with it to eventually get to the bottom to discover the reason for such an occurrence to be experienced in the first place. In other words, some modalities may be too aggressive for sensitive hearts and unawakened souls, and as such, the experience may include heavily suppressed, oppressed, and repressed psychic material that is unprocessed. When they have a negative opening or awakening, too much may come out too fast and overwhelm the life-forms. Much of it is judged out of fear as something negative, which may include life-forms associated with the unprocessed material. Therefore, they may be unable to heal it and may get stuck with a far more limited perspective than before they had the experience, which thereby produces an apparent negative experience and outcome.

The purpose, however harsh, is to begin the process of cleaning out and clearing up one's internal house or environment to make way for the light of awareness and one's soul and spirit, whole and complete. The process will lead directly to the point at which the life-form first had a positive experience with the light of awareness or Christ, such as in the Catholic church, with the seven sacraments associated with the church and its religion. As the life-form remembers and reconnects with its complete past item by item, God the Most High reveals each time the light was brought into them first by believing and now through the soul by faith, making the two one heart and soul, head and heart, and now adult and child.

During this self-reflective evaluation and contemplation, all the shame, guilt, and negative feelings are revealed and released after the life-form becomes conscious and aware of them, creating a path from the inside out. Life-forms then connect to where they left off or got stuck both as children and as adults, when they were overwhelmed, unconscious, unaware, or unequipped to effectively cope and deal with working through and processing experiences for healthy, functional growth; learning wisdom in the process; and reuniting with love. This process explains the extremes in behavior, mood, and feelings experienced in going through it, which reflect that the life-form is trying to balance itself out. Because the life-form appears disconnected from its feelings when stuck, there is no coherence with head and heart or harmony between inner child and soul adult, which therefore explains why the life-form is depressed or, worse, without feeling altogether. Divine alchemy is in feeling the feeling completely and grieving the limits of the depths the feeling is trying to reach to breach the border of the love found not only within the feeling but also in the depth from which it cries out to be healed, receive love, and be the love that was there the whole time before the illusion was created.

True heart needs to realize itself apart from the ego so it can let go of dysfunction and embrace the soul and spirit with wholeness, knowing the difference between dysfunction and wholeness, pleasure and pain, and where they originate.

Realization that the inner child did not ruin its life on all accounts is key. Through illusion, it may have appeared that way, but that is not true. It also realizes that its initial response to fear with fear was not its own but came from outside itself, spiritually violating its boundaries.

Greg Braden makes a solid case for literal interpretation of scripture in his book *Wisdom Codes*. He posits that the words from scripture lead to the transformation of people's hearts, giving them perspective from their perceptions, and indeed, they do. However, true perspective, or God's view of perspective, includes the symbolic, metaphorical, and figurative meanings as well. A focus only on the literal interpretation will lead to more questions than answers and feel incomplete. Transcendence has two stages to go through from the literal interpretation. First, it becomes a hybrid of literal and transcendence or literal transcendence, and then it becomes transcendent. If persons are looking to only validate the literal with the literal, then they may have a quasiawakening, realizing they are identifying with something that is the opposite of what their soul deep down is seeking, and then they have to go deeper till they discover transcendence.

The literal interpretation of perception by perception is a hurdle in growth if a life-form has this as its perception about itself, God, and the world. Those who seek validation of the literal for the literal by the literal are the furthest from God's perspective, which is love. To positively validate their perception and present the truth with love, they must find the perspective that is real, which is based in the reality of God's love.

There is a difference between what is literal (perception) and what is real (perspective). To validate individual constructs and constituents of the ego's mindset, one needs to gently dissolve it a little at a time, allowing both realization and integration of the process, to be able to learn and grow accordingly. This will heal the mind and the brain as well as the heart and, eventually, the soul. This process will culminate in one's becoming and being real from the perspective of love, or the Most High God. This awakens the wisdom within the life-form and will establish the perspective for it to become real not in worldly terms but also in God's abundance and love.

The Holy Bible is given in chapter and verse to coordinate and integrate the number of the chakras involved in the life lesson to be learned and, once learned, realized and integrated back into time and space for a time to realize the significance, context, and meaning of the lesson of an individual nature as it relates to the whole, returning understanding back to love from the origin of where the lesson began. Thus begins the sequence of the experience leading to wisdom during and after such experience.

The Old Testament represents people's pasts, including past lives. The prophets represent the ability to move along the continuum of time and go into the future from the standpoint of the soul. The New Testament represents the soul's and mind's ability to be in the present moment while accessing the past and future. The book of Revelation represents the fulfillment of past, present, and future through the soul, body, and mind one with God, both the infinite and creation, in the one eternal moment, representing the beginning and ending and, once through it, then without beginning and ending and a beginning of a new beginning or cycle of spiritual growth.

For example, in Matthew 18:21–22, Peter asks Jesus how many times he must forgive his brother. Jesus replies to Peter's offering of seven times with seven times seventy. This is how interpreting scriptures from the Bible works with numerology and the chakras:

1. Survival/family
2. Sexuality/materialism
3. Personal power/shelter
4. Love/heart
5. Understanding
6. Wisdom
7. Connection to God
8. Infinity
9. Completion

Numbers are added together and then reduced down to the lowest-value figure. For example:

18 is 1 + 8 = 9 (9 is the lowest value or figure, which represents completion)
18 reduces to 1 + 8 = 9
21 reduces to 2 + 1 = 3
22 reduces to 2 + 2 = 4
9 (heart)
3 + 4 = 7 (soul)
9:7

Let's look at Jesus's reply to Peter:

7 × 70 = 490
490 reduces to 4 + 9 + 0 = 13, or 1 + 3 = 4

At chakras one through eight, a heart that is wise and connected to God will be complete after learning the lesson of forgiveness of chakras three and four in another. Adding and reducing chapter and verse (9 + 7 = 16 reduced to 1 + 6 = 7) reveals connection to God. The lesson to be learned is of the heart (4). Forgiveness or revenge is the choice. Completion (9) of this lesson (4) leads to understanding the other and oneself as oneself.

This leads to completion (9) of connection to God (7) and understanding completely the heart of another all levels.

The heart is completed, understanding its connection to God of the soul, and the soul completes its understanding of the heart's connection and completion of God. This brought Jesus's experience of the transfiguration to reality after realization of this lesson.

Another aspect of Bible interpretation is to gain perspective regarding disease, death, and sin, in addition to what has already been included in this paper. Wayne Dyer, in his book *There's a Spiritual Solution to Every Problem*, quotes Joel Goldsmith on these topics in the review of literature.

Denial is the acceptance of the illusion as real versus what is real, which is the reality of God as God's love from God's presence. It doesn't mean the persons are necessarily conscious of this, but at perhaps an earlier time in their lives, trauma was a factor emotionally, spiritually, and perhaps physically as well. This means that what needs to be acknowledged as illusion needs to be validated so they can understand, forgive, and let go of it so they can accept, embrace, and realize or reawaken to the truth that only love is real and that God wants the best for His creation. He wants us to be free from disease, death, and sin.

The Art of Spiritual Healing by Joel Goldsmith quotes supply versus lack as supply is as a person's developed state of consciousness and that this is the real reason people seek out help: they perceive themselves to be lacking or unworthy in some capacity in relation to their experience of what they are dealing with or suffering from. "Infinity is the measure of God. ... The Presence of God does not manufacture some form of harmony. ... The Presence of God is itself the form of all good" (157). Wisdom, love, and God don't get any higher or wiser than this. Connecting to it is key to resolve the issues involved so healing can lead to a change in beingness, giving birth to a new perspective, a new reawakening that will stay with the person and stand the test of time and the person's own belief system. Real growth and understanding become self-evident, and people realize the truth that they are love, whole and complete, as they were created to be.

Don Miguel-Ruiz, in his book *Mastery of Love*, sums up God's reality of what we are: "You can be so strong and so powerful that with your self love you transform your personal dream from fear to love from suffering to happiness" (197). People have an innate ability to heal and transform themselves from whatever disease or sickness they may be experiencing. It doesn't matter how big or how small the problem is; they have to not only understand with their soul but also believe in their true heart for it to align and become their reality.

Whether a person believes in something or not doesn't necessarily make it true, but in reality, this is releasing the fear that is preventing such yearnings from becoming true if operational from the ego and includes the fear of death or a death that didn't allow for such fears to be worked through and processed, as in a sudden end to life, such as an accident or crime. If operational from the soul, then as persons believe, they receive that which has been already placed in their lives and are willing and able to receive and accept it. They're able to love and care for it in a positive, appropriate way that benefits whatever or whoever is involved, and it is a win-win for both.

Dr. Masters, in his book *Mystical Insights*, comments on, as far as science is concerned, why relying on the intellect and five senses is not good: because it provides an incomplete perception of what is being observed or studied. To inquire about such a potential paradigm-shifting event within one's self would create a conflict that produces opposition to one another thus unresolved. To resolve the conflict, one must apply what is learned, and when the person does this with God's presence or Christ, he or she learns wisdom in the process. Then the person will have a more complete perspective on what he or she is studying or observing and be able to draw inferences and subsequent conclusions related to phenomena, instead of ignorant, unconscious, uncommunicative speculation.

Understanding of science, scientific theory, and subsequent laws is subject to change, based upon the consciousness-awareness level of the researchers and whether or not their perceptions or biases have been figured into the design of the experiment along with appropriate variables and controls necessary to the experiment to determine if the phenomena they are observing have merit to what is being experienced via the phenomena and what conclusions can be drawn upon such observations. All too often, there are not enough variables or controls established, along with checked experimenter bias (oftentimes ego), which skews statistical interpretations and observations, which may inadvertently either support or invalidate the theories and outcomes being tested. This accumulation of rhetorical data, not science, leads to doctrine that becomes outdated over time and dogma that is simply not true. Perceptions oftentimes are clouded with unseen issues, and theories are often looking for validation to make a name for themselves in certain circles, sacrificing true science to begin with, so the experimenters will find acceptance rather than the science, oftentimes from their own dysfunctions. They use so-called science to justify the conclusions they conjure to justify their own ego's existence, which is not science by any stretch of the imagination or mind. Science is only truthful and reliable, standing the test of time, when done by those who are coherent and congruent with the truth. They're aware of their perceptions and biases and can successfully filter them out of the experiment altogether. What they find in the final analysis will ring true, leading to sound scientific laws and, more importantly, providing insight into the mysteries of the universe's laws or God's laws, which benefit all life-forms and not just a select few.

Science changes because revealed truth is expanding and filling gaps in understanding in fields of study, because doctrine is outdated and needs updating, and because people in institutions want to make names for themselves, using science as a means to do so. Why is any of this important to this paper? Because perceptions cloud both the mind and the workings of the mind, leading to erroneous conclusions that are not true. Perspective, on the other hand, is needed to begin with, not only to come up with the proper scientific theory but also to create the scientific design of the experiment to produce a phenomenon that stands the test of time and peer review. People know beyond a shadow of a doubt it is true, and the only disagreements to be found expose experimenter bias within individuals who do not wish to accept the results based upon the merits of the experiment.

Perspective allows for and includes its own as well as others' perspectives to be of benefit to all and is not biased, except to the truth. The reason for the experiment is to learn primarily why and how it works or doesn't work, and if not, why not? Bible interpretation is similar. As people consult the Bible, they are searching for truth that is valid to their process and rings true that will prove to them something so they may understand something better to help them with a perceived perception that is not allowing the proper perspective into their consciousness to become clear so the above-mentioned questions may be answered to resolve the perception and establish perspective. This leads to an appropriate outcome or conclusion for them: changing their mind and the way their mind works so they can learn and grow according to their needs as determined by God in what they need to do to be coherent and congruent with their new perspective regarding important decisions to be made in their lives. Bible interpretation with the appropriate perspective fulfills the law, meaning it fills in the gaps of differing perceptions and perspectives and unifies them in a common universal law based in wisdom, which is love. From the layperson to the scientist or the fundamentalist to the metaphysician, things may appear different at face value, but a deeper level reveals the truth: they were merely different expressions of the same thing, and that thing is God, or love. True science would welcome the changes necessary and brought about by true scientific endeavor. However, politics often gets in the way and makes the process of growth slow and arduous.

Any credible profession has science, art, and philosophy as a triune approach to existence, practice, and sustainability. Science is used as a guide to aid the profession as to what has been tried, what the results and outcomes were, what worked, and what didn't.

Art is the practice of applied science, which goes beyond science and is further developed through philosophy, which is developed by the investigation of natural phenomena and includes God, creation, wisdom, ethics, and conduct. All three—science, art, and philosophy—dovetail into one another and are not separate from one another. Philosophy influences science, and both are used to determine the practice or art of bringing the process together in the real world.

Today there is a big push for evidence-based outcomes to supplant and take away the professional's clinical judgment through overemphasis on one part of the triad. This is politically motivated to control and, through this guise, to establish science as the science, art, and philosophy of practice itself. Without the God mind discerning truth, truth is speculation at best.

When in need, people seek the professional's clinical judgment based upon experience guided by science and interpreted through the art. People are pragmatic and practical to a fault, which means they go where they can get the help they need with what works. Gifted people do not currently fit into the evidence-based model, because they may be further ahead of their prospective field, who try to penalize them for it, which is unfair to them and the people they could potentially help, whom evidence-based professionals may not be able to help. This is to create an idol out of science and remove God out of it, making it secular, which is why people consult such things as the Bible: not only to get guidance but also to ascertain and discern truth from what is false and how it applies to their lives and whatever issues and circumstances they seek help with. True scientists often do the same, as ultimately, science was created to prove the existence of all things true, including God, so doubt would not have a hold on a person's mind. Science illuminates truth so people can be free to share the discovery with others and help the world in the process.

If in ego going to soul and observed by the ego perception, then they could, by that perception, be seen as hypocrites to the ego, labeled as being political. If they are in soul consciousness, reconciling their ego, then, from a less-evolved soul, they could be seen as hypocrites labeled as being holier than thou. The word *hypocrite* means a person who stands for one thing and does another that is opposite of what he or she stands for. If persons discover for themselves enlightenment leading to wisdom, then the appearance of such things leads them to truth because they decided to find out for themselves if it is truth or not. They, in fact, have, because they tried and discovered something that either worked and is true or didn't and isn't, beginning by choosing to follow the path of wisdom. What worked or didn't work? What was hoping for it to work or not work? What was inquiring? What was learning? What was learned? If persons are open to learning the lesson presented to them, they will no longer be seen as or be hypocrites but, rather, people of value to God to learn wisdom and how to love.

Experiential Process of Wisdom

Heart   Soul

Rejection   Sadness

Regret

Missed opportunity. Guilt over doing or not doing something

Awakening

Realizing that it wasn't mean to be and that another opportunity will come along at the right time

Pain too great for childhood understanding leads to repression, suppression, or oppression until a time when it is meant to be healed and understood. Kings in the Old Testament were given concubines to offset this pain. This was allowed because Jesus Christ's incarnation came many years later to solve the dilemma. If that hadn't been the case, negative behavior would have been the end result. If persons are doing their spiritual growth work and this happens, then there are mitigating circumstances, but if they are not, then that is a more selfish act that has to be accounted for. However, once people learn the wisdom of Proverbs 3:5–6, which, reduced down, equals five (3 + 5 + 6 = 14; 1 + 4 = 5), or understanding that leads to freedom for heart and soul, understanding chakras one through four, then they will realize that transcendence takes time, energy, and effort to reach those levels, which are materially, energetically, and consciously lower energy. It will be revealed that the past, where the conflict was or is from, has been helping the offended party who needs healing, and the one doing the harm needs help with the ego or soul. If unhealed, emotions cause it to sin or offend love.

This goes on until the ones being harmed learn to love themselves, stick up for themselves, and realize that the one doing the harm to them is being abusive, selfish, and blameful about the conflict. Once abusers process their emotions and feelings, they will learn that they have been doing so for some time and that the source or origin of the conflict resides within themselves. They will realize where it came from and can no longer wrongfully blame the one being abused. In addition to revealing these things, it will reveal what actually happened to cause the conflict in the current lifetime and any links or associations to past lifetimes as well.

At this moment of realization and revelation, people are furthest, apparently, from themselves, thinking they are lost from God in fundamentalism. Jesus Christ's death on the cross was true, and He really was the son of God. Many immediately had regrets for contributing to that outcome. The mystics and believers would wait until Easter to be treated and rewarded for their faith and hard work of following Jesus Christ's message of love.

After Jesus Christ arrived at the realization of choice, knowing His free will still needed to be used, He used it after His suffering was concluding, becoming love. He chose love after becoming love and laid His life down for others, which is where the power of forgiveness comes from. He chose out of love, being love of love; became one with God at the personality level; and laid down His life to be raised up in three days on Easter Sunday, fulfilling the scriptures, leading to freedom of His spirit, soul, mind, and body, free of all karmic responsibility to self, others, and God.

Fear ends at the foot of the cross, and decisions are now given meaning contextualized from the perspective of choice from the viewpoint of love. The motivation, which started long ago out of fear, ends to resolve it, as it was from the consciousness of the abuser on the abusee, and love is the wise choice to free them both if that is what is chosen by either one or both. Forgiveness, letting go, self-love, including one's self as other, or another loves thy neighbor as thyself. No more negative, dysfunctional projections. It ends with this contemplative revelation and realization and epiphany. One sees others as representations of oneself. At that time, the literal spirit transforms into literal transcendent and then transcendent spirit and is released to fly and ascend. The soul knows now that both the spirit and itself are free from illusion of death and sin, and the soul resurrects, learning that the wisdom of wisdom being wise is love.

Love the Natural Order and State of Order and Being

The belief in love must be stronger than the belief invested in the illusion or false belief. It requires no effort but to be pure in intention to affirm and realize the truth for what it is, which speaks for itself. The belief in love is true belief because it is real and one with the reality of love itself, which is based in wisdom and truth. It is one with the light itself, including its shadow, experientially fulfilling the essence of the holy Trinity: Father (love), Son (truth), and Holy Spirit (wisdom). It knows how to operate and navigate in the light and the dark, or day and night, in peace, harmony, and tranquility of knowing, realizing and living as one with it, being part of it. This is the birthright of all of love's creations and what the indwelling life force seeks and attempts to achieve with all life-forms or creations of God, because it knows deep down that providence is its inheritance from the Most High God.

> Deep level of the mind: soul to heart.
> Surface level of the mind: heart to soul.

Perspective is the same, not to be feared but to be embraced with love. Emphasis is on either heart or soul, with its complement complementing the other for total, complete, comprehensive experience of the human condition reconciled to God.

Those who don't deal with their issues blame others for them, and when others point out the truth to them, they twist it and turn it around in blame, once again creating an illusion, which they incorrectly interpret as having dealt with the issue they projected through blame originally onto others. This is known as the illusion of resolution. This only hurts the persons projecting negatively, until they awaken and realize the error of their ways. Coming from love (Word of God as directed by God) leads to fruitful discussions with no projections, only reflections of what is contained in a life-form's beingness. Heart and soul, done in such a way (reflection), neither threaten (refraction) nor diminish (refraction) either life-form in the process, and as a result, the process leads to positive growth for each in recognizing the negative and choosing not to follow it anymore.

A Shadow of Light

In the beginning, there was light, and from this light, all things came. The big bang expanded, contracted, and expanded again. During the expansion, light illuminated the darkness, and during contraction, the darkness (shadow) condensed, becoming darkness in the light, casting a shadow upon itself and into the light. Contraction led to another expansion, in which more of the shadows were reabsorbed by the light, accounting for all condensed light and shadows. When light is condensed, it forms life-forms and objects of contraction and of the light. Refracted light, as apparently opposed to reflected light, is the light that is condensed, giving off a shadow of darkness and of light. Refracted light is not reflected light and, therefore, is searching for light and love uncontracted or condensed outside itself, because that is where the shadow of light is directed. This contraction or condensation is the densest substance or part of matter and spirit and, in reality, is always in flux, moving to and from awareness and consciousness to this densest form of spirit, which is the physical reality of the world and universe we live in.

Once the light starts to congeal, it forms perceptual limits or boundaries based upon shadows and the condensation of these shadows. Once a limit has no more to teach or learn from itself, the light within, which is now pressurized, expands, absorbing all the contents that were condensed, so it may know itself through the process of expansion (perspective) and contraction (perception). Breathing in and out with a rhythm and the impulse of life that started it all, monitoring the process as it unfolds in the process of creation and of life itself, is a dance between the heart (personality cleansed of the ego) and soul.

CONCLUSION

The wisdom of wisdom being wise is love. It is the process of life and life-forms evolving spiritually, mentally, emotionally, and physically and healing their life wounds or perceptions through an ever-evolving frame of reference leading to a cosmic, infinite understanding, using the Bible and God's presence within themselves and to God, others, and themselves. One is both human and deity as it relates to the human condition and how the human condition relates to God. This provides the appropriate perspective from which to make decisions based upon understanding the choices being made in and with life. We are energy forms and, as such, exist in the seen and unseen worlds and have an understanding through consciousness and awareness of this dynamic phenomenon and connection. Through this study, we have learned how important meditation and breathwork are in communing with God for proper interpretation and comprehension in using and applying scripture. We have learned about the limitations of perception and the importance of perspective for overcoming perceptual limits and experiencing and realizing the truth of who and what we really are, which is love.

We have learned that in order to accomplish the proper perspective, the appropriate energy's words and relationships need to be communicative to have the essential communication to obtain it. We have learned how this takes place in people as individuals as well as in groups of people or societies. In addition, we have learned the importance of one's developed consciousness and awareness regarding love and what can happen when it is missing from a person's life developmentally and in general.

Contemplation

Reflectively reflecting on one's life as seen by God, man as God, and man from an integrative perspective is necessary to ascertain one's position in the flow of life from a growth perspective for the purpose of understanding God's will for one's life. This deepens faith within the heart, and one learns wisdom in the process of continually discovering God's love, or love's love, and its infinite, creative infiniteness, realizing there are no limits as far as application of lessons learned from the process. This includes application to one's life and others' lives. In whatever environment people are in, they can follow and carry out God's will for their lives. Meditate, contemplate, integrate, assimilate, renew, and regenerate, becoming whole and complete.

Love validates and affirms others' perspectives, creating reassurance and well-being, and provides clarity, insight, and foresight. It shares wisdom and knowledge, as well as helping itself by helping others to free themselves from limiting beliefs, unhealthy emotions, and physical distress. It has no agenda but to love, spread joy, and illuminate the heart, mind, soul, and spirit so it may know the truth and, therefore, be free to be all that it can and was created to be.

Love and truth are the foundation and building blocks of reason. Reason defines the law, and the law establishes wisdom. Reason gives definition, usage, context, background, logic, precedent, and inference, relating to God and creation. In other words, it explains why something exists, how it is to function, when it may do so, where it is to do it, and what it is to do. The law interprets this relevant to its relation in time and space, compared to reality with the conditions and circumstances present at the time the matter for consideration is considered. Reason and law change over time. God is always busy upgrading life-forms. The means by in which all that has been stated here are carried on and carried out in a timely fashion. This is relevant to the needs of the life-forms carried out in relation to their apparent limitations, which need and require God and creation to gather the application of reason and law with intelligence and common sense, to establish genius.

This genius is to be implemented to solve the problems or challenges of each species and life-form to evolve them to a greater state of being alive and in harmony with the universe and God. The practice of this spirituality and spiritual practice is the essence of wisdom, which is love. A life-form provides for itself to maintain itself until its higher purpose is obtained, sustained, and maintained so the life-form may grow, learn any lessons to be learned, and eventually culminate in being that higher purpose, becoming the evolutionary spark or impulse of creation and life, joining others who have achieved it, serving it, and surrendering to it in love with love, being love, loving love itself or God.

WORKS CITED

Amen, Daniel. *The End of Mental Illness*. Carol Stream, IL: Tyndale House Publishers, 2020.

Arya, Usharbudh. *God*. Honesdale, Pennsylvania: 1979.

Bock, Darrell L. *The NIV Application Commentary (Luke's Gospel)*. Grand Rapids, MI: Zondervon Publishing House, 1996.

Braden, Greg. *Wisdom Codes*. Hay House, 2020.

Brown, Raymond, Joseph A. Fitzmyer, and Poland E. Murphy. *The New Jerome Biblical Commentary*. Englewood Cliffs, NJ: Prentice Hall, 1990.

Caponigro, Andy. *The Miracle of the Breath*. Novato, CA: New World Library, 2005.

Dalai Lama. *Dzogchen: Heart Essence of the Great Perfection*. Boulder, CO: Snow Lion, 2000.

Daniel, Alma, Timothy Wyllie, and Andrew Ramer. *Ask Your Angels*. New York: Random House, 1992.

Dyer, Wayne. *There's a Spiritual Solution to Every Problem*. New York, NY: Harper Collins, 2001.

Goldsmith, Joel S. *The Art of Spiritual Healing*. New York: Acropolis Books, 1959.

Good News Bible. New York: American Bible Society, 1978.

The Holy Bible. New King James Version. Thomas Nelson, 1984.

The Living Bible: The Way. Wheaton, IL: Tyndale Publishing, 1971.

Klotz, Neil-Douglas. *Original Prayer.* Boulder, CO: Sounds True Publishing, 2000.

Levi. *The Aquarian Gospel of Jesus the Christ.* Marina del Ray, CA: Devorss and Company, 2001.

Masters, Paul Leon. *Mystical Insights.* Arizona: University of Sedona Publishing, 2016.

Mays, James L. *Harpers Bible Commentary.* New York, NY: Harper and Row, 1988.

McKenzie, John L. *Dictionary of the Bible.* Macmillan, 1965.

McTaggart, Lynne. *The Field.* New York, NY: Harper Collins, 2008.

Rama, Swami. *Meditation in Christianity.* Honesdale, PA: Himalayan International Institute of Yoga Science and Philosophy of the USA, 1983.

Ruiz, Don Miguel. *The Mastery of Love.* San Rafael, CA: Amber-Allen Publishing, 1999.

Strong, James L. *Strong's Concordance of the Bible.* Thomas Nelson, 2010.

Upledger, John. *Cell Talk.* Berkeley, CA: North Atlantic Books, 2003.

Webster's Dictionary. Barnes and Noble Inc., 2003.

8

Within the Spirit, by the Spirit, of the Spirit

A Dissertation Submitted in Fulfillment of the Requirements for the Degree of Doctor of Divinity, Specializing in Spiritual Healing, on Behalf of the Department of Graduate Studies of the University of Sedona

RAMON LAZARUS
DECEMBER 1, 2022

INTRODUCTION

This dissertation will explore, examine, and explain the spiritual aspect of the process of spiritual healing as it relates to and works with the densest part of spirit (the body) as well as the guiding intelligence that oversees the process to become a realized divinity in oneness with God with no ego. This is important because without spiritual healing, which restores vitality and well-being, life-forms would not have their health or be able to thrive, evolve, or change for the better. This results in an environment not conducive to life or positive outcomes and possible extinction.

Within the spirit, by the spirit, of the spirit is the phenomenon of God in all dimensionality and is the viewpoint of the observation, observing itself being observed, or God looking at God as a life-form in existence and beyond as God. This is the experiential viewpoint of God after mystical union with God of a life-form. It becomes the goal or purpose of life over and through time to integrate the rest of its beingness. This is the primary purpose of spiritual healing: to help life-forms to determine if that is how they wish to use their free will, following God's will.

The viewpoint and interpretation will utilize divine, metaphysical intuition and divinely interpreted metaphysical science from God's viewpoint in the spiritual healer's oneness with God and will be the orientation and inception point of this paper.

The goal of spiritual healing is to help other life-forms to obtain an improved or higher-energy vibration to evolve into a higher state of experience for the purpose of fulfilling their destiny and becoming one with God in the process. This allows their soul to experience itself as God, and God can experience God as the life-form in human form, with both the soul and God fully aware and conscious of each other in harmony with each other, learning from each other in order to continually evolve and help others in a positive way.

This is both a privilege and a reward for the life-form to achieve and obtain. It is an acknowledgment from God recognizing the life-form's soul for its evolution since its being spoken into being. It has graduated from the wheel of karma to the cycle of eternal life, and this is a time of celebration to share with others.

REVIEW OF LITERATURE

According to *Webster's College Dictionary*, the definitions of *health*, *vitality*, and *well-being* consist of the following interpretations and meanings:

- Health: "The condition of being sound in body, mind or spirit; freedom from physical disease or pain" (407).
- Vitality: "The peculiarity distinguishing the living from the nonliving; animated" (1031).
- Well-being: "The state of being happy, healthy or prosperous" (1047).

In the process and practice of spiritual healing, the spirit is of the highest priority and is essential to the flow and steps of spiritual healing.

From *The Dictionary of the Bible* by John L. McKenzie, SJ, comes the definition of spirit:

- "Spirit is the principle of life and of vital activity" (840).

The process of healing involving spiritual healing focuses upon healing the spirit of the life-form seeking the treatment. The spirit is either the indwelling literal spirit or the soul that is to be healed. From here, mental, emotional, astral, and physical are the next levels of healing to heal.

Spiritual healing is needed for spiritual growth. This process requires spiritual healing so it is not an excruciatingly painful process. The spirit provides vital activity, which is life-force activity, and animates the life-form. When trauma occurs on any level or age, it can, and often does, disrupt the flow of life-force activity and cause the spirit apparent injury, therefore limiting its divinity of expression, resulting in lower spiritual activities with lower thoughts, feelings, and emotions of the consequences that caused the trauma to be experienced by the life-form and resulted in the dilemma to begin with. If the trauma is not spiritually healed and regulated at the age and level it was originally experienced at, then the life-form will be limited to the construct of the consciousness that caused it. This will lead to an unfavorable outcome for the life of that life-form.

Jesus Christ referred to the living vitality of the spirit and its life force in the New Testament, when grieving the dead. Jesus said to let the dead bury the dead. In other words, those who are not fully living in the full vitality of the spirit should undertake the task of burying those who lacked it. This was early on in Jesus's ministry, and He later realized He was to help these people who lacked vitality, teaching them how to recover it in His many healings, miracles, and teachings.

Joel Goldsmith, in his book *The Art of Spiritual Healing*, states that different people seek spiritual healing for different reasons: "Some seek it because of physical illness, or because of mental, moral, or financial problems; others because an interval of unrest that gives them no peace regardless of how much outer satisfaction and success they may have found" (3).

Goldsmith continues, speaking about spiritual healing and how peace plays a vital role in it: "finding ourselves in a spiritual peace, an inner peace, an inner glow, all of which comes to us with the realization of God with us. The Presence and power of God felt" (3). Resting in that peace, "the body resumes its normal functions and those functions are carried on by a peace not our own. The body then begins to show forth, perfect, complete health, youth, vitality and strength all gift from the Lord" (3).

Greg Braden, in his book *Wisdom Codes*, articulates the components that constitute a human being or life-form. This information is key to spiritual healing, as related in his book about grief, the process of it, the pain we feel at the loss of a loved one, and the love that appears to be lost in the process. "When a loved one is with us in the body, there is an energy that we create from the merging of our awareness, consciousness, and feelings for one another. More than a metaphor, this very real measurable field of energy results from the bioelectric, bio-magnetic, and photonic fields that we emit from the cells of our blood, organs and tissues" (73).

Braden concludes, "And it's precisely because of this field of energy is so very real that when it dissolves with their passing we experience so much hurt" (74). Grief is part of spiritual growth, and depending upon the circumstances involved, as each person is unique, complications may arise that need spiritual healing to allow feelings to untangle, pain to lessen and diminish, consciousness and awareness to increase, and assimilation and integration to occur through peace and contemplation, leading to increased vitality, well-being, health, and wholeness.

Wayne W. Dyer, in his book *There's a Spiritual Solution to Every Problem*, has this to say about healing: "Healing occurs when we approach our own healing power through faith in our spiritual perfection and an abiding sense of unconditional love" (187). This, used as an intention, can be powerful. Dyer comments on healing coming from God or Source as one with it as well: "When you touch the illness of another with the energy of spirit or the source, you activate the connection and facilitate the healing process. In that sense yes you are a healer, even though you (ego) heal no one" (188).

Goldsmith has this to say in addressing healers and healing: "The spirit of God that is generated in us, which we have either brought with us to this earth experience as a divine gift or have attained through the cultivation of it, is that which does the healing" (173). It is clear that Goldsmith and Dyer agree regarding healers and what the healing is: direct God Source contact or a realization of that contact or connection. It is not of the egos of the individuals involved.

Elizabeth Targ, daughter of Russell Targ, a scientist with patented laser technology, along with Hal Putoff, developed remote viewing and studied healing in her experiments, as chronicled by author Lynn McTaggart in her book *The Field*. Russell Targ developed a reputation for his highly and tightly controlled scientific studies, which produced exemplary qualitative and quantitative analysis of data found and extrapolated in his experiments. Elizabeth Targ applied even tighter controls to the rest of the studies that examined such phenomena. Her background in education included being a psychiatry major. Elizabeth studied different types of healing, employing different types of healers. She mainly focused on prayer and intention, usually involving getting in touch with "a Higher Power or Infinite Being ... Giving thanks to the Source whether it was God or some other Spiritual Power" (McTaggart 186). The healers involved had diverse backgrounds from a wide spectrum, from Native Americans to Christian and Buddhist backgrounds. The only criterion the healers needed to maintain was to believe what they did or were using would work. Her experiment was to treat AIDS patients and verify if healing would work, to what degree, and how effective it would be. The experiments were a success. "At the end of the study, the patients had been examined by a team of scientists and their condition had yielded one inescapable conclusion: the treatment was working" (McTaggart 190).

Another study mentioned in McTaggart's book, done by Elmer Green, shows that experienced healers emit high electric-field patterns during healing: "Studies of the nature of healing energy of Chinese qigong masters have provided evidence of the presence of photon emission and electromagnetic fields during healing sessions. These sudden surges of energy may be physical evidence of a healer's greater coherence, his ability to marshal his own quantum energy and transfer it to the less organized recipient" (194). Elizabeth's study, along with William Braud's work, shed light on the nature of illness and healing. "It suggested that intention on its own heals, but that healing is also a collective force" (194).

Richard Gerber, MD, in his book *Vibrational Medicine*, comments on holistic healing and the role of spirit in it: "The realities of spirit do not negate the laws of science. They only extend existing laws to include the higher frequency dimensions of matter, even as Einsteinian physics incorporated the earlier discoveries of Newtonian mechanics but went far beyond" (418). Gerber then defines what holistic healing is: "The term holistic, in reference to the health and wellness of human beings implies not only a balance between aspects of body and mind but also between multidimensional forces of spirit that until now have been poorly understood by the vast majority" (419).

Gerber then proposes the new paradigm to emerge: "For truly, it is the endowing power of spirit that moves, inspires and breathes life into that vehicle we perceive as the physical body. A system of medicine which denies or ignores its existence will be incomplete because it leaves out the most fundamental quality of human existence—the spiritual dimension" (419).

Gerber then mentions why healing is so important and how it works with spiritual growth: "We are often afraid of owning up to our fears, anxieties and shortcomings. To cope with this frightening inner environment, we begin to project our fear and insanity onto the world, making it seem that the problem is coming from out there when, in fact it originates from within our egos" (482). Gerber then concludes his point: "The only way to break this vicious cycle of confused thinking and illness is through love and forgiveness and a greater awareness of the healing potential of love" (482).

In the book *Meditation in Christianity*, Father William Teska Arpita, PhD, comments on the journey through the unconscious and the times of difficulty in spiritual practice or growth: "The process of making the unconscious conscious entails the surrender of defense mechanisms that have been habitually and subliminally employed to protect the ego from emotionally charged and personally incompatible contents" (93).

This material then is sent to the unconscious mind because the ego is unable to cope with the suppressed and repressed psychic material. Arpita describes the purpose of defense mechanisms in the psyche in relation to spiritual growth concerning the true personality: "The defense mechanisms were designed to protect us from realizations harmful to the ego's identity, but as the personality grows and strengthens, they are no longer needed. When they become barriers to further growth, they must be torn down and the fears they protected released" (93).

It is important to note that when the aspirant is truly ready for this part of the journey of spiritual growth, the ego surrenders itself because it is outgrown, has lived its purpose, and is ready to surrender to one's inner divinity.

Arpita validates achieving oneness with God by following the Word within: "The transformation that occurs through turning within to the word 'that enlightens all men' (John 1:9) is called self-realization. This state of experiencing one's perfect union and oneness with the divine is the ultimate purpose and outcome of meditation, and Jesus was living evidence that this state is possible" (103). Meditation is a growth process and a healing process at the same time and culminates in mystical union or oneness with God. The freedom within equates to how much of God can come through the life-forms for healing both recipients and practitioners alike, as well as in individual healing sessions in meditation.

Pandit Usharbudh Arya, in his book *God*, identifies the deity that the soul becomes one with in mystical union with God: "Yoga-Vedanta, Buddhist, Christian, Brahman, Dharma Kaya, God, the father logos The transcendent reality Hiranya-garbha or ishavara, sambhoga kaya, Holy Ghost, the teaching Spirit in the universe. Avatara, Nirmana Kaya, Son, God in history" (102). Arya concludes that in all three of the religions or philosophies that involve or comment on meditation, it is the same God for all three. Arya also describes the meaning of Siddha and Avatara regarding divinity: "The difference between an incarnation and a Siddha is that in the former, the divinity has descended into humanity where as in the latter, humanity has ascended to divinity. … In the tradition that recognizes and reveres such divinity, both the Avataras and Siddhas are addressed as Lord Bhagavan" (99).

The ego is based in fear, and in *The Living Bible*, the Book of Wisdom 17:11 says, "Fear is nothing else but a surrender of the aids of reason." When a life-form is unable to cope on a spiritual and emotional level, reason and truth, accompanied by love, are surrendered because the life-form is unable to regulate its response or lack thereof to what it perceives it is experiencing, allowing the experience to define the life-form as the experience.

Cyndi Dale, author of *The Subtle Body: An Encyclopedia of Your Energetic Anatomy*, reports on the histories of the chakras, which are widespread and diverse throughout the world. Most notably, they are historically associated with Vedanta philosophy, dating back to written knowledge in about 800 BC. "Vedanta Philosophy, which was written down in the Upanishads around 800 B.C. Vedanta means 'The end of the Vedas,' and refers to the name of four sacred Hindu texts originating in 1500 B.C. These texts are called Tantras. In general, the chakra system branched into two sections: The Vedic and Tantric" (Dale 239).

"The term Tantra comes from 2 words: Tanoi, or to expand and Trayati, or to liberate. Tantra therefore means 'to extend knowledge that liberates.' Tantra is a life practice based on teachings about the chakras, kundalini, hatha yoga, astronomy, and the worship of many Hindu Gods and Goddesses. Tantric yoga originates in pre-Aryan India around 3,000–2500 B.C." (240).

Since energy cannot be destroyed but only changes form, the life-forms of the time periods mentioned above could do the following: "Through the optical glass of intuition, they were able to describe and work with the energy bodies that could turn gross (physical) matter into subtle energy and subtle energy into gross matter. The chakras were clearly central to this conversion process" (239).

Cyndi Dale's book *The Subtle Body* mentions the work of a Shinto priest and scientist named Dr. Hiroshi Motoyama, who investigated the science of the chakra system. Dr. Motoyama discovered, through his experiments, several key findings, such as the following: "Mental concentration is represented in the central nervous system by the brain and nerve plexuses, as well as meridian acupuncture system points. Though the chakras are separate from the CNS and the meridians, Motoyama considers the chakras as superimposed upon these two systems, rather than occupying the same physical space" (250).

Dr. Motoyama explains, "The chakras supply the physical body with outside energy through the nadi system, a circuitry that spreads subtle energy throughout the body. Motoyama states that the 'gross nadi' equate with the meridian system, and together they represent a 'physical but invisible system of physiological control' located within the connective tissue" (Dale 250). Chakras can be evaluated by shape, spin, speed, and size to determine vitality and well-being.

Cyndi Dale, in her book *Advanced Chakra Healing*, reveals practical, insightful ways to evaluate and treat the chakras to restore vitality, well-being, and health. According to Dale, there are twelve chakras total in the human dimension. Chakras one, two, and three deal with the physicality of the first three dimensions. Chakras four, five, six, and seven deal with mostly spiritual issues and connection to God. Chakras eight, nine, ten, eleven, and twelve deal with God as the universe and associated topics and issues.

Dale comments on the imagination pathway with a profound realization regarding one's humanity and one's divinity in her book *Advanced Chakra Healing*:

> Jesus and other Ascended Masters- including Elijah of The Old Testament and The Chinese Hsien who ascend in their bodies or immediately after death- remain in human form even after completing transmutation to the divine. If

human and divine are both equally unreal, then both are equally valid expressions of the other. If you only own your divinity, your humanity exits through the imagination pathway. If you only own your humanity, your divinity leaves through the imagination pathway. If you own both, you'll become both. You can remain in human form and be equally divine. You don't have to choose. Twelve is the last number of the human dimension and a place to celebrate the human experience. (330)

Much has been written in the ancient through the modern era on the chakra system by various authors from various cultures around the world. There is more to the chakras than can be applied to the study of them here in this paper, but for purposes of this paper regarding spiritual healing, I will discuss and further develop the practical integral workings of them in pathology and in health, vitality, and well-being

Chakra 1: Muladhara: "Represents the ground of existence" (Dale 255).

Chakra 2: Svadisthana: Creativity.

Chakra 3: Manipura: "Health of the body and mind" (Dale 257).

Chakra 4: Anahata: Love and compassion.

Chakra 5: Vishudda: Communication of truth.

Chakra 6: Ajna: Bridges the subtle realms that form the entirety of the subtle body.

Chakra 7: Sahasrara: Transcendence. Samadhi. Oneness with God.

In the book *The 12 Stages of Healing*, Donald M. Epstein, DC, describes the process of healing from a seeker's perspective: "For those of us seeking spiritual enlightenment healing or a sense of connectedness with all of creation, the consciousness and rhythms of stage 10 are usually the highest expressions of what we are seeking. ... Stage 10 is the reward for our efforts. It is the stage when we relinquish our sense of self completely and merge with Universal Consciousness" (166).

Epstein further describes the attributes of the resulting process of "being filled with energy and consciousness" (167). We become the energy and consciousness, in which we become love. "Instead of a conceptual understanding of our oneness with this divine source, we know it to be true at a cellular level. We incorporate this understanding into the deepest aspects of our being" (183).

A Course in Miracles discusses at length the process of healing and why it is important: "Healing is the one ability everyone can develop and must develop if he is to be healed. Healing is the Holy Spirit's form of communication in this world" (Foundation for Inner Peace 120). "Healing always produces harmony because it proceeds from integration. ... Healing can be counted on because it is inspired by His Voice, and is in accord with His Laws" (121).

The text also addresses the perspective of God, who performs the healing and inspires miracles: "The miracles the Holy Spirit inspires can have no order of difficulty, because every part of creation is of one order. This is God's will and yours. The laws of God establish this, and the Holy spirit reminds you of it. When you heal, you are remembering the laws of God and forgetting the laws of the ego" (118).

Healing is important to reverse the mindset of the ego so it may be transformed and integrated into the light of God's presence within the soul and Source of God within the life-form. Because of the human condition and how humanness is experienced, healing is essential for growth and positive outcomes in people's lives. When the time comes for growth, it requires transformation, healing that reminds life-forms to remember their Source, or God, and that their true identity in God is love. All life-forms have the capacity to heal. However, there needs to be a willingness to grow and become an instrument of the Most High God. The life-form must become aware and conscious of itself in God so that it can find healing within itself as it heals others, so it can accept it and learn from the process and apply it to itself.

Authors Danah Zohar and Dr. Ian Marshall, in their collaborative effort *Connecting with Our Spiritual Intelligence*, address the topic of healing and why it is important: "The Soul itself ... is nothing but this channel or, better still, this dialogue, from the inner to the outer, the spontaneous communion of the rational, conscious mind with its center and with the center of all being. When this channel or dialogue is broken ... the soul is broken. We are fragmented and spiritually ill" (184).

Zohar and Marshall reveal the remedy or healing necessary to reverse the previously mentioned pathological condition: "When insight and energy flow freely through the channel from inner to outer ... the Soul can heal us and perhaps those with whom we come into contact. We become centered and whole" (185).

Wholeness is spiritual health, and spiritual healing gathers the parts or pieces of ourselves that have been fragmented by becoming human and any other trespass or injury we may have sustained along the way leading up to the chance and opportunity to heal.

Spiritual healing involves all aspects of beingness and all levels of being and ages of development. Eckhart Tolle, in his book *The Power of Now*, gives the example of the pain body as an illustration of the soul that needs healing: "The pain body, which is a dark shadow cast by the ego, is actually afraid of the light of your consciousness. It is afraid of being found out. Its survival depends on your unconscious identification with it, as well as on your unconscious fear of facing the pain that lives in you" (31). The pain body, composed of psychic, unhealed, unwhole material, is an overlay on the soul, with its composition consisting of all the moments of the life-form's history with pain, brokenness, and abuse. These fragmented pieces are all haphazardly joined to one another in the ego, and that is why the illusion of separation is so convincing to the life-form it is in. Becoming aware, the light of consciousness dissolves the pain body, allows the pieces to reassemble, transforms the undigested psychic material, integrates it, and recycles the rest each time a growth sequence takes place. Sometimes the feelings can become so entangled and complex that miracles are needed to help a life-form heal, which leads us to our next two sources, which address the topic of miracles.

Paul Ferrini, in his book *Reflections of the Christ Mind*, states the reason and purpose for a miracle occurring: "The real miracle does not lie in the outer event. The real miracle lies in the spiritual purpose behind the event. The purpose may be to strengthen your faith or to challenge it. You cannot judge the meaning of an event until you know what its spiritual purpose is" (123).

Ferrini defines what a miracle is and what it does: "Miracles help you break through the limits of your own mind. They challenge your world view. They urge you to let go of your interpretation of life so that you can see the possibilities of life that lie beyond it" (123).

Michael J. Tamura, in his book *You Are The Answer* addresses the topic of when a miracle happens and how to identify it: "Yet if you were to examine it more closely, you may discover that it is precisely when you open your heart and mind to Divinity that you experience the true miracle. For miracles do not speak to you in the language of your mind but of your soul. Your intellect may not be able to explain them but you can intuit their reality" (180–81).

Tamura then defines what a miracle is and what to do to make people more receptive to have one occur in their lives: "Miracles are God's answers to your every need, dream and prayer. And you must be there to catch them. God may be the one who produces the miracle, but you must create the space within you to receive it" (182).

Miracles occur inwardly as well as outwardly, in both the seen and unseen worlds within and among life-forms on a daily basis. Inwardly, they provide the necessary stimulus to free up, disentangle, and provide light of a magnitude more than sufficient to successfully eliminate the condition and free the life-form. Outwardly, they may be viewed as improved circumstances combined with synchronicity and serendipity of those circumstances, resulting in and appearing as good fortune. Miracles are a result of spiritual healing, and spiritual healing is a miracle itself.

In his book *Mystical Insights*, Dr. Paul Leon Masters comments on the life of Jesus Christ as a healer and whom He gave credit for the healings performed through Him: "Consider the way of example, Jesus, who had seemingly—at least in appearance's sake—performed miracles of healing. When credit was directed toward him, he responded... Why callest me good? It is not I (Ego), but the Father which doeth these good works'" (171).

Dr. Masters then describes the role of healers and the perspective they have regarding healing: "Mystically awakened healers—and there are but a few—realize that they are part of the illusion of life through the physical senses; They have their roles to play in the universal process" (172). "They (Healers) realize that if a healing takes place from a physical sense perspective, it is because it is the appropriate time and place in the universal process; the healing is something that has already taken place... in the one eternal moment that is God's Presence" (172–73).

Charles Whitfield, MD, in his book *The Power of Humility*, lists and diagrams the four stages of humility and recovery from the false self (ego) to true self (soul) and, finally, oneness with God.

Merging   Creator (God)   Higher Power

4 (oneness with God)
Unity, Holy Spirit
Christ Consciousness Vibratory Bliss (Whitfield 146).

Inviting Trusting   Creativity   Higher Self

3 Co-Creator
Love   Energy, Movement
Expansion   Vibration (Whitfield 146).

Both /And   Empowered Self   True Self

2 Co-Committent
Nurturer   Motivator (Whitfield 146).

Either/Or   Victim   False Self

1 ego
Rescuer Conflict   Persecutor (Whitfield 146).

DISCUSSION

Spiritual healing involves healing or making whole that which was perceived to be incomplete or not whole in becoming human and then realizing divinity in human form made whole, or the Word made flesh. Spiritual healing is the repair, renewal, regeneration, and transformation of a life-form containing a spirit and a soul. Transmutation of outgrown feelings, thoughts, and emotions that have affected the life-form on a spiritual, mental, emotional, or physical level in consciousness may manifest as dysfunction anywhere within the life-form or organism. This manifestation may have or has produced an apparent limitation of function on at least one level or age of being or more. Thus Spiritual healing transforms it into divine consciousness and awareness.

It can be a present issue or a past issue that was unresolved due to the functional capacity of understanding of the life-form at the time of perceptual dysfunction. This is caused by the inception of the ego formation when a life-form is first faced with the life-form's negative karma combined with the world's negative karma and how the life-form reacts or not to the phenomenon and deals with it or not at the moment when it's first exposed. This can be classified as spiritual fear.

Love is the catalyst for transmutation, leading to transformation, producing a revelation or realization, and answering questions associated with phenomena, such as the following: Why? Where? What? Who? How? Love heals on a soul or spiritual level or both soul and spirit, as some complex illusions may reach the level of the soul, depending upon the level of consciousness and understanding of the life-form. One may need to heal both to heal overall and become whole and complete.

Although time and space are factors in wounding, spiritual healing is not necessarily linear but, rather, is based upon intensity or severity. Amplitude and wavelength of the emotional energy of a lower vibration and how it affects the sensitivity of the lifeform's spirit and soul are based upon the lifeform's understanding of it or lack thereof (complications), how the life-form reacted to experiencing the lower energy, and what associations were made, along with whatever dissociation may have occurred with the experience or trauma.

As Goldsmith states in his book about the importance of peace for healing, it is important to mention that clients who seek help have lost contact with that part of themselves for some reason. Yes, it is still within them, but perhaps the level and age needed for healing happened so long ago that there is other psychic debris in the way, preventing them from their consciousness and awareness regarding this presentation. God provides the internal and, if needed, external environment, including the attributes of God. The God mind provides the peace, love, joy, hope, and understanding needed to heal. It also organizes past lives and their gifts through the soul and spirit. It also organizes the unfinished business of the unhealed psychic material to be healed and integrated into wisdom for learning and educational purposes for both the spiritual healer and the patients or clients. The pain body overlay on the soul illuminates it to make it conscious and aware and begins to heal it, until eventually, it is completely immersed in light.

Spirit, in its totality of beingness and expression, covers the full spectrum of light and its associated human qualities at the low end and the attributes of God (Most High) on the other. It, like God, is continually refining itself from lower-consciousness emotion and feeling to higher-consciousness emotion and feeling until it discovers and becomes love and God.

Braden's description of what constitutes a human being is accurate, precise, and correct. The soul is one with God's presence and the kingdom of heaven. The divine spark within it contains all three. These provide photonic light to the life-form, providing for its awareness and the photonic light it emits. The spirit provides for its consciousness and feelings, which, when combined, form the mind and body and give it beingness, until the mind and consciousness (emotions) are purified and the components individually and as a whole are healed, integrated, and made whole and complete.

When a life-form transitions, the spirit, after learning about finishing up its unfinished business—if it's not a traumatic, unexpected passing—will release from the body with joyful feelings, free to appear and create as directed by God's love. The soul resurrects, and the photonic light of the soul and the magnetic properties of the spirit form the electromagnetic charge of the life-form. The intersection of these substituents can be felt and palpated through therapy localization involving touch to a disharmony or chaos state through its biofeedback loop—spiritually speaking, through photonic, bioelectrical, magnetic impedance or touch. This is what creates a life-form and establishes vitality, well-being, and health, giving the perspective of life the life-form identifies with and witnesses to itself, others, and God. The phenomenon of bioelectrical magnetic impedance or touch can also be felt and sensed through the heart (spirit), soul, consciousness, and feelings. The components combine to create life-forms of light, and when they transition, they discharge and release from the body to re-form from and return to light and spiritual properties, which are infinitely creative.

Spiritual healing can be through physical or spiritual touch, by intention through prayer, through meditation, or by all of them in combination. God's presence, Jesus Christ's love, is the carrier energy, substance, frequency, and vibration in which the metaphysical bodies are used to transmit healing through the chakras, nadis, meridian system, and cells of the mind and body simultaneously when healing is applied. Regeneration is the creative cycle, or cycle of creation, that balances until harmony with the recycling apparatus of the mind and body is established, and its mechanism for achieving balance is free of the illusion causing imbalance and any subsequent potential impending pathologies.

Spiritual light, as Source, is emitted, transmitted, and received by the life-form whose awareness and consciousness are aligned and coherent. As such, the being is able to transform itself and others who appear to suffer as a result of not being able to evolve according to the application of their free will to their life and circumstances.

Dyer and Goldsmith agree on the origin of spiritual healing. The spiritual healing comes from God; however, the soul that becomes one with God's spirit experiences itself with God, being part of the whole process. The primary reason for this is so the life-form does not get overwhelmed or have any adverse reactions to the healing. In spiritual healing, communication takes place between God, who's one with the healer, and the intelligence of God in the client or patient. At all times, there is communication. God in the healer, and the healer in God, is sensitive to the condition the life-form is in to receive the healing and the life-form's free will. God does not violate free will, nor can God do so, as it is a promise God makes with each life-form. God monitors both the condition to be healed and the client's free will and works with it in each session to bring balance, healing, and harmony back to the life-form to reestablish vitality and well-being, resulting in good and restored health.

Spiritual healing is not limited to a healer and a client. It can be in other forms or modalities. Meditation is a form of spiritual healing that can take place within an individual life-form or a group of life-forms. Prayer is another form of spiritual healing that, like meditation, can take place within an individual or a group of individuals. Intention that is positive and God-based may spiritually heal as well. Combined with touch and voice (spoken Word of God), it acts as a catalyst to expedite healing, based upon the comprehension and understanding of the life-form, its level of beingness to heal and integrate the healing it receives, and its ability to assimilate it. Touch develops consciousness and awareness specifically in the area in the body mind to be brought up for healing. This helps the client to feel again. The voice of the healer allows clients to hear within their inner world and helps them to give a voice to the event or psychic material so it may be heard. Intention from Source or God connects these two, and since it is based upon the first cause of creation, it establishes communication within them and initiates a rapport with the healer to cognitively heal the central nervous system, the autonomic nervous system, and their related networks with other structures in the body, both the lower and higher energies thereof.

In other words, does the experience make sense to both the spiritual healer and the client during the healing, and does it agree with what was found, discovered, recognized, understood, integrated, assimilated, and, most importantly, healed?

Lynn McTaggart's book is a groundbreaking work that scientifically proves that healing works even under tightly controlled double-blind clinical trials and that many forms of healing are not only valuable but also viable to acute as well as chronic states of disease and stress. However, more research needs to be done to establish how and why it works.

Therapy localization is a *how* in the healing process. TL is closing a circuit whose resistance to flow or impedance is open, creating a short circuit of a functional level, decreasing energy of vitality and electricity, detecting where it is at, and using the appropriate circuit breakers to reset the circuit so it once again flows with energy to sustain the vital function of optimal health and well-being. Well-being is spiritual, mental, emotional, and physical coherency and congruency with one's Creator, or God. A why in how it works is, as previously mentioned, is the intricacy of the design of the higher expression of a human being or realized divinity. Its main constituent components are the soul and spirit and when healed and integrated are capable of not only healing but much more, including the miraculous.

Gerber's *Vibrational Medicine* is a groundbreaking book regarding the workings of holistic healing. It proposes both the theory and plausibility of how and why it works.

Spirit, consisting of soul and spirit, is the software, and the mind body, through the mind, is the hardware, to use a computer analogy. Any type of spirit can affect the body through the mind and cause potential problems with either if the life-form does not get the right help it needs to effectively mitigate the negative, dysfunctional phenomena. Abuse that is physical, emotional, mental, or spiritual affects both the body mind and the spirit of a life-form. Through repression, it gives the illusion of experiencing what the abusers experienced to make them the way they are and also where the abuse originated, resulting in a limited perception that is not based in the reality of who they really are and were created to be.

It will give insight into the conflict, its origin, how it has been applied in the present moment, and how it relates to the past and the potential future it might create. This dynamic can transcend lifetimes as well as take place as the current lifetime. All conflict is based upon ignorance (negative emotion), miscommunication (unconsciousness), and misunderstanding (hurt feelings of brokenness) in the issue at hand between two life-forms. Deterioration of relationship leads to base mortal consciousness, prompting one or both life-forms into survival patterns and modes, leading to control to contain and dominate the other to eliminate the perceived threat to their lives and existence.

Father William Teska Arpita briefly explained some of the issues that can come up during spiritual growth or practice in the book *Meditation in Christianity*. The negative dysfunction projection begins to diminish with both God's presence and Christ's light and love. The idol that was cleverly devised to confuse, manipulate, and control lessens, losing its allure, transforming its selfish way, reducing it to what it is: an illusion of what the ego thinks it needs to be fulfilled and whole in the area of its beingness where the woundedness is. Its pride comes from its marvel of having created something so elaborate and convincing that it convinces the ego that it is God, which is another illusion that it thinks is real because it appears real to it and is able to occupy the body mind in a way that mimics creation but is far from it. It is a false representation of the life-form's self.

The idol is made of and from the feelings experienced and the perceptions they carry from the consciousness of the offender's trespass either directly in life or indirectly through one's karma that is negative and unresolved. The feelings have components of brokenness, unconsciousness, and humanness, which subjugate communication and understanding, therefore not allowing wisdom and subsequent connection to God. The feelings' components program whoever is not strong enough to withstand them, with brokenness as the program, unconsciousness as the limiting parameter of belief (feedback cycle of negativity), and humanness as the emotional energy to carry out and run the program of dysfunction in the means of the idol created to successfully secure the ego its desires or dysfunctional needs to keep the cycle of dysfunction or sin and death going. This goes on until the soul becomes strong enough to overcome it and become who it really is and was created to be.

Chaos is the sum repository of all the lifeform's unresolved, unfinished business or feelings contained within the body mind (in the ego) over a period of time. There is disorder through the ego but perfect order from the lens of God's perspective and the soul. The ego likes to be distracted and forget its pain. The soul lives, moves, and has its being to restore order, process, integrate, and make the life-form whole and complete.

In unconscious formation, an idol is formed from the sum of all fears and suppressed, repressed, undigested psychic material, including pain from all previous forms of trauma and drama that is judged by the inner child to be bad as an overlay on the actual psychic consciousness contained within the psyche. This material, when compressed through suppression or repression, is judged by the inner child to be the worst possible thing it could be. The continued judgment of it gives it power—not in the usual fashion, but it can be empowered to become an entity-like existence psychically within the psyche.

This entity-like formation is the figurehead or representation that can form and be triggered when the life-form's inner child or adult gets overwhelmed. If the child or adult or adolescent can process the material when this happens, he or she will mitigate the consequences of it being acted out. If the life-form cannot successfully work through it and process it, then destruction is likely to occur as it is acted out. Its supposed power is based upon the inner child's inability to self-regulate when first contact with such material is experienced and unsuccessfully processed. The ego of egos looks to consume light and conquer it, which is an illusion, and convert as many as it can to its agendaless agenda of purposelessness, which is to create chaos and fear by first judging itself and then judging it again to create the illusion on top of the illusion of doing something about it to appear to deal with it, which subsequently creates more chaos and fear and, thus, more illusions.

Conscious formation of an idol is consciously imbuing an image of something deemed valuable to the life-form that is a distraction to the wounding and pain. The greater the pain is, the more powerful the idol is. The image is imbued to the point where it projects outward into the life-form's life, and this is when it becomes real to the person. Once this happens, life-forms begin to give their power away to it so it will take care of them and protect them from the harm of how the original pain came to be in the first place.

Pandit Usharbudh Arya, in his book *God*, lists the components that make up God from three primary religions or philosophies. From these religions, Arya has determined that the components and the deity are the same. The following graph will show respectful perspectives of God as reflected in it, showing their relationship to each other as well as the energy to consciousness relationship itself, and how by increasing both energy and consciousness leads to growth and God.

Consciousness is focused, concentrated energy propulsion by an originating thought, directed in creating something or improving something already created from the field of infinity and creation. It is created and applied by intelligence and common sense and abides and complies with the laws of God, the universe, nature, and science.

	Eternity Transcendent Spirit Oneness with God	High Vibration
High Chakra		
7 Observations	Observation	Observing being observed
(Subconscious mind)	(Conscious mind)	(Superconscious mind)
Heart 6 Lives	Moves	Has its being
Energy 5 Within the Spirit (Conscious awareness)	By the Spirit	Of the Spirit
4 Before	During	After
3 Past	Present	Future
2	Time	Space
	1 Literal Spirit Separation	
Low _____ High		
	Awareness Consciousness (Energy)	

This graph depicts the perspective of God once oneness with God is achieved, as God sees the life-form as God (the Word made flesh). Chakras one through four show the densest part of spirit, and chakras four through seven show the evolved higher vibration of spirit or God, with its respective perspective at each level, representing the component associated with deity overall.

The Book of Wisdom in *The Living Bible* defines fear as nothing more or else than a surrender of the aids of reason, which are love and truth. As briefly mentioned in the review of literature, this scripture applies to what happens during the unregulated response to opposing consciousness on a psychospiritual level. This page will discuss this process in further detail to show how and why it happens.

During unregulated response, opposing consciousness will not let up until it has lowered defenses of its target, until the victim has given his or her power away. This happens so it can completely dominate its targets and control them, making them into a version of itself, and the victims will be at its mercy. An unregulated response or reaction occurs when the inner child's boundaries have been violated, resulting in shock and post-traumatic stress disorder. If it continues further past this point, it becomes a potential pathology within the psyche.

The child will internalize what it is feeling, not knowing the feeling is because its boundaries were violated and because of the bond the child is supposed to have with its parents. It thinks it is OK to take on the feeling violating its boundaries. But at the same time, it's confused because its boundaries were violated, leaving the child with an inability to discern, comprehend, and understand its own feelings, because opposing or foreign feelings in consciousness are there to cause confusion.

This confusion can lead to irritability, agitation, uneasiness, and mental and emotional problems. Blame is therefore set up to be directed first at the child for having allowed it to begin with and then the parents and family. The illusion of betrayal begins the state and emotion of fear and leads to other illusions, which lead to miscommunication, misunderstanding, and disconnection on a heart level. The child's developmental, conceptual models of God in human form are its mother and father. Betrayal by either or both causes a distortion of perception and affects the child's image of itself, its parents, and God. This distortion of perception affects it to the point that its images of itself, its parents, and God transform into their shadow opposites, unless they're otherwise regulated and understood regarding the misunderstanding that caused the pain.

The feelings of a trespass impose to the point of violating boundaries, creating an illusion of admission, allowing the feelings to enter based upon the child's reasoning that the parents, through their bond, know about it, and that because they know about it, it is OK. If there was a problem, they would have helped the child to regulate his or her response to it. However, the confusion from the boundary violation persists unless the child can get the help he or she needs to regulate it or develop a way to cope with it or until it gets oppressed or repressed, and the child will act out the feelings and patterns associated with it until it becomes a problem in the child's development at some point in life.

If the feelings in this process are negative and affect the child, causing a significant loss of vitality and well-being, then the frequency and vibration of these negative feelings in question can cause mutations to become active in either a conscious or an unconscious way, signaling and feeding back to the inner child that it is time to heal from the event where the boundaries were originally violated and regulate and process the event to completion to stop the depletion of vitality leading to poor health or the absence of well-being.

Embodiment is important for the previously mentioned reasons and marks a culmination point for the life-form to heal from. With embodiment, the life-form gets the chance to use its free will and regulate a psychospiritual, neuroemotional response to the stimulus that resulted in the wounding. Regulating its response using free will frees and heals the life-form spiritually, mentally, emotionally, and physically. There may be a realization of the construct involved or grief work associated with it to engage in before one is able to effectively process feelings about it.

When a person takes back their power from the collective unconscious, every time in life it was given away from them by manipulation or unconsciously or any other way it may have been taken, it is returned and signifies completion of the growth process through dysfunctional darkness.

The metaphysical bodies—astral (dark), light (soul), etheric (transparent), and spiritual body (gold light)—are spirits. They are in different frequencies, amplitudes, and wavelengths of energy, light, and intelligent information, vibrating at different levels to give the appearance of perception and perspective to each end of the spectrum of experience of the human condition. They service the experience of phenomena of life from each unique, divine design of individual DNA, have since the beginning, and will to the end of time and beyond. Together they represent the software and hardware for beings and existence and the level of consciousness, whether they are awakened or not. They work together with and within all levels of mind and beingness and in all dimensions and beyond them at the same time.

Spirit-mind and body are created when the spirit and soul merge into life with innate intelligence, an extension of universal intelligence. This synthesizes the two as one being, but they retain individuality at the same time for the purposes of learning and growth in an environment inhabitable to the life-form. Both soul and spirit have feelings that are unique to them to provide dimensionality and depth through all dimensions on a feeling level, which is the life-form's designed level of learning.

Chakras service these bodies and their energies to synthesize and project a construct that is interactive, is detectable by the five senses, and feeds back to the mind through the afferent pathways of the central and autonomic nervous systems. This is the basis of perception-perspective pathway learning created by the organism. This is stimulated by the evolutionary impulse given by God to the heart and mind of the parents of the offspring at or around the time of sexual intercourse to hopefully create a life with context, meaning, and purpose to contribute to the human condition and to enjoy and be part of creation and God's plan to make whole and complete. This takes place so that all the life-forms in spirit in the universe can return to God when it is time to do so.

Cyndi Dale, in her books *The Subtle Body* and *Advanced Chakra Healing*, offers a variety of ways and insights into how to work with the chakras from a mostly traditional methodology regarding treatment, working within and with them. In this discussion, I will share a practical application of familiar concepts, simplifying complex presentations to make sense as far as context, meaning, and purpose.

How Chakras Work

Chakras integrate the information of mind from the merging and combing of the spirit and soul to form the mind and the body. The chakras integrate the mind with the spirit, the soul with the mind, and both to form the body. The chakras do this via the subtle electromagnetic energy system (mentally), the nervous system (emotionally), and the DNA system astrally (physically).

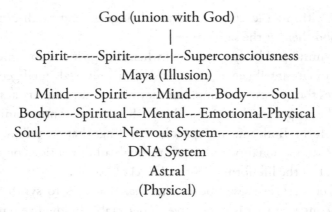

Chakras download and manifests contents (integrated) of the psyche. They constantly monitor and transform from spiritual to physical and physical to spiritual simultaneously from outside time and space into and through it. Chakras are dynamic and active and, when in a state of well-being, high vitality, and optimal health, provide for an optimal expression of the life force from the spirit and soul. Part of their nature is their spin or lack thereof, which determines the quality and quantity of vitality, well-being, and health.

Chakra Spin

- Stuck: Spiritual cessation of life-force energy results in mental or physical disorder.
- Clockwise: Natural flow and function synchronize simultaneous integration of experience.
- Counterclockwise: Reverse flow and function access past issues out of body and trying to get in.
- Too Fast: Anxiety. Unable to appropriately comprehend its feelings or issues environment. Comprehension issue. In body trying to function.
- Too Slow: Depressed. Can't get out from under its feelings or is too slow in processing them.
- Just Right: Optimal vitality and well-being in an organism in harmony with itself, others, its environment, and God.

- Clogged: Psychic material needs to be broken down. Spirits and entities need to be healed, forgiven, and released.
- Front of the Body: Conscious mind.
- Rear of the Body: Subconscious material trying to become conscious.
- Superconsciousness: All body-related chakras are healed, integrated, and incarnated, as well as those above the head. All become one in mystical union with God. Releases soul to ascend and integrate into and with God's heart and spirit, becoming one with universal God mind's universal spirit.
- Light: Shines in the heart into the mind, resulting in illumination of the organizing internal environment (chaos to order). This creates awareness of issues that are unresolved or unexpressed feelings of refracted light seeking to resolve and become whole by knowing self and gaining wisdom and connection to God.
- Alchemy: Prevents pathology transmutation into golden awareness, consisting of infinity and creation. Patient will feel better when being treated as well as after treatment.
- Power Spirit and Divinity Spirit: Personality and soul, respectively. Personality strengthens from learning about forgiveness and the power of love. Spirit is divine infinite, and soul represents eternity and creation. Together they power and make divinity, a human being (realized divinity) made by God, speaking it into being, being fully human and fully divine.
- Spiritual Coherence: Densest part or vibration of spirit is coherent (connected) and congruent (works with) transcendent or purified spirit. This provides the greatest full-spectrum versatility of the soul and spirit to experience the complete, full experience of being a realized divinity and a human being simultaneously, instantaneously contemplating both at the same time, thus honoring their true heart (spirit), soul. Positive expression of humanity and divine design of God, free of the ego.
- Art: The expression of the spirit. It uses the faculties of the soul's eternal oneness and beingness with God, with its light, to convey all its wisdom it has accumulated since its inception. Its knowledge comes from how to apply its wisdom to current events and how

to do that through science based in love and truth. Its philosophy is based upon the creative impulse of life to evolve and grow with God.

Donald Epstein, DC, in his book *The 12 Stages of Healing*, mentions the reward for one's efforts to heal and what that is like, as described in the review of literature: receiving God's perspective or the truth with love in a profound peace that continually heals. It is important to understand the components that contribute to dysfunction to fully appreciate the healing and oneness with God when they occur.

Transcendent Spirit> consciousness>awareness>function> health.

Literal Spirit>limitation of consciousness>limited awareness>dysfunction>disease.

- Spirit: The primary building block of life-forms and life. In its purest form, it is one with and connected to God Most High.
- Limitation of Consciousness: Limiting feeling, emotion, and thought by a spirit of limitation that is searching for light, love, information, knowledge, understanding, wisdom, and connection to God, ultimately seeking mystical union with God.
- Limitation of Awareness: Limited awareness limits a life-form from its Source, God. There is a propensity to give up trying because limited consciousness limits the mind, perceptually speaking, making it entertain negative outcomes in favor of positive ones.
- Dysfunction: Dysfunction of the mind is unconsciously accepting negative outcomes as valid or true. The mind affects the body, and the body affects the mind.
- Disease: Results from the mind believing the negative outcomes as valid or true. They are unchallenged in the mind and are based upon the invalidations of life.
- Pain or Dysfunction Generator: The loop or cycle of karma, sin, and disease, which leads to illness and eventual death. The literal spirit's limitation of consciousness leads to limited awareness, which creates dysfunction, which the mind, by believing in it,

makes real, making sense to the ego. It manifests as disease in the body of the life-form, unchallenged by positive thought or power from God.

- Two-Step Process to Healing: Healing spiritually one's own karma (negative) and healing the karma of others (negative projections of abuse) through their trespasses over the course of life as they arise.

A Course in Miracles mentions four significant points regarding healing. Everyone can both heal and be healed. The Holy Spirit communicates this in the world. Healing produces harmony, and remembrance of God's laws leads to order. The healing process will be described here in this paper as it applies to and works with spiritual healing.

True healing takes place first on a spiritual level with the release and healing of the spirit on a spiritual level, transmuting and transforming it into light and love, with the primary feeling associated with the corresponding configuration of lack of vitality and well-being. This is commensurate with how the life-form feels regarding both the toxicity before healing and the relief obtained after or during the healing. After healing on a spiritual level, next, according to the associations and constructs involved in the disruption of life-force energy, is healing of the mental, emotional, and physical levels.

Mentally, thoughts that are poisonous will dissolve into the love and light of the life-form and be transformed, leading to insight about where the toxicity came from, how it came to be, the circumstances involved, and how it applies to the life for learning purposes. Next, there will be healing experienced on a physical level, and relief of pain or discomfort will be experienced on a feeling level and with the thoughts and emotions that developed as a result of the trespass or wounding that apparently took place.

This will then scan the life-form for other spiritual, mental, and emotional comorbidities through the life-form's past, leading to being present in the present moment. This process extends to the soul, heart, mind, and body as well and will heal each corresponding component of being as it applies to and with emotional logic and emotional intelligence.

Emotional logic is the systemic process of how the toxicity formed to begin with, and as it is healing, the pieces of the narrative of the ego from which it came will make sense to the life-form's experience of it, validating it and increasing consciousness and awareness. This leads to emotional intelligence and healing according to the life-form's mesenchymal matrix to alert and notify the life-form of how the poison crossed the life-form's boundary, causing instability and an imbalance of harmony and altering its perception from its perspective.

Danah Zohar and Dr. Ian Marshall describe the pathology that spiritual intelligence, a component of universal intelligence, works with to heal in spiritual healing. When the pathway from within to without gets obstructed from freely expressing the spirit's and soul's life-force energy, it results in fragmentation or brokenness.

The dysfunction will affect the mind and, when a conscious decision (based in ego or dysfunction) is made to follow in its direction, will signal to the body that something is off as far as life purpose is concerned. If ignored long enough, it will feed back to the cells of the body specific to the issue, causing the dysfunction and subsequent ignorance to download a mutation from the specificity of the dysfunction in the body. This informs the life-form's attention of the body as validation that something is off and out of alignment with its life purpose from a perspective of healthy function and well-being. The mind affects the body, and the body affects the mind.

This creates a cycle of dysfunction or a pain generator and symbolizes the circle of sin and death. If intervention is not taken seriously in getting the appropriate help to mitigate, it can result in disease or an impending or potential pathology or disease.

Spiritual healing breaks the cycle of disease and pathology on the level and age at which it was created in dysfunction, stopping illness in its tracks. Since the spirit and soul combined create the mind and body, it can influence both in a positive way, whatever the imbalance causing fragmentation of being and subsequent dysfunction. Spiritual healing will remedy and mitigate it and begin the healing process, working with clients' free will to help them complete the process, heal, and recover, including regeneration and renewal of the body, mind, spirit, and soul if necessary and if it is in alignment with God's will to do so, which most are.

If the spirit, soul, mind, and body are involved in dysfunction and illness, then spiritual healing will be needed to heal life-forms, and they may need a miracle as well if circumstances require it for their spiritual growth and well-being to be recognized, realized, integrated, regenerated, and restored to health. At the cellular level, this will activate stem cells for regeneration following the renewal of the mind after the apparent limitation is healed, revealing the spiritual purpose behind the illness and dysfunction and the reason for the healing.

Eckhart Tolle's pain-body concept is based upon the ego and what makes it the way it is. It is composed of brokenness, unconsciousness, and emotional dysfunction and toxicity, which can lead to greater problems the longer one identifies with it.

Emotional toxicity can lead to a toxic spirit contaminating the life-form spiritually, mentally, and emotionally, and if it becomes chronic enough, it may affect one physically as well. Primary negative emotions of fear and anger will alter physiology of detoxification of the kidneys and liver primarily and can impact the adrenal glands (cortisol-DHEA axis) and thyroid glands, respectfully. This may impact other organs and channels of elimination, such as the large intestine, bladder, lungs, skin, and lymphatic system. Love and light are the answer to toxicity on all levels of being and all ages of existence. Love and light, in the form of forgiveness, will, in many instances, transform and release chronic toxicity from the life-form, allowing healing to take place, releasing the toxicity from the body and life-form on all levels of being and all ages of existence.

Chronic toxicity of an organ system on a spiritual level can become systemic, altering functional awareness on a cellular level, affecting DNA and cell-nucleus mutations and a lack of discriminating, selective permeability of the cell membrane, allowing mutations to be activated. With healing, this process is reversed, and vitality, well-being, and health are restored. This is validated by the patient's feeling better as well as other indicators and markers of recovery and healing, both during and after the healing session. The feeling of joy felt throughout the life-form's being, as well as improved function of affected areas, will be reported by a successful healing by the life-form and will agree with the findings of the life-form performing or assisting the healing to take place. DNA translation goes from negative to positive with spiritual healing.

Toxicity activates mutations and alters cell respiration to favor mutation and pathogens that are routinely, in a healthy life-form, effectively discarded by a healthy, well-functioning immune system. Toxicity causes and is caused by low energy and, as such, creates by pathophysiological decay and an internal environment that favors other low-energy pathogens, such as viruses, bacteria, and fungi.

Loss of vitality is directly proportional to expansion of the ego and its lower-energy vibration and favors expansion or spread of a potential pathology to form or proliferate. Spiritual healing neutralizes this phenomenon and restores the life-form as quickly as its vitality, well-beingness, understanding, and intelligence will allow. Characteristics of toxicity will be low energy, lethargy, weakness, confusion, negativity, brain fog, low self-esteem, heaviness, contraction, and disconnection. Character-based characteristics of spiritual healing include high energy (transcendence), joy, lightness, strength, positivity, mental acuity or sharpness, healthy self-esteem, expansion, and connection.

Paul Ferrini and Michael Tamura are cited in the review of literature for their insightful comments on miracles. Ferrini focuses on the greater purpose of them besides the remediation of symptoms or restoration of health. Instead, he focuses on the spiritual purpose of a miracle to challenge or restore faith, including hope. Tamura gives detail on how to receive a miracle by opening to divinity with one's heart and mind. Tamura adds that the soul can understand miracles by intuiting their reality of God's love and sovereignty.

Miracles can happen when there is coherence established within the life-form receiving healing or having assistance from a spiritual healer who is spiritually advanced for the presence of God from the God head (which determines the *who, what, where,* and *when* for a miracle) and can transmit the miracle to the recipient. Miracles work on any level of age of development or level of consciousness or awareness. They happen in life-forms' lives when circumstances, through no fault of their own, present in such a way that the life-forms may not be able to lovingly, intelligently respond, because of the depth of the cascade of negativity (associated with a toxic emotional attachment) they may be caught up in. The miracle, in this case, cleans the slate; reestablishes vitality, well-being, clarity, and hope; and restores health. This allows life-forms to respond intelligently from love and learn how to heal and grow to walk with God in faith confidently to fulfill their lives and responsibilities in peace, love, and truth.

Dr. Masters comments on, in the review of literature, an example of perhaps the most prominent life and person in the Bible: the personage and deity of Jesus Christ. Jesus exemplifies all that is within here in this paper and more. Jesus's connection through His soul to the God presence within Him provided the healings and miracles in the scriptures of the New Testament Gospels. Jesus practiced functional medicine on a spiritual level by incorporating the ancient ways of the past, with His life and beingness, into the modern day of His time and brought them together in the one eternal moment of time, which is experienced and found in the present moment.

Spirits come and go. Spiritual healing releases literal spirits that are limited or unliberated. With every healing, both the literal spirit that is unliberated and the literal spirit of the life-form need healing to successfully evolve. Once released, each goes through healing from the cycle of negative karma, sin, and death to the cycle of eternal life. Sometimes with complex issues and tangled feelings, more than one healing treatment may be necessary, unless both spirits experience a miracle so that only one time is needed. How long it takes depends on how conscious and aware both spirits are and how quickly their hearts can learn and process their feelings, transmuting them and transforming them into their highest expression of spirit.

In spiritual healing, there are different spirits in the process that may leave or come and go before the business is finished and the lesson is learned, completed, and integrated. Knowledge is gained, and wisdom is derived and converted from the experience or event to allow one to make a different conscious, aware, coherent choice in the hope of a desired outcome instead of one based in fear.

Spiritual orbs are spirits associated with the personality and possibly the ego and are the basic spiritual support system for the human being or life-form. These may contain, like the pain body defined by Tolle, overlays of projections from others' hurt feelings, primarily from their family-of-origin experience. They communicate through the life-form through consciousness and awareness, and they interface and download through the CNS, ANS, heart, and periventricular system components of being and then manifest their beingness in the mind and body.

Liliths are spirits that are karmic and are associated with emotional energy that is low-density frequency and vibration. These are involved in learning and knowledge to inform life-forms how and why something happened to them, as well as the *what*, the *who*, and when it occurred.

Shadow spirits' purpose is to veil an issue until it becomes conscious and aware to be healed and then departs. Like liliths, these spirits may come and go until the lessons are learned and their purpose for being is fulfilled, when they're needed no more by the life-form. Shadows are an extension of the unconsciousness of the life-form about its issues that are either a projection or hybrid of the offender who was involved with the issue. These vary tremendously as far as karmic, emotional makeup or design and are specific to the life-form's experience of dysfunction.

Entities, if they become denied or repressed, can influence the life-forms they are attached to and engage in the lower, harmful behaviors toward others that caused the original event for them. Grief work associated with the spirit and soul may be required, along with spiritual healing. In complex issues with tangled feelings, they may appear as the offenders' inner child or adult, representing the age at which they were offended themselves with the same or a similar issue or feelings and emotions.

Charles Whitfield's work on the inner child's importance in recovery, to this day, still vibrates its magnitude of relevancy and has stood the test of time with its truth.

The diagrammed charts in the review of literature illustrate the progression of how consciousness evolved with awareness from dysfunction (at the bottom) to the intermediate stages in between to eventual oneness with God, the goal of spiritual healing and spiritual growth. Stage four (oneness with God) is the harmony and balance of the holy Trinity of God (Creator), Christ consciousness (unity), and Holy Spirit (vibratory bliss). We are born in this state and return to this state at some later date, with karma and life lessons in between to learn from.

The spirit of a developing embryo and then fetus and then birthed human being is supplied by the male during fertilization of the female ovum within the female's uterus, about mid–fallopian tube before it implants in the uterus to grow. The soul enters just before birth, signified by the organism's transitioning from a fluid environment to an environment where it is able to breathe on its own, using oxygen. The spirit and the soul form the body and the mind, and all four together make up the life-form or human being. The introduction of being to one's karma is a process that takes place for many when the life-form or organism is young, usually within the first year or so after birth. With the introduction of karma, the process can, and often does, contribute to trauma for the life-form or organism. This trauma must be overcome for the life-form to be able to function; learn to cope; and, eventually, feel and heal from the event.

The karma provides contrast to experience later life experiences judged as good or bad based upon the life-form's or organism's impression of them or their perception, which can be pleasant or unpleasant to the life-form or organism. This karma provides as well the fuel for the holy spiritual fire in the transformation process of divine alchemy, leading up to and through enlightenment and culminating in mystical union with God, wherein the soul and spirit heal themselves through spiritual healing, preparing the soul to become one with God's spirit in the heart of the almighty and all-merciful Most High God.

Mystical Union with God

God's Spirit

Highest-Frequency Vibration

Mind

(Energy, consciousness) Spirit ←-----→ Soul (light, awareness, information)

Body

Lowest-Frequency Vibration

Within the spirit, by the spirit, of the spirit—this is the phenomenon of God in all dimensionality as the observations of the observation observing being observed, or God looking at God as a life-form in existence and beyond as God realizing the observations and the observation all the while as it lives, moves, and has its being in itself or God.

The spirit's essence congeals, entering the influence of time and space and the interval or delay of the congealing, creating the phenomenon as it maintains its frequency and vibration as it assumes formless form and then form. This form occupies space within time and creates a distance within time and space to produce perception, which contributes to a basic level of interaction and understanding with an environment that has apparent limitations created by form and now has boundaries. The boundaries give shape to the essence of spirit now in human form and produce consciousness because it is able to interpret this from the shapes of other life-forms as well.

These boundaries form in the levels before entering time and space and through time and space. When violated, they cause pain to other life-forms, because the life-form violates or crosses the boundary, not recognizing its shape or respecting its divinity, which encompasses the life-form being violated as a whole. This causes trauma to other life-forms, and drama is the way in which the trauma is induced. That which causes trauma to others has had its spiritual essence congeal to the point where its perception causes it to believe the boundaries of its essence have become hard and rigid. The mind develops from this perceptual belief in limitation, and from this limitation, it furnishes other beliefs of further limiting itself, becoming denser and denser in its form, and then concludes, because now it thinks it is the form the mind created.

Reason is the deduction of environmental data based upon its limitations compared to what the life-form thinks is reasonable to accept versus what is possible. The denser the form becomes, the more it diminishes its flexibility to reason within itself and reaches the limit of limitation, in which it has formed the form that will form its base model of understanding. Although primitive, this is needed as a basic function of mind to operate base mortal consciousness.

The journey to enlightenment starts from here, travels to God or Source, and returns here. Spiritual healing is necessary for the base mortal consciousness to heal so it can come alive and feel and heal its boundaries and form. This becomes the Word made flesh and experiences its divinity fully in human form without limitation or a thought process that is limited in any way. Otherwise, limitation of base mortal consciousness, left to itself, would lead to more trauma among life-forms and eventual extinction.

The remainder of this dissertation's discussion will evaluate the risks of uncertainty that exist in the collective ego and why spiritual healing is important to remedy and heal them so the risks are not incurred individually or collectively.

There is risk because those who don't want to change for the better don't want to take the risk, because of what their ego is telling them, which is to be perfect according to the ego's illusions of life and self. They want the benefit without the risk (pain or circumstance). They want others to experience it so they feel safe, and they do not want change, even though life may require it. They base their science on this false feeling of safety when going over their data, interpreting it as safe from any harm because their ego is going by its literal feelings, with no alternative to them, and the feelings that are unresolved terrify them. The only way, they think, to follow them is to change this narrative to something false, not honoring God, because the ego is incomplete without God in the process or equation. The ego eliminates God from their perception, flawing their perspective; this is how dysfunction works. God, on the other hand, would correct this mess by using faith, love, courage, recognition, understanding, and transcendence to help those for whom this applies to understand and work with their light in the darkness and, with Christ's help, eventually heal their beingness to reflect the reality of God's love for them and all people, unifying them in love instead of dividing them in its opposite.

When the collective ego acts out its agenda of denial, deflection, and blame, it causes destruction, first upon others and then upon itself. This takes place in the literal spirit, which is the ego connection to the heart and is a lower vibrational frequency. Because the ego deems it real, it must suffer the consequences of its actions if those actions are not of God or not of love. Sin's payment is destruction and death of the spirit to cleanse it of its negative contents so it may be restored with God's goodness of light from the soul, thereby creating a new spirit, one that is much better than the one before the sin took place. One becomes holier, and with God's correction, there is an emphasis on inner renewal of the heart and spirit through symbolic understanding to balance out its negative perception, leading to perspective to take responsibility at the emotional level of the personality, which, in astrology, is where the ego will be located (moon sign), and its reigning need to be healed.

The ego controls and manipulates because it does not want to be controlled. It fears this and doesn't know the truth. It thinks it is separate from God, because it is not healed and integrated with the soul and made whole. It thinks it knows what it knows, but it really knows only what it fears. If these fears are taken away from it, it fears having nothing to look forward to. The ego needs to get to this place to realize the truth: the reality of love is what it really is. Once this is realized, it moves from a fear-based reality of having nothing to look forward to to having everything it ever has dreamed of having with love. This is accompanied by our choice to love self as the antithesis of love, being honest with experiences both light and dark, both fulfilling and disappointing; focusing on God's presence; forgiving what was done to us; and asking for forgiveness for not being who we were earlier in our lives.

Love is realized at both the soul and heart levels, transforming and renewing the mind, free of the ego and its fear of being afraid. This transforms the addiction from fear and stress and leads to freedom of the heart, peace for the soul, and clarity and cognition of the mind (brain, CNS, and ANS), restoring, regenerating, and renewing vitality and well-being to the life-form.

When a life-form is feeling feelings within or outside itself, if a life-form has not made peace with its so-called enemy, then the feelings are being judged and not discerned. Judgment is fear-based, and discernment is spirit-based. Judgment reacts to protect itself from the perception it perceives. Discernment realizes it is a spirit or feeling and acts out of love. Perception has feelings associated with it as well, to communicate and understand. The enemy demands attention because it has been judged so much and denied its voice to express itself. Judgment leads to conflict and escalation out of the underlying fear playing out with it. Discernment seeks to allow and tolerate, giving both a safe space and a place for the enemy to relax and establish communication within the self and with others. The enemy is now seen as he or she really is: a life-form asking for help because no one has helped or is helping it through its difficult time, perhaps because others didn't know how to help it. This doesn't justify trespass or subsequent abuse if the situation is highly volatile.

However, discernment out of love knows where the line of sanctity, sanctuary, and demarcation is, not only within themselves but also within the enemy's perception, and realizes this is a boundary to be respected within the perception and perspective. Discernment, using love and high vibration, will elevate the situation to where it can be viewed objectively from the perception's flaw or link to its own spirit and communicate with it on a conscious and unconscious level.

Once the flaw is discovered, then life-forms will realize they have a choice to either deescalate and realize the solution within themselves or realize its alternative, which brought it to perception to begin with.

Discernment will further realize that the so-called enemy was a result of past trespasses in which the life-form was not able, for some reason, to stand up for itself on any or all levels. It needs to forgive itself and the perceived perpetrators so it may heal and be free of the pattern of its beliefs and belief system, its unhealed emotions, and underlying feelings, forgiving, releasing, and blessing them, as they have been outgrown to God, which transforms and renews the mind, heart, and spirit. This creates a new perspective that needs nurturing to be maintained, nourished, loved, and cared for. This is everything the perception perceives that it didn't get in its perceived time of need when the trespasses or offenses were perceived to have occurred.

The illusion of attachment (addiction) consists of fear that a life-form has lost its heart, soul, and mind, creating an illusion that it is no longer divine in its resulting perception about itself and its inner and outer environments. This is fear of being afraid. This creates a three-dimensional illusion or interactive interface with itself and others in the environment called the culture or the world. This is based upon the first humans to go through this experience and the mating rituals of attraction between male and female gendered life-forms. This illusion creates emotional instability and turbulence and is stabilized by whatever the life-form needs to do to stabilize itself. The feelings involved are considered real by the experience of them felt by the literal spirit, are unique to each life-form's DNA configuration, and are uniform to what is deemed the human experience and what subjects of this culture refer to as the *real world*, which is described by its inhabitants as a fallen and broken world. Life-forms mate by comparing their compatibility in the contents of their literal spirits that have gone through this process.

If they stay together long enough, can handle and endure the emotions, feelings, and brokenness that spirituality is a part of the marriage, then they can go deeper to reveal their souls' purpose, heal their hearts, be given a new spirit, and renew their minds from that phenomenon to health, wholeness, vitality, wellness, and well-being. Spiritual healing assists with these conditions, illusions, and more to help life-forms heal, recover, and make sense of their lives and the experiences of their lives to realize where they have been, are now, and choose to go from here, being unlimited and one with the Creator of life, or God.

The degree of difficulty is commensurate with what the soul knows and how intelligent (willing) it is to work with the heart to solve and eventually outgrow its problems and challenges to become unstuck and move forward. Anxiety attacks and panic attacks have roots in one's being stuck and unable to move forward and grow to bring part of one's self furthest from God into alignment and eventual integration, where the rest of one's beingness is in aware consciousness and awareness. This is the reason for most, if not all, relationship impasses between a man and a woman. Working through this will lead to reconciliation and a new beginning for both in the relationship or will end with no regrets, as everything that could have been done was done to reconcile it, but one or both parties were unwilling to do the work necessary to achieve that.

Anxiety is not knowing what the fear is or what one is afraid of, along with not being able to figure it out and not knowing what to do about it.

In the final analysis, karma is a check on God's transformative power in a human sense to balance that power in human terms and experience. This eventually arrives at a place of peace, following God's will, as God has the final say on all things and matters regarding what is best for the life-form. It is a prerequisite for being included in God Most High's plan and being given a future, hope, an opportunity, and happiness to be content to learn God's higher ways of love. It is the quintessential definition of integration.

CONCLUSION

Within the spirit, by the spirit, of the spirit—this is the experiential experience of God experiencing God's creation of a life-form from God's perspective after a life-form becomes one with God in mystical union. Recognition and realization of the life-form's soul one with God's spirit and the perspective it creates, is now beingness and beyond, recognizes and realizes deity or oneness with all that is, was, or will ever be. This is for the purpose of fulfilling God's and the life'form's purpose to contribute to love in human form while simultaneously expressing divinity. This is so God may, as completely as possible, experience in the flesh and directly or indirectly influence the human condition to become a higher vibration and an improved version of its condition and experience thereof. Ego is nonexistent as far as negativity or dysfunction is concerned.

Spiritual healing works on any level or combination of the spirit, soul, body, and mind, regardless of the age of the life-form, to alleviate suffering, pain, and dysfunction. This happens so it can heal, integrate, assimilate, recognize, understand, and use free will to make a conscious, aware choice regarding the circumstance or situation that developed from the original choice not made, in the hope of learning wisdom in the process.

Spiritual healing uses the mind, body, spirit, and soul to heal through the chakras, nadis, meridians, and fluid-based systems of the body, downloading the healing through the central nervous system and the autonomic nervous system for optimal health, vitality, and well-being. This provides for optimal expression, efficiently providing animation to the body and giving it life, breath, brain waves, rhythms, a pulse, and a heartbeat. All of this is realized internally by life-forms, especially humans, as the Great I Am, one with God's presence as expressed through infinity and creation. The impulse that started it all is the divine spark that lives within each life-form in the holy of holies within the heart, deep within the soul.

The body is the conductor of current and is the effective grounding apparatus of the organism. The initial impulse from the divine spark within is the initial thought God has of us in His mind and heart at the moment of conception of the thought being created by God from infinity and creation into and upon the canvas of time and space in the world and gives it life with a spirit and soul from God itself. This transmits the divine blueprint of the original or initial impulse, imprinting the DNA and translating it into the organism as a body, mind, soul, and spirit to become aware and conscious. This is to discover and realize God's thought that inspired its creation and purpose for being created. God contemplates life, and that life contemplates God, being God's creation, realizing being God's creation, and being God in human form.

The purpose of spiritual healing in the final analysis of wisdom, connection, and oneness with God is for a life-form to become liberated literal spirit and transcendent spirit at the same time. When this happens, the realm of limited experience disappears, and the cosmic sea of infinite creative potential opens up and can work through the life-form and organism. This happens so it can have and create any kind of experience to experience its oneness and connection to God, achieving rapture, reaching the glory of God in the highest, recognizing the highest expression of the divine, and having a revelation that was occluded by the dysfunction. This allows life-forms to feel fully the love God has for them and share it with others. This leads to understanding in cognitively recovering from and with the whole process; learning wisdom; being able to reclaim violated boundaries on all levels; making them safe, whole, complete, and restored; connecting that aspect or part of themselves back to God; and healing and renewing the mind.

Spiritual healing is accomplished through any and all of God's messengers, including mystical union within the life-form. One's touch, voice, sight, intention, and prayer are the most widely used to accomplish it. Holistic healing is here to stay, and the trials of spiritual growth are like built-in continuing education classes to help those who are part of it go further with themselves and their clients. God is the ultimate journey and destination, visited many times through the process. Mystical union with God brings supreme security and safety; knowing beyond belief; and, later, belief in knowing that God's heart and mind fulfill the scripture that a place has been prepared for you.

Although the science proving and validating spiritual healing is valid as a modality for restoring health, vitality, and well-being and is more than twenty years old, more research needs to be done to validate or inquire about other spiritual forms, methodologies, or philosophies that may develop in the future.

The moment divinity is realized in healing the human condition ends the ego portion of the heart and begins the true heart, which lives by faith and knows and realizes it is divine as a realized divinity in the sacred heart as the amygdala, anterior cingulate gyrus, and prefrontal cortex of the brain clear.

WORKS CITED

Arya, Usharbudh. *God*. Honesdale, PA: 1979.

Braden, Greg. *Wisdom Codes*. Hay House, 2020.

Dale, Cyndi. *Advanced Chakra Healing*. Berkeley, CA: Crossing Press, 2005.

———. *The Subtle Body*. Boulder, CO: Sounds True, 2009.

Dyer, Wayne. *There's a Spiritual Solution to Every Problem*. New York, NY: Harper Collins, 2001.

Epstein, Donald. *The 12 Stages of Healing*. San Rafael, CA: Amber-Allen Publishing, 1994.

Ferrini, Paul. *Reflections of the Christ Mind*. New York, NY: Doubleday, 2000.

Foundation for Inner Peace. *A Course in Miracles*. 3rd ed. Mill Valley, CA: 2007.

Gerber, Richard. *Vibrational Medicine*. Santa Fe, NM: Bear and Company, 1988, 1996.

Goldsmith, Joel S. *The Art of Spiritual Healing*. New York: Acropolis Books, 1959.

McKenzie, John L. *Dictionary of the Bible*. Macmillan, 1965.

Masters, Paul Leon. *Mystical Insights*. Arizona: University of Sedona Publishing, 2016.

McTaggart, Lynne. *The Field*. New York, NY: Harper Collins, 2008.

Rama, Swami. *Meditation in Christianity*. Honesdale, PA: Himalayan International Institute of Yoga Science and Philosophy of the USA, 1983.

Tamura, Michael J. *You Are the Answer*. Parker, CO: Star of Peace Publishing, 2002.

The Living Bible: The Way. Wheaton, IL: Tyndale Publishing, 1971.

Tolle, Eckhardt. *The Power of Now*. Novato, CA: Namaste Publishing, 1987.

Webster's Dictionary. Barnes and Noble Inc., 2003.

Whitfield, Charles L. *The Power of Humility: Choosing Peace over Conflict in Relationships*. Deerfield Beach, FL: Health Communication, 2006.

Zohar, Danah, and Ian Marshall. *SQ: Connecting with Our Spiritual Intelligence*. New York, NY: Bloomsbury, 2000.

Printed in the United States
by Baker & Taylor Publisher Services